ligion, Media
and
Public Sphere

Religion, Media and Public Sphere

Nilesh Kumar Singh

MD Publications Pvt Ltd
New Delhi
www.mdppl.com

Published by :

MD Publications Pvt Ltd
"MD House", 11, Darya Ganj,
New Delhi - 110 002
Phone : +91-11-41563325 (Customer Service)
+91-11-41562846 (Editorial)
E-mail (orders): order@mdppl.com
Website: www.mdppl.com

ISBN: 978-81-7533-227-0

Published and Printed by Mr. Pranav Gupta on behalf of **MD Publications Pvt Ltd** at Times Press, Delhi.

Preface

Religion seems to be a subject that is vitally important and yet little understood. And the media, which are both the context of such conversations and the central source of our information about religions other than our own, seem often ill-prepared for the role they play.

In the media age, religion can no longer control its own story or its own symbols. In times past, clerical authority could more or less dictate where, when and how religious ideas, symbols and claims would surface.

Religion and the media are today linked in powerful and profound ways. The sex-abuse scandals in the Roman Catholic Church, the consecration of a gay bishop in an Episcopal diocese, the Ten Commandments monument in the Alabama Supreme Court building, and struggles over the constitutionality of "faith-based initiatives" are only the latest ways that religion has emerged into public debate.

The process of privatizing the media offers a particular model of communication that, undoubtedly, will affect all religious expressions, in public service the supreme criterion is the presence of society and its institutions and respect for religious and cultural traditions. In private service the objective is to reach the largest audience in order to obtain the greatest profit.

The audio-visual media (cinema, television, etc.) populate their hours with an immense number of people in an endless attempt to excite our senses. Very deep areas of the human being are reached by the senses. The media invade our privacy, and we still do not know the effects that such a multiplicity of stimuli has on us. Religion and affectivity are closely related and all religious expression in the media is stamped by its affective impact.

The mass media have shown signs of producing, above all, the destructuring of the human being. The fragmentation of the image, of information, the manipulation involved in 'montage', creates a kind of partial 'truth', which prevents authentic communication. Mina Ramirez, a sociologist from the Philippines, reminds us: "The most subtle form of dominance is that of the mind. The most detestable sort of dependence is not material but spiritual: people have lost the power to think critically for themselves. The moment people lose this power, they are not able to communicate. They can only ape."

I am very grateful to Mr. Pranav Gupta, Director of MD Publications Pvt Ltd, New Delhi, for his kind cooperation and support for this book.

Nilesh Kumar Singh

Contents

1

Introduction

A religion is an organized approach to human spirituality which usually encompasses a set of narratives, symbols, beliefs and practices, often with a supernatural or transcendent quality, that give meaning to the practitioner's experiences of life through reference to a higher power or truth. It may be expressed through prayer, ritual, meditation, music and art, among other things. It may focus on specific supernatural, metaphysical, and moral claims about reality (the cosmos, and human nature) which may yield a set of religious laws, ethics, and a particular lifestyle. Religion also encompasses ancestral or cultural traditions, writings, history, and mythology, as well as personal faith and religious experience. The term "religion" refers to both the personal practices related to communal faith and to group rituals and communication stemming from shared conviction. "Religion" is sometimes used interchangeably with "faith" or "belief system," but it is more socially defined than personal convictions, and it entails specific behaviours, respectively.

The development of religion has taken many forms in various cultures. It considers psychological and social roots, along with origins and historical development. In the frame of western religious thought, religions present a common quality, the "hallmark of patriarchal religious thought": the division of the world in two comprehensive domains, one sacred, the other profane. Religion is often described as a communal system for the coherence of belief focusing on a system of thought, unseen being, person, or object, that is considered to be supernatural, sacred, divine, or of the highest truth. Moral codes, practices, values, institutions, tradition, rituals, and scriptures are often traditionally associated with the core belief, and these may have some overlap with concepts in secular philosophy. Religion is also often described as a "way of life" or a life stance.

The Public Sphere

The "public" is distinct from community or even civil society in general. Publics connect people who are not in the same families, communities, and clubs; people who are not the same as each other. As such, they are central to the functioning of modern societies. What are the forms, locations, and conditions of public life? How do publics work, how are they supported by different kinds of physical and virtual communicative spaces, how do they figure in political and cultural life? And what are the consequences of the unsettling of familiar boundaries between the public and the private as we begin the 21st century?

Media, Technology and Culture

Changes in the technologies and structure of the media are transforming public life in the U.S. and around the world. These changes affect not only the ways in which media content is delivered—via digital broadcasting, the Internet, and other new channels—but more fundamentally the ways in which we understand the world, communicate with each other, and participate in public discourse. Advances in digital technologies, the concentration of media ownership, the privatization of communications infrastructures, and the expansion of intellectual property regimes are underlying features of this global transformation.

Religion and the Public Sphere

Among the striking but not always recognized dimensions of globalization is a more or less simultaneous revitalization of religious engagement. This includes private devotion and renewal of theological study and debate, but it is also, centrally, a claim to public relevance. The prominence of religion in American public life has grown, as have the religious dimensions of international conflicts and terrorism.

Religion has also increasingly offered resources for resolving conflicts and seeking reconciliation, through the efforts of international movements of peace and the work of faith-based nongovernmental organizations, and, controversially, in the functioning of state-sponsored truth commissions. The SSRC examines these and other changes in the relationships between religion and the public sphere.

The Privatization of Risk, Catastrophes, and Inequality

Efforts to replace public institutions with private sector mechanisms shift the burden of life's many risks disproportionately to those without substantial private wealth. This is a pressing concern not only with regard to natural disasters and "homeland security" but with regard to pensions and social security, the availability of health insurance and health care, and the stability of financial institutions and markets. In a cluster of related projects, the SSRC seeks to advance work on different dimensions of the privatization of risk, catastrophes, and inequality.

Strategic Emphasis

In addition to programmatic work on the public sphere, a strategic emphasis of all the Council's activities is to bring the expertise and insights of social science to bear on current and pressing issues of public life. This commitment is reflected in our "Real Time Social Science" initiative, which includes online Forums where some of the world's premier social scientists examine contemporary issues such as debates over immigration policy, the privatization of risk and the social and political implications of Hurricane Katrina. The SSRC also has a long history of publishing the best social science through major university presses. Building on this tradition, recent publications make the expertise of social scientists quickly available and intelligible to a wide reading public. The Council produces a variety of books and digital products that inform and shape public debates, bringing timely and necessary knowledge to the public sphere.

Religious Media

Focusing on the circulation of religious media and their emphasis on religiously grounded notions of the common good, this chapter addresses the importance of a media-sustained public sphere for the modalities of ethnic pluralism in Mauritius. Contextualize uses of religious media against the background of a dominant discourse of pluralism, which identifies successful coexistence with moral and social values emerging from the negotiation of orthodoxy and authenticity in religious traditions. The media driven dynamics of ethnic and religious pluralism also highlight the affective and emotional dimensions of the public sphere, as they are evident in Mauritian engagements with religious media.

Media, Muslim Publics, and Piety

Recent comparative work on Muslim publics has emphasized the significance of new media in shaping public spheres. The main stress has been on a democratization and fragmentation of such publics engendered through the capacity of new media to undercut the dominance of established powerful players, such as the state and the 'ulema. Eickelman and Anderson, for example, claim that the rise of a new class of "interpreters of Islam" throughout the Muslim world has gone hand in hand with the spread of new information technologies, such as audiocassettes, audio-CDs, satellite television and the internet (Eickelman and Anderson 1999, Eickelman 2005).

These new participants in public debates about Islam and the common good (Salvatore and Eickelman 2004) often lack traditional or other formal credentials as interpreters of Islam in exchanges about public morality. Because such media circulate discourse and images in different ways, they create new media producers and audiences and therefore have a fundamentally transforming impact on the shape of the public and its limits. They have the potential to empower previously disenfranchised actors and enable interventions in public exchange on their part while largely evading the control of the state and established religious authorities. A second, primarily anthropological focus on new media in Muslim publics is the intersection between media practices and personal piety.

Here the emphasis is on how uses of electronic media become part of regimes of pious discipline. Electronically mediated sound and images have recently been described as playing an increasingly important role in the production of religious sensibilities and sentiments within the context of turning embodied listeners and viewers into religious subjects. Highlighting the visceral dimensions of religious experience, this strand of research asks how uses of electronic media have shaped or have even become constitutive of these aspects of religious practice and belonging. Coinciding with a growing interest in sensory experience in media studies, the intersection of electronic media practices with embodied religious subjectivity has therefore emerged as a second site in which media practices articulate both with the making of Muslim subjects and debates about the common good.

Recent work on Muslim publics above all poses the question of how uses of electronic media impact Islam as a religious tradition and Muslim notions of personal piety. However, such processes also have important consequences for the dynamics of ethnicity in plural societies, especially where there is a strong correlation between religious and ethnic identities. In Mauritius the morality of ethnic and religious pluralism and piety often converge in notions of peaceful coexistence. The latter is seen as a supreme common good, which many Mauritians in turn associate with moral conduct conforming to religious values.

Moral values and sensibilities influence how subjects participate in publics, thus shaping the very sense and limits of the public sphere. Moreover, the reproduction of pious dispositions in the contemporary world depends to a considerable degree on the public circulation of discourse and images. Electronic media practices intervening in this interrelationship between pious subjectivities and public spheres concerned with notions of the common good are therefore highly significant for questions of ethnic and religious pluralism. First, how to shape the pious subjects is one of the central themes in a public discourse of tolerant coexistence as the key common good in Mauritius.

The importance of moral values and dispositions for this particular notion of the common good emerges from a postcolonial Mauritian politics of promoting official ethnic "ancestral cultures" that are in turn centered on religious traditions. The cultivation of religious traditions embedded in different "ancestral cultures" is a particular way of managing religious pluralism centered on a distinction between "true" religiosity and destructive religious "communalism." From this Gandhian perspective, task of tolerant coexistence, since they are guided by what some believe to be "true" religiosity and moral rectitude. Thus, the internal debates and social processes among people following a particular tradition are of particular importance in this regime of religious pluralism.

Following this observation, my second point addresses the importance of electronic media practices for the making of subjects imbued by such presumably benign religiosity among Mauritian Muslims. The effect of such media practices is not reducible to an extension of preestablished devotional discourse to new contexts, nor do its effects emerge directly from the formal and material properties of media technology. Instead, locally ascribed characteristics of the electronic medium inform the public circulation and consumption of electronically mediated devotional discourse as it shapes a Mauritian Muslim public centered on the notion of coexistence. In a third step engage the issue of affective and sensual experience for both the shaping of pious subjects and the formation of a Mauritian public concerned with successful coexistence in an ethnically and religiously plural polity.

Describe how among many Mauritian Muslims piety is inseparable from the cultivation of affective stances, in particular a feeling of overwhelming love and attachment for the Prophet Muhammad. These feelings for the Prophet are regularly produced in religious speech events known as mahfile mawlûd, in which na't, a particular devotional genre of poetry in praise of the Prophet is recited. Electronic media practices have recently become important for the production of affective stances through reciting and listening to na't, as audio cassette and audio CD recordings of this genre have become very popular. Affective dimensions of religious experience are often important for the public circulation of religious discourse and images. Following this observation, my case here poses the question of the relationship between religious affect and ethno-religious pluralism. Recent anthropological studies of religion, media and the public sphere have highlighted the significance of affective experience for the interlocked processes of mediatized religion and the transformation of public spheres.

In a move away from a Habermasian understanding of the public sphere as primarily deliberative, several analysts have portrayed publics as shaped by sensory dispositions and engagements and have highlighted the role of electronic media in blurring the boundaries between religion, entertainment, and consumer capitalism. One consequence of this is a new interest in the affective dimensions of religious experience and religious practice, as they are increasingly inflected by the desires of commercial entertainment and commodity consumption. In other words, since religious traditions are part of public culture circulated by electronic media, one also has to pay attention to how media practices contribute to the modeling of the affective and corporeal dimensions of religious experience. Moreover, according to some writers, the affective dimensions of public culture have a tendency to constantly exceed the various ideological and other political projects to which they are often harnessed.

An important question these contributions raise is the significance of the affective and sensual dimensions of publics for the problem of ethnic and religious pluralism. Most discussions about ethnic and religious pluralism and equitable and nonviolent coexistence have so far focused on the deliberative aspects of justice, political representation, and administrative practices. But if we agree on the centrality of the public sphere, and therefore also of modern media practices for negotiating and shaping such pluralism, we cannot afford to ignore the sensual, pleasurable and visceral dimensions of such publics, whose importance in practice often overshadows the rational, argumentative, and ideological strands of public exchange. Paying attention to affective and corporeal aspects of publics is indispensable, if we want to get a sense of how pluralism is actually lived, and not limit our understanding to its analytical and abstract characteristics only. This applies in particular to the sort of pluralist public, which is primarily concerned with religiously inflected notions of the common good.

In contrast to a recent tendency arguing for"autonomy of affect" and the primacy of the sensory over the conceptual and deliberative dimensions of publics, stress that affective and the meaningful dimensions of piety have to be understood as mutually constitutive. The role of electronic media practices in a public concerned with a morally inflected notion of the common good also rests on a tightly interwoven relationship of both poles. The analysis of the circulation of cassette and audio-CD na't as part of a Mauritian public concerned with piety as guarantor of successful coexistence points to the pitfalls of privileging either the affective or the deliberative elements of these processes.

Coexistence and Piety as Common Good

Mauritius is a former plantation society in which almost 70% of the approximately 1.2 million populations are of Indian origin. Members of the middle class among Hindus, 52% of the population, in particular those of north Indian background (approximately 41% of the total population) have dominated the Mauritian government and state institutions since independence from Britain in 1968. They have established the hegemony of a notion of cultural citizenship according to which Mauritians are subjects with origins in other parts of the world and ongoing commitments to diasporic "ancestral cultures" with colonial genealogies. These officially recognized ancestral traditions are in turn largely identified with different religious traditions, as religious difference is of supreme importance in the making of boundaries between the "communities" distinguished both by the Mauritian constitution and the larger public.

The cultivation of officially recognized ancestral cultures with religious biases is nowadays supported by dense transnational networks, and above all strongly encouraged and supported by Mauritian state institutions, and for Mauritian Muslims who constitute 17% of the population and who are like Hindus also of Indian origin, Islamic traditions represent their official "ancestral culture." The management of religious pluralism is one of the chief public concerns in Mauritius, as many fears that political competition and power struggles could quickly slide into destructive religious "communalism" between members of different ethno-religious communities, a worry heightened by violence between Hindus and (Christian) Creoles in 1999.

Mauritian politics of "ancestral culture" and ancestral religious tradition are officially presented as engaged in a combat against "communalism," as they emphasize a normative contrast between destructive religious communalism and "true" religiosity. While the former is the curse of a plural society, encouraging violence and intolerance, the latter makes citizens capable of coexistence and respect for the other, enabled by the moral guidance of "genuine" moral values. According to Mauritian state institutions and many Mauritians in everyday contexts, authentic ancestral cultures with their religious traditions are the chief source of such moral values. In this, the Mauritian politics of coexistence through promotion of ancestral religious traditions resembles a particular strand in Indian debates about secularism, in particular a Gandhian critique of modernization according to which the destruction of "authentic" religious traditions of coexistence among the populace in a process of modernization and secularization are the principal culprits for the recent rise of violent Hindu nationalism in India.

Religious Pluralism and Secularism in India and Mauritius

In some countries, such as France and Turkey, secularism has involved separation of state from religious institutions seeking to confine religious practices and identifications to a sphere of the "private," thus creating a secular public sphere. Indeed, it can be argued that the modern category of "religion" as a area of life distinct from politics, society and law, and the emergence of the "secular" as a particular type of public sphere or as new techniques of social transformation have emerged simultaneously and are mutually dependent. However, this separation is not the only way in which the problem of equitable coexistence under conditions of religious pluralism has been approached.

In India, for example, the postcolonial state has heavily intervened in religious institutions with the aim to suppress practices deemed as "backward" and to ensure that religion does not interfere with the production of modern, progressively minded citizens, a project that has run into considerable resistance when addressed to religious minorities. Indeed, a discursive distinction between secular elites and masses easily consumed by religious passions is fundamental for understandings of secularism in India. The latter also helps to explain why the state seeks to regulate religious tradition in order to foster the emergence of rational citizens inclined towards coexistence with others. The creation of a public sphere from which religious symbols and identifications are absent is not considered a feasible project, as the latter are expected to be very visible in the political process and in the public sphere.

As they cannot be eradicated from a public sphere of political discourse and performance, still less from popular culture, and constitute a danger for peaceful coexistence in the from of uncontrollable religious passions, control and regulation of the religious by a secular elite dominating state institutions is essential. Closely related to the distinction between regulated and enlightened religion and backward and violent religious passions mentioned above, another key theme in discourses of Indian secularism is a Gandhian perspective on religion, according to which there is an opposition between "true" religiosity and violent religious communalism. While the former fosters nonviolent coexistence and mutual respect among followers of different religious traditions, the latter is the product of a cynical instrumentalization of religion for political gains, encouraging violence and intolerance.

Accordingly, those favouring this vision of Gandhian coexistence and nonviolence do not favour a politics free from the use of religious images and discourse but have appealed to Gandhian nonviolent and "true" religiosity supposedly inherent in Indian popular religious traditions in order to fight violent Hindu nationalism. Understandings of the secular in Mauritius share several of these themes prominent in Indian politics. In particular the theme of "true" religiosity as an antidote to dangerous "communalism" is important in Mauritius, where the citizenry is not only officially differentiated in terms of religious identification, but where the public salience of such identifications is also encouraged in the context of a state-sponsored policy of "ancestral cultures" above all equated with different religious traditions.

In comparison to Indian discourses of secularism with their suspicion of religious passions among the masses, religious values and identifications feature as more positively valued elements of a politics of secularism. Instead of being concerned about an excess of religious passion among the populace, Mauritian state authorities appear to be more apprehensive of a decline of religious values among citizens in a process of modernization and rapid economic transformation. While recent economic success and relative prosperity in Mauritius are of course welcomed, these economic transformations are also accompanied by a concern about unbridled competition and moral corruption that many believe have accompanied the "economic miracle" since the early 1980s. As a consequence, Mauritian state institutions have sought to mobilize "ancestral cultures" and the religious values presumed to be inherent in them in order to combat social anomie and moral decline.

Mauritian politicians have also invoked these ancestral traditions in order to foster peaceful coexistence among Mauritians of different religious communities, while conversely the recent changes in Mauritian society and economy are portrayed as undermining "true" religiosity ensuring nonviolent coexistence and mutual respect among Mauritians. Both Mauritian state institutions and many Mauritians in everyday contexts cast secularism understood as equitable and peaceful coexistence in an officially multireligious polity as a moral problem. In this, secularism becomes a field of values and dispositions conducive to coexistence and to be inculcated into citizens, and these dispositions are in turn inseparable from religious themes and discourses. One way in which this identification of religious values and traditions with the common good is manifest is in mediatized political performances on state-controlled Mauritius Broadcasting Corporation (MBC) television. On occasions such as the numerous official religious holidays, or inaugurations or anniversaries of religious centers, representatives of the Mauritian state frequently make this connection explicit.

For example, the annual Hindu pilgrimage to the temples surrounding Grand Bassin, a mountain lake, on the occasion of the festival of Shivratri is also major political event during which the prime minister and other senior dignitaries give speeches centered on religious themes, and participate in ritual. State television coverage of such events is extensive and demonstrates quite clearly that an orthodox liberal separation of state from religious institutions and relegating religious practices and identifications to a sphere of the "private" is not the way religious pluralism is accommodated in Mauritius.

There is, however, another level on which the intersection of the common good and religious tradition is manifest. Media practices intervene in this issue not only because they circulate images and discourse demonstrating how Mauritian secularism and religion are not in an antagonistic zerosum relationship, even though this aspect may be the most obvious. This is because the use of electronic media has also become part of religious practices. Such uses of media have turned into one of the chief battlegrounds on which contests over authority and authenticity in religious tradition have played themselves out. The most significant aspect of this Mauritian politics of coexistence through the proportion of presumably genuine and authentic ancestral religious traditions is that this notion of the common good ultimately locates the task for ensuring successful coexistence in the formation of piety among Mauritian citizens.

It does so by placing particular stress on the authenticity and validity of religious traditions, as only they can shape Mauritian citizens in a spirit of moral virtue and rectitude, and thus enable successful coexistence in an officially multireligious polity. Thus, in this state-sponsored vision of pluralism, the internal politics of religious communities bear most of the responsibility for the making of good, tolerant citizens. As a consequence claims to piety also become part of political struggles over inclusion and citizenship. For Mauritian Muslims, Islamic traditions represent their officially recognized ancestral culture. Therefore the cultivation of "genuine" Islam and the shaping of pious Muslims are of supreme importance in their claims to be good citizens who contribute to the task of coexistence and the fight against "communalism" as the central notion of the common good in Mauritius.

Devotional Genres and Electronically Mediated Affect

In contemporary Mauritius the listening to cassette and audio-CD devotional discourse and poetry is one of the key ways in which electronic media practices and the formation of Muslim piety intersect. The particular genre concerned with is *na't*, devotional hymns and poetry in praise of the Prophet Muhammad, and also of other Muslim authorities such as the prominent Sufi teachers Mu'inuddin Chishti (popularly known as Khwaja Gharib Nawaz), 'Abd al-Qadir Jilani, and even in praise of members of the ahl-e bayt (the family of the Prophet and their descendants) such as the Prophet's son-in-law 'Ali and his grandson Husayn, a practice recalling Shi'ite traditions. Na't is usually performed in Urdu and is very popular among Muslims in South Asia and its diasporas.

In Mauritius, as in also often the case in South Asia, the performance of this poetic genre takes place in religious speech events known as mahfil-e mawlûd on auspicious occasions, such as the birthday of the Prophet and prominent saint teachers, as well as key events in life such as weddings or moving into a new home. Performing na't has been an established practice usually confined to these performative occasions, but starting in the 1980s, the circulation of cassette and later audio-CD recordings of this genre has not only extended the practice to new contexts of audition, but has also begun to shape how na't is performed in mahfil-e mawlûd. Cassettes na't from India and Pakistan, as well as live recordings of visiting na't khwân (accomplished performers of na't) from both countries have emerged as authoritative models for local performances of the genre.

At the same time, a few Mauritian na't khwân who received training from Indian and Pakistani Imams have also started to produce recordings of the genre, and their cassettes and audio-CDs are now the most commonly used in Mauritius. Na't is a key practice in a larger complex of spiritual mediation characteristic of some South Asian traditions of Islam. In particular the Ahl-e Sunnat va Jama'at (Barelwi) tradition emphasizes the role of the Prophet as a mediator between Muslims and God. According to this tradition the Prophet continues to have a spiritual presence of his own manifest as pure light (*nûr-e Muhammadî*) and his powers of intercession can be appealed to by the performance of na't poetry in praise of the prophet. The performative dimensions of the recital are of supreme importance for the act of spiritual mediation.

This is because in reciting the poetry, the performer becomes immersed in love for the Prophet and a better Muslim. Given the transformative qualities of practicing na't, its adherents consider that great spiritual benefits derive from the act of reciting and listening to this genre of praise poetry. In other words, na'‘t is a performative technique creating pious dispositions in its practitioners. More in particular, it is a technique for producing certain pious affective stances, especially deep affection and love for the Prophet, resulting in a sense of visceral closeness to him. Na‘t is a controversial genre, because for some the exuberant praise and description of the Prophet's attributes is going too far, approximating the Prophet Muhammad to a God-like figure.

Practitioners of na‘t are keenly aware of the delicate status of the genre, which in the eyes of most Muslims should never suggest equivalence between the Prophet and God. Therefore the authoritative status and the authenticity of the recited poetry, ideally traceable to scholars and poets of repute, is of great importance for the performative efficaciousness of na‘t. Performing poetry that steps over the acceptable boundaries of praising the Prophet would turn the perceived benefits of na‘t into their opposite, instead of enacting a pious transformation of the self or the successful enactment of spiritual intercession.

Against the background of controversy around Na‘t, uses of electronically mediated na‘t have interacted with Mauritian Muslims' practice of the genre in shaping notions of textual and performative authenticity. Concern about the correctness and faithful reproduction of Na‘t has invested na‘t recordings from South Asia or those of local performers trained by South Asian Imams with particular authority. From the perspective of many of its users, electronic reproduction of voice facilitates authentic textual transmission.

Audition of cassette or audio-CD Na‘t is thereby domesticated into an established tradition of recitational logo centrism also attested for other Islamic traditions. Even if recitation of scripture directly summoning the presence of the divine is not at issue here, the concern for the authentic presence of the "correct" text through long chains of interlocutors is also important in other engagements with

Islamic traditions in Mauritius and elsewhere, such as in the faithful transmission of hadith, the record of the words and deeds of the Prophet and his companions, or as in the case here, the authentic transmission of na't.

But the faithful transmission of text through long chains of interlocutors and performers is not the only aspect addressed by media practices such as cassette and audio-CD na't. Equally important is the safeguarding of a particular performative style, which is as decisive for the pious transformations sought in the practice of na't as the "correctness" of the textual dimension. The affective dimension of the practice of na't is at the forefront of concerns about the faithful transmission of a particular performative style, which is as significant for the efficaciousness of na't as the authoritative transmission of texts.

According to interlocutors, the recitational style in the expression of love and affection for the Prophet should never remind one of Hindi film songs in a setting such as Mauritius where the consumption of Bollywood entertainment is extremely popular. There is no use of musical instruments and there are no female voices. Also, unlike in Hindi film songs, recitational qualities should be emphasized, with moderate speed and rhythm. The expression of overwhelming affection should be balanced with the decorum, the restrained conduct and absence of agitation many conceive as iconic characteristics of a pious Muslim, compare. Unlike the transmission of the "correct" text, this performative dimension cannot be effectively mediated by print, but by techniques of sound reproduction. There are only a few accomplished na't khwân in Mauritius to serve as examples in live performances. However, in the eyes of many Mauritian Muslims, circulating audiocassette and audio- CD recordings can provide the guidance necessary for the successful performance of na't.

The successful performance of na't with its production of the "right" kinds of affect within a framework of spiritual mediation depends on the "right" way of performing, and also listening to na't. This entails the ability of the performer to move his audience towards the experience of strong love and affection for the prophet, and for the audience the capacity to hear in the right way, against a background of shared knowledge of spiritual mediation and of the generic conventions of na't. Cassette and audio-CD na't are treated as enhancing this process, as for many Mauritian Muslims listening to na't recordings ensures not only the faithful transmission of text, but above all provides guidance in matters of performative style.

Despite the popularity of cassette and audio-CD na't, many reject the practice of this devotional genre. This is related to the antagonism between adherents of the Sunnat Jama'at, as the Mauritian followers of the Ahl-e Sunnat are locally known, and the local representatives of the Deobandi tradition. The latter, in Mauritius above all the followers of the Deobandi-connected global missionizing movement Tablighi Jama'at, reject the former's openness to Sufism as well as their veneration of saints and their perspective on the Prophet as a mediating figure that can be appealed to for intercession. They regard these practices as illegitimate innovations that they attribute to the Indian environment in which they arose, and seek a "return" to the original society of the Prophet.

The collective recitation of na't as an invocation of the Prophet and saint-teachers is part of this complex of spiritual mediation the Deobandis reject from their purist perspective. As such, the differences between Deobandis and the Ahl-e Sunnat or Barelwi tradition has so far been above all understood as a matter of different philosophies of spiritual mediation and different understandings of what the original society of the Prophet was like. But disagreements about na't among Mauritian Muslims show that these differences are not only a matter of conflicting perspectives on the authenticity of certain Prophetic traditions. They are also concerned with the role of affect in devotional practice. This in turn has also led Mauritian Muslims to develop different perspectives on the electronic medium in this devotional practice, the one more optimistic, and the other more skeptical.

Religion and the Aesthetics of Communication

The relationship between nationalism, religion and communication in India has been altered by history and context, personalities and technologies. Gandhi's famous 'Salt March' and Bollywood mythologies, along with current attempts by the Hindu Right to fuse together a highly exclusive Symbolic of religious nationalism, have each sought to reconcile the public and the private, politics and morality, in the cause of a larger Nation.

However, present-day attempts at forging a majoritarian national identity through the use of communication have been characterised by crass manipulation of religion in the interests of an ascendant Hindu Right. The paucity of concerted counter-responses towards the making of inclusive futures is a sign that all is not well with civil society in India. Religion in India is a capacious experience. It accommodates within itself a range of activities and ideas, including those we would usually associate with the secular realm. Let us consider the phenomenon of the Elephant God that drank milk. It was a superb media event that happened simultaneously all over the country and yet retained for the curious viewer a credible degree of spontaneity. The idea seemed to be to convey to a jaded public the assurance that the age of miracles was not yet past and that God's ways are still mysterious.

But that is not all. Given the fact that for the past few years the Hindu right has been working hard to press the claims of religion on the public sphere, it is obvious that religion or rather religious structures - of feeling, organisation and communication - have rather consciously adapted themselves to contingent needs. This is not to be wondered at. Religion in the Indian context provides, fills out and enables an entire aesthetics of communication. That is, religious lore, symbols, ideas, practices, principles and all else go to structure, shape and even direct forms of communication in modern India.

As with everything else, there is a history to this. Here concerned with the role of religion in communicative practices during various times in India's rich and layered past, but with a relatively modern practice of religion and one that we associate with a politics made famous for its piety by that 'saint' of modern India - Mahatma Gandhi. Famous 'Salt march' he undertook, along with thousands of other Indians protest against the rapacious tax policies of British rule. The campaign was not only well planned, but it was organised in very specific ways: religious metaphors were liberally used to compare the proposed march with a pilgrimage; the media were informed well in advance of what they might expect and Gandhi's act of picking up a fistful of salt, in defiance of laws that forbade such things, was endowed with an aura of classical and austere simplicity that called attention to its constitutive value, to its poetics, so to speak.

Gandhi undertook to imagine a nation that would derive its identity from its past and seek legitimacy for its existence from a religious world view. He managed to inflect traditions in characteristically ingenious ways so that change and transformation were made to appear as if they were mandated by a pre-existing religious imperative. Gandhi's genius lay in imagining an India that was simultaneously 'Bharath' of the glorious days of yore and a land of the poor, the meek and the marginalised. His success lay in communicating the worth and validity of his vision to large sections of the populace and winning their consent. This was possible because he took over from religious experience structures of faith and belief that were now given expressive power in particular contexts. It would not be amiss to refer to this imagined India as a 'Hindu' India. In addition this was also a 'Hindi' India, since it was assumed that Hindi, held to be closest to Sanskrit, the language of ancient Indian culture, was a natural national language. This 'Hindu-Hindi' India was imagined within the confines of an old unequal order, the caste system.

Shaping Popular Culture

The aesthetics of communication afforded by religion also came to shape popular culture during this period. Even the new art of cinema - which reached India in the early decades of the twentieth century - originally had recourse to themes from religious lore. Mythic figures were played by popular heroes and the patois of everyday speech commingled easily with the classicised talk of the protagonists in these films. It did not seem unnatural that tales of another time should thus be represented to a modern audience and through this most modern of the communication arts.

The verisimilitude that the camera enables laid itself rather effortlessly over the mythic content of many a tale, so that protagonists were at once Everyman as well as larger than life. The homology that comes to mind is of course from the political realm; for here too, the needs of the people were represented but in and through the modality of a discourse that was saturated with the mythic and other worldly dimensions of experience.

It is not to be wondered at then that in recent times, India has witnessed a sort of Hindu resurgence and this has been heralded by and acted out in daily instances of the everyday by the party of the Hindu right, the Bharatiya Janata Party. This latter organisation has acquired great public and political visibility and relies chiefly on its communicative endeavours to forge a constituency for itself. It is obvious that the rise to public visibility of the Hindu Right has happened in a global and national context which is haunted by the growing and menacing shadow of economic liberalisation.

The Hindu Right has managed to capture the attention and represent the concerns of the class that is most at home in this conjuncture: the middle class. In India this is still largely upper caste in its composition. As far as this class is concerned the aesthetics of religion is significant in as much as it enables them to practise religious faith as a style. The Hindu Right has worked at rendering religion a matter of deportment and discourse through its reliance on rites, festivals, reenactments of old tales. The milk drinking elephant god emerged out of this milieu.

The Hindu Right's efficacy has been due to the fact that it has broadened the spectrum of accepted religious expression and communication. Technology is used to advantage by the conscious and the unconscious ideologues of the Hindu Right, such that one can meaningfully talk of the manipulation of belief and of faith as techne (the promise of technology, its aura and ambience). Ever since the Hindu Right demonstrated its will to power with the destruction of the mosque at Ayodhya, the religious imagination it has constructed and deployed in several and diverse realms has come to govern all forms of communication. Thus not only do political leaders seek for themselves the kind of legitimacy that religious faith confers on its devotees, but religious leaders have come to represent their interests in the public sphere and have sought to promote themselves as worthy as any secular purveyor of the common good.

The Hindu Right's strategies of communication rest on a set of evocative symbols, the most important of which is the icon of the beleaguered motherland, at once the repository of glory and heroism and yet, being female, always vulnerable. The idea of doomed womanhood has long lent itself to verse and song and as far as Mother India is concerned, she has roused many a Hindu male heart into valour and (misplaced) anger at the thought of the Muslim marauder who is biding his time to spoil her.

In such a context, where religious sentiment has become captive to the hegemonic ambitions of a cynical and powerloving class-caste combine, counter-public spheres have been slow to emerge and where they have, they have not proved effective. The secular imagination is drab and bereft of ideas and though the Hindu-Muslim riots inspired many protest art exhibition, films and plays, the efforts have been few and far between. As E V Ramasamy Periyar, the great anti-caste radical of our times, has said, the peddlers of religion have vast resources at their command to gather assent for their views, since all forms of communication and all forums for communication are available to them: from song and dance associations to theatre groups to temple festival committees, etc.

But what is perhaps most worrying is not even the paucity

of responses to the Right but the rise of leaders with a cult value and power that will stop at nothing. Such leaders win constituencies through their ability to represent their concerns as universal and through the appropriation of all visible signs of the common good. They are, more often than not, great communicators who eventually come to define all meaningful political interaction in extremely functional and manipulative terms.

The point is that their emergence has been due to the association of ideas of piety and sacrifice with notions of power, politics and the public good. Gandhi began this process but while he was able to render the association meaningful and authentic (even though the terms on which he achieved this need to be interrogated) others who came after him and lived (and continue to live) at a time when the public sphere is being transformed in unprecedented ways have stolen piety's aura and located it in their own persons.

As far as India is concerned religion is not peripheral to the everyday lives of the people. It is their solace, their source of entertainment and also their notion of proper and admissible behaviour. This being the case, one should assume that just as media manipulate religion, the latter also functions to supply themes and ideas for communication. The problem lies in staying clear of manipulation and seeking out more nuanced and resistant strains of articulation.

2

Media and the Public Sphere

Among the institutions that contribute to the makeup of a public sphere in society, the media perhaps perform the most critical function. In the transactions in the public sphere, the media are not a neutral participant or an impassioned chronicler. Instead they are either a legitimiser of the status quo or an innovator of the existing social equilibrium. The conflict or collaboration of the media with forces that attempt to colonise the public sphere materialises in this context. The mutual relationship between the state and the media, either as oppositional or as complementary, is influenced, among others, by the nature of intervention of the state in the public sphere. The former goes back to the 18th century when the Bengal Gazette trained its guns on the British administration and was mauled in the process.

Since then, the endeavour of the press to imbue the public space with a critical culture has been consistently curtailed by the state, both by legislative interventions and by administrative interference. For liberal democratic practice such measures of the state have serious implications, as restrictions on the media are bound to affect the ambience of the public sphere. The Indian intelligentsia realised this as early as the beginning of the 19th century when Rammohan Roy, acclaimed as the father of modern India, publicly denounced the attempts of the British government to curb the freedom of the press. Following the lead set by Rammohan, freedom of expression and civil liberties became two key issues of the anti-colonial struggle.

In fact, the history of both the national movement and of the press can be read as the history of the struggle for these two rights. The legacy of this struggle has great contemporary value, as the freedom of the press and civil liberties continue to be under strain due to the restrictions imposed by the state. The recent action of the Tamil Nadu Government against, both in its nature and execution is perhaps the most glaring example. But violations of the freedom of expression are taking place in varying degrees all over the country, particularly against those scribes whose reports adversely affect the dominant forces in society or expose the initiatives of the state, which are not in the national interest.

Herbert Schiller, a theoretician of repute, has ascribed to the media the role of mind managers. Implicit in this description is the ideological function of the media in society. As such, multiple social consequences could ensue as a result of the intervention of the media. For instance, it could generate a sense of fatalism. It could also create nonconformism. The first relegates the media to the status of an adjunct of the dominant interests whereas the second provides them the possibility of influencing the course of history. There are several occasions in the life of a nation when the media are called upon to make a choice. In India such a situation arose in the 1990s when a massive, emotionally orchestrated religious mobilisation was attempted around the issue of the construction of a temple at Ayodhya.

The response of a large section of the media to this coercive and antidemocratic movement was ambivalent. Many chose to swim with the tide. In justification the editor of a reputed national newspaper advanced the rationale that the media are bound to reflect the sentiments of society. By doing so he was renouncing the leadership role of the media — of that of an intellectual, if you like — which the nationalist press had so admirably performed. It also relegated the media to the status of a helpless victim. The consequences were grievous and such a sense of fatalism led a section of the media uncritically to accept the communal discourse, and some others to remain as neutral observers and 'objective' reporters. The intellectual atmosphere thus generated by the media considerably contributed to the undermining of the secular and the success of the communal was among the few honourable exceptions who boldly and consistently championed the secular cause.

During the last two decades, the Indian media have undergone a sea change, particularly in their intellectual content and cultural ambience. There are two sources from which the transformation draws sustenance and inspiration: one emanating from outside and the other internally generated. The first, which seeks to subordinate the media to global control, comes with a variety of promises — of development, technology and internationalism — extremely appealing to the modernising quest of the middle class. The baggage also includes access to the advanced frontiers of knowledge and the cultural avant garde. The political and intellectual discourse, which it might generate, is likely to influence the nature and direction of social transformation. Whether it would lead to an intellectual climate in favour of a mode of development that may not address the problems of the nation is a fear entertained in many quarters. Even without actual control, the Indian mainstream media appear to have succumbed to the cultural imperatives of a developmental paradigm that leaves out the poor from its concerns.

Internally, the media confront a powerful communal discourse generated by a variety of political, social and cultural organisations. The media, at least a major section of them, have over the years internalised the logic to such an extent that it has become the instrument of its reproduction. If communal stereotypes like 'Muslim rule' and 'Hindu rule' or the 'fanaticism of the Muslims' have become part of the common sense, the public discourse created by the media, even if unconsciously by some, is to a large extent responsible. The communal categories are rampant in reporting and communal assumptions inform news analysis, even in newspapers that are otherwise secular. The colonial ideologue, James Mill, who characterised Indian society in terms of religious communities in conflict, still appears to exert influence on our minds.

Consequently, the secular space in the media has considerably shrunk. Not because of the secular-communal divide that indeed exists but more because the communal has succeeded in replacing the secular. The logic of the communal is increasingly becoming respectable in almost every newspaper establishment. The legitimacy thus gained by the communal, often through crude and false repre-sentations, helps to change the popular commonsense about key concepts like nationalism, secularism and communalism. This tendency has considerably impaired the fundamental commitment of the media to truth. The truth, however elusive it is, is not an avoidable luxury, as is believed at least by certain sections of the media, particularly the communal.

Despite these developments, the media are privy to an intense ideological struggle that Indian society is currently witnessing, between secularism on the one hand and communalism on the other. Secularism is the source of India's inclusive nationalism, based on historical experience and enriched by the anti-colonial struggle. Communalism, on the other hand, draws upon religious and cultural exclusivism and seeks to deny all that is meaningful in our tradition. While secularism stands for mutual respect, togetherness and enlightenment, communalism is characterised by intolerance, hatred and ignorance. The contradictions between the two have set the stage for contestation in the public sphere, either for its eventual secular reclamation or its communal transformation.

The struggle between secularism and communalism is not purely a fight for political power, but a clash between two different systems of values, both trying to bring the public sphere under their hegemonic control. The outcome to a large extent depends upon the manner in which the media intervene in the public space and mould its character. On it also depends whether the Republic will be able to preserve its foundational principles. Hence the importance of the media remains secular.

Being secular, however, does not mean being insensitive to tradition. In the past Indian intellectuals have invoked philosophical traditions like Vedanta to erase social divisions and appealed to universalism to bring about religious unity. Taking a leaf out of the past, the media can contribute to the ongoing efforts to halt the unfortunate tendency of communal appropriation of the past by adopting a critical but creative attitude towards tradition.

Over the years, the character of the public sphere in India has undergone a qualitative change. There is a discernible decline in the intellectual content of its transactions. Moreover, the culture of public discussion it promotes has lost much of its sanity and social purpose; the self rather than society seems to dominate in it. As a consequence, informed interventions by institutions like the media have become exceptions rather than the rule, in contrast to the era of the national movement when such interventions contributed to the emergence, evolution and vitality of the public sphere. The resulting intellectual poverty of the public sphere has made it vulnerable to the influence of forces seeking to undermine the fundamental principles that have molded the character of the nation. Although the media currently function under severe compulsions, both ideological and financial, a critical introspection is in order.

Expanding Media Market

The media industry produces peculiar commodities. At one level they are goods and services like any other. But they are also something more. By providing accounts of the contemporary world and images they play a pivotal role in shaping social consciousness. It is this 'special relationship' between economic and cultural power that has made the issue of their control a continuing focus of academic and political concern. The media are important in a situation where most of the citizens never meet their fellow citizens and the media serve as a kind of proxy. The media perform many functions. They provide a link to the larger society and in varying degrees a sense of connectedness and solidarity. They provide information and play a central role in working of democracies. They create what calls as 'public sphere' enabling discussion and debate on issues vital to the community. The public sphere is part of that space which is beyond the influence of systems such as economy, religion and the state.

Public sphere works most effectively for democracies when it is institutionally independent of the state and society's dominant economic forces. Though there are many other instruments of public sphere the media are the preeminent vehicles of communication through which the public participates in the political process. How effectively they participate determines how effectively a democracy works. If their performance is poor, people will be ignorant, isolated and depoliticised. As a result small elite will easily capture and maintain control over decision-making.

Although both government control and private media systems threaten the public sphere, the private media empires that have emerged in the recent times pose a greater threat to the public sphere than the state. The agenda setting hypothesis argues that ideas and images that mass media disseminate largely determine what citizens think about and the importance they give to the issues. A few corporations that dominate media market build up a dominant discourse and expand the 'spiral of silence' on issues critical to the people. They tend to present one side of an issue to the exclusion of others which further encourages those people to keep quiet. If various viewpoints on the issue are ignored, maginalised, or trivialized by media reports then people will be reluctant to talk about them. Instead of moving people to speak up the corporate media silence them. Concentration of ownership endangers plurality, diversity, risk taking and dissent. Privately owned media depend on advertising revenue and must therefore compete for advertisers' attention and serve advertiser interest to prosper.

This results in a preference for entertainment over controversy, serious political debate, and discussions and documentaries that dig deeply, inform, and challenge conventional opinion. The media keep audiences in a passive, non-critical state of mind. The last decade saw increased commercialisation of Indian media with the entry of multinational media corporations. Media ownership is getting concentrated in the hands of a few big conglomerates. Programme content is narrowing down to mere entertainment. Contrary to the claims of free-market advocates competition among the media hardly exists.

Given the small number of major media players, there is very little competition in the media industry and the major media companies use a variety of strategies to try to reduce the limited competition that does exist. Intercorporate investments and interlocking of directorships between media companies have been common. Increasing media monopoly in India has raised questions about the erosion of public space. The dominant economic forces are using the media to set their own agenda and to marginalise independent voices. Instead of providing voice to the voiceless the media operate as propaganda tools of the dominant economic and political forces. Dissenting voices are rarely heard. In fact, The Press Council of India, a body set up with the objective of safeguarding press freedom, has been advocating a system of cooperative ownership as an alternative ownership structure to ensure that media operate in public interest.

Media-Government Relations

Among the institutions that contribute to constructing a public sphere in society, the media perhaps performs the most critical function. In transactions in the public sphere, the media is not a neutral participant or an impassioned chronicler. More often than not, it either legitimizes the status quo or the change. And it does soon the basis of information accessed, processed and disseminated. The conflict or collaboration of the media with forces that attempt to control the public sphere materializes in this context. The media, therefore, works in a fragile environment and can be easily compromised, as in India, the largest functioning, or as some put it, "dysfunctional" democracy in the world.

Perhaps the most illustrative example of this conflict in India is the, till very recently, tightly controlled access to information. This is in the main due to the laws on the right to public information that combine legacies from the British colonial era with a more contemporary technocratic secrecy. First, it ensures that citizens make responsible, informed choices rather than act out of ignorance or misinformation. Second, information serves a "checking function" by ensuring that elected representatives uphold their oaths of office and carry out the wishes of those who elected them. It's a well-established principle in Indian jurisprudence that the media enjoys rights coterminous with the public.

This is quite unlike the situation in the United States, for example, where the First Amendment to the Constitution ensured that the "Press" enjoys rights that go beyond the public right to free speech. The US First Amendment prohibits the federal legislature from making laws that establish religion or prohibit free exercise of religion, laws that infringe the freedom of speech, infringe the freedom of the press, limit the right to assemble peaceably, or limit the right to petition the government for a redress of grievances. Thus, media freedom in India is derived from the right to free expression, which in turn is related to the public right to information.

"Nothing shall affect the operation of any existing law, or prevent the State from making any law, in so far as such law imposes reasonable restrictions on the exercise of the right conferred by the said subclause in the interests of the sovereignty and integrity of India, the security of the State, friendly relations with foreign States, public order, decency or morality, or in relation to contempt of court, defamation or incitement to an offence. And since a right of access to information can only be implied from the guarantee of freedom of speech and expression, the clauses just listed out worked as disabling clauses to this right, especially in their interpretation by government, most notably when rights were suspended during the declaration of "Emergency Rule" between 1975 and 1977.

The Threat of Defamation

A few words, on that journalistic bugbear when it comes to the dissemination of information accessed—defamation. Now the Indian Penal Code takes cognizance of defamation as a criminal offense, and criminal proceedings can be initiated against a newspaper, TV or radio channel if the complainant is able to satisfy a magistrate that a statement made about him/her was prime facie defamatory. Civil—or money—suits for defamation are also possible under Indian law wherein the individual or organization that files the suit must deposit 10 percent of the total damages claimed with the court before the suit is admitted. Two significant aspects of the defamation law impact on the media in its interface with government.

First, once a case of defamation is taken to trial, the matter is deemed sub-judice and cannot be commented upon. Second, where the person claiming to be defamed is the prime minister or the chief minister of a state (i.e. province), the public prosecutor can launch the prosecution; in other words, at the state's expense and presumably on behalf of the "people." There can be little doubt that the intention—in the real world of the Press in Asia despite country specific variables—behind government using the law on defamation against media is to use it in a debilitating way to create roadblocks in accessing and disseminating information. This is especially true when it comes to smaller media entities that may not always have the financial wherewithal to slug it out in court. But the whole issue of defamation is a tricky area; the devil, as always, is in the intentions. In theory, a law on defamation is an essential tool in curbing malicious and concocted stories or even plain lies.

Especially, from those working for a selfserving agenda that plainly falls outside the public interest paradigm. And often it's the only tool for individuals to protect their professional and personal reputations. Yet governments have been known to use defamation to harass media organizations, often with malice aforethought. Perhaps that's where there is work to be done—in discussing and then making a distinction, in law, between the right of an individual to pursue a case of defamation and the propensity of government to use defamation as a tool to harass media.

Two obvious criticisms of such a suggestion would be: (a) implicit in this suggested decoupling of an individual's right to sue for defamation and a government or its functionaries' right to do the same against a media organization it feels hard done by is an appeal for the Press to be accorded some sort of "special status"; and (b) it is unworkable because it would be bad in law as it goes against the principle of natural justice. But a solution has to be found given the realities of the day. Unlike, say, in Singapore, where the allegation is that defamation has been used as a tool by the influential to bring newspapers to heel and thereby restrict the flow of information, in India defamation does not impact on that scale. At least not on the larger, mainstream media entities because, in the main, it takes years, if not decades for a court verdict.

Islamism in Popular Media

A good deal of literature, before and since the publication of Edward Said's *Orientalism* and then *Covering Islam*, has taught us the myriad ways in which Islam has been represented negatively in the West. But long before the spectacular and specular violence of the exploding World Trade Center in New York City, many countries in the Arab Middle East had within their midst Islamist political groups that were oppositional to the regimes in power. In Egypt during the 1980s and 90s, for example, there was a sharp sense in elite circles and a widespread discourse disseminated through popular media that the nation was in danger of being torn apart from within.

The state was portrayed as facing a political-cultural crisis, one that it dealt with mostly by force—through arrests, executions, and the arbitrary powers of a continually renewed state of emergency. The problem was represented publicly as religious extremism. The villains were the members of Islamic groups. In the early 1990s I embarked on an ethnographic project to understand television's place in the Egyptian national imagination and in the everyday lives of people who are somewhat marginal to the nation— people who are neither middle class nor urban. I focused on the most popular genre of television programming, one for which Egypt is justly famous across the Arab world: the dramatic serial.

Unlike soap operas, Egyptian serials are finite, consisting of 15 or 30 episodes, shown on consecutive evenings. And, because until well into the 1990s there were only a few television channels and first-run serials aired on only two of them, they were watched by a majority of the population and were often the subject of discussion in homes, and in the public sphere—in newspapers, magazines, and elsewhere. I was intrigued to find that television serials were often the vehicles for national debate. One of the big debates that television became part of in the mid-1990s was about what was called "extremism" or even "terrorism." Television drama in Egypt in the 1990s reflected, if unevenly and with certain lags concerns about the place of religion in society and nation.

In keeping with its self-consciously pedagogical mission, it condemned, preached, and offered alternative models for the future. Accordingly, this research raised questions such as: Were television serials effective in their missions of smoothing over the divisions that, in the name of religion, threatened the Egyptian national body? Did media management of religion help create national community? Did mass media participate in the configuration and reconfiguration of "religion" and "nation" in Egypt? How did media representations of Islamic groups and "terrorists" operate in a Muslim majority context where, unlike in the West, the civilizational discourse of West and East could not be mobilized, Islamists or terrorists could only partially be represented as an outside enemy, and Islam could never be the alien other?

Good and Bad Islam

Beginning in the late 1970s the rising visibility on the streets of Cairo and provincial cities and towns of a self-conscious Islamic identity represented a phenomenon that was noticeable to everyone and troubling to some. The movement ranged from increased piety among educated youth to some more sensational acts of violence committed by militant Islamic groups. The broad piety movement and the wide widespread feeling against cordoning off religion as a private matter of faith led television to capitulate to the desire for more religious programming and to try to appropriate for itself the role of supporter of a legitimate Islam. In 1994, just after a new policy of confronting terrorism with media was announced, the serial *The Family* (*al- A'ila*), was produced to great fanfare, and some controversy.

Written by Wahid Hamid, it showed, in its assessment by critics, how educated youth from disadvantaged backgrounds were drawn into terrorism, and how corruption was rife in these groups. Public opposition to the serial, not surprisingly, came from wellestablished moderate Islamist thinkers. In their jockeying in the press, both the moderate Islamist thinkers and government and television officials tried to align themselves with the religious authorities of al-Azhar. The Islamists stressed the number of letters and phone calls al-Azhar had received, urging them to take action to get the serial off the air. Controversy over a scene in which the enlightened modernist protagonist challenged the extremist on the doctrinal basis of certain beliefs had led to calls to halt broadcast of the serial.

The Mufti, the leading government religious authority, used the press to clarify doctrine and offer a set of phone numbers for the public to use if they had questions about religious matters. The Minister of Information, however, speaking about a television broadcast that followed the serial (a documentary in which Islamist prisoners spoke about the error of their ways), responded with a statement that points to the heart of the official construction of religion. He said, "[T]here are repenters who speak with remorse and ... discuss how it was that they came to ...lose their faith in those erroneous ideas that led them to commit deviant terrorist activities..."

Serials like *The Family* contrast the good, correct, and reasonable Islam of the people, the cultured and educated, al-

Azhar, the state, and television with that of the bad, violent, misinformed, and twisted Islam of the extremists. Many television writers claim to be secularists—that is, to believe in a separation between personal piety and the state, a legacy of their intellectual and political formation in the Nasserist period of the 1950s and 1960s that pushed secular ideals. Yet, despite the objections of such prominent television personnel and their own relative silence on religion in their serials, Egyptian television continued to increase religious programming in the 1990s, adding to the popular shows featuring Quranic exegeses by religious authorities big budget serials about the history of the Arab-Islamic world.

These were broadcast alongside many more serials with plots or subplots about violent militants and serials explicitly about terrorism. There was good Islam and bad Islam and these judgments were made, ultimately, on the basis of how Islam related to the nation and social responsibility. They were not, as they might have been in the past, part of the struggle among religious authorities. For more than half a century, revenge killing, or the vendetta, has been in the national imagination the cultural trait most associated with Upper Egypt. The obsession of northern, urban, educated people with the horrors of honour feuds and their condemnation of Upper Egyptians as backward and unenlightened can be found everywhere, from film to social science.

Without denying the existence or importance of this practice to communities in the region, one must still be suspicious whenever a cultural trait is singled out and made to stand for a whole region or community and one must be even more suspicious when such a region is mapped as a place of new forms of violence: in the 1980s and 1990s Upper Egypt was linked to religious extremism. However, a major shift occurred in the second half of the 1990s in television representations of Upper Egypt. The most popular of the serials to represent Upper Egypt balanced the theme of revenge with that of authentic values such as honour and integrity. The recent spate of serials set in Upper Egypt that depict positive qualities of the region are mostly the work of one writer, himself originally from Upper Egypt. Although based in Alexandria, Muhammad Safa' 'Amir makes much of the fact that he was born in an Upper Egyptian town not far from Luxor.

Even those from the south single out his work as not stereotyping them negatively, describing his serials as realistic because they focus on their "true" characteristics: generosity, courage, honesty, and valour. What these serials suggest is that Upper Egyptians are part of the nation; they do not live in a closed society and do not constitute a backward or frightening "other." The most important message is that they are by no means all religious extremists. Upper Egyptians, on the other hand, are being told through the serials that they have within their own traditions important values worth preserving and nurturing, values that are social, cultural, and regional, not particularly tied to religion. In other words, their true identities are not as Islamists but rather as people with an indigenous regional nobility and code of honour. The attempts of the media to promote a culture stripped of religion may be even less healing of the torn civic body than its attempts to turn religion into a cultural system linked to the nation. This is because it bears little resemblance to local experiences. But insofar as regional values are offered as cultural ideals, the serials invoke a national frame, since regions are primarily defined by national territory. Upper Egypt only has meaning as a distinct region if understood as part of a larger Egyptian nation. And so again, the serials offer support for a united nation and a placing of religion within that nation.

Media Violence

Over the last quarter century, while some industries polluted our air, water, and food, the entertainment industry increasingly poisoned children's cultural environment with violence carried by television programs, video games, and movies. While society has agreed to regulate the pollution of air, food, and water, governments have been unable to regulate the use of violence in entertainment products for children. The increasing power of the media on public opinion has inspired such fear on decision makers that when having to choose between children's rights and accusation of censorship, none dare to put their political party at risk. This lack of moral fortitude has left the media free to decide what our children will watch, what values will be pushed down their throats, and what cruelty will be used to feed their fantasies. George Gerbner used to call the big media the Secret Ministers of Global Culture.

The executives of a handful of big media conglomerates think they own the freedom of the press and that it is their privilege to decide alone what will be aired to children on the global market, "with little to tell but a lot to sell." After witnessing the increased amount of violence carried by entertainment products for children, more citizens ask why they should let children be abused by the media. Not all TV and other entertainment programs are toxic for children; some informative and even inspiring programs provide positive stimulation and help children and teens to understand the world. In fact, though, an increasing number of programs and movies do exactly the opposite. As a result, parents and teachers have searched for, lobbied, petitioned, requested, and finally created ways to protect children against mental manipulation and emotional desensitization. Fortunately, some of these efforts have allowed discoveries to help reduce the impact of pollution on the cultural environment of young people.

Influence of Toxic Culture

Since the 1977 LaMarsh Commission Report—where the analogy to environmental contamination was first drawn in Canada—well over one thousand studies have routinely confirmed that violent entertainment influences children. In 1995, University of Winnipeg researcher Wendy Josephson, author of *Television Violence: A Review of the Effects on Children of Different Ages*, found more than 650 studies linking real-life violence by children to violence watched on TV. In 2001, the

Media Awareness Network found that "only 4% of violent programs have a strong antiviolence theme [and] only 13% of reality programs that depict violence present any alternatives to violence or show how it can be avoided." University of Washington epidemiologist Brandon Centerwall estimated that TV violence could account for 50% of real-life violence. Violent entertainment has three kinds of influence on children, depending on their age, how much they watch, and whether they watch alone, with adults, or with peers.

Research has revealed that children mimic TV violence because they perceive it as approval for hitting, bullying, and humiliating their peers. It also encourages between 5% and 10% of victims to accept the treatment they suffer without seeking help. Finally, it reduces empathy in the witnesses, who then prefer ganging with the aggressor instead of helping the victim. With increasing exposure to violence in entertainment, children become mentally altered and physically inclined to commit, accept, or enjoy watching real-life violence.

World Congress

The world congress on "Media and Religion: Risk or Opportunity?" held at Sherbrooke in Canada provided great insights into the way the media deals with religion, especially in Canada as well as in other parts of the world. The keynote speakers explored the impact of new media technologies on the way news and events are presented, perceived and judged by people worldwide. On the one hand, it is true that the media and religious landscapes are being totally reshaped by endless possibilities, but on the other hand, less and less freedom and more and more financial constraints do not allow the provision of complete backgrounds and comprehensive information on events. Though it is theoretically possible to access all news at any time anywhere in the world, technological shortcomings, the limitations of search engines and difficulties in assessing the truth of the content, hamper many people worldwide from obtaining even vital information. Some of the congress resource persons were of the opinion that though a huge amount of information on practically anything is stored somewhere on the worldwide web, there is a great lack of information diffused or made available to the general public.

Traditional media, especially print, still plays a major role in democratizing information and getting it to out to most people, without incurring major financial, technological, political, religious, social and other constraints. Another major aspect of the theme analysed during the congress was the way in which religion is interpreted, made to be understood, propagated and even fabricated by the media worldwide. The congress found that more and more people worldwide especially in developed nations understand religion through the media rather than through childhood education or the practice of a religious faith. Thus for many, religions are a source of conflict, scandal and sects rather than inspiration, guidance or a reference for everyday life and decision-making. The resource persons also stressed the necessity of respecting the sensibility of all religious groups worldwide, while making reports or covering events. This requires one to go beyond one's own religion-based attachment and emotions.

Many of today's conflicts have originated from a lack of respect for people's sensibilities, aspirations and expectations. The congress also studied the ethical and moral challenges of the media in the new era of globalisation where there is a growing tendency to avoid discussions or debates on the fundamentals. In a superficially globalised world, information on religion, religious ideas, convictions and practices are often inadequately or defectively propagated through all types of media. In this diffusion of religious content, the aim is not always the betterment of humanity at large, but the vested interests of media owners who are still a very small but highly powerful group. All the keynote speeches of the congress will be published online in the coming months.

Cultural Perspectives on Media and Christianity

Belief in the Media is an intriguing journey into the realm of religion and the media (both broadly construed). The edited volume developed from the International Study Commission on Media, Religion, and Culture, and all but one contributor, Jin Kyu Park, were core members of this seven-year commission. The contributors hoped that this volume would provide a new perspective on the study of religion and the media, which would challenge the existing paradigm that focuses on how institutional religion deploys media technology. Rather, the contributors seek to move from an institutional frame to a frame that embraces cultural studies, the importance of lived praxis, and an emphasis on individuals. The work, however, primarily focuses on Christian traditions and their relationships with media.

Moreover, the contributors represent a wide array of experience with media and religion from theologians to producers to art historians to former journalists. Thus, the essays sometimes feel a bit uneven in their coverage of the subject matter. The volume is broken down into four parts: the cultural perspective, mediated Christianity, media culture and Christian institutions, and an overview of the field of religion and media. In his introduction to the volume, Editor Peter Horsfield explores the importance of media in religious and social changes beginning with the importance of printing for the Reformation. More importantly, Horsfield examines the desire for the reenchantment of the world in the twentieth (and now twenty-first) centuries. Media have been essential to the desire for reenchantment.

Horsfield writes, "Media have become the practical marketplace where individuals gather, converse, gain information, communalize their concerns, and build identity and worldviews" (xix). Additionally, Horsfield lays out the issues that concerned the commission: how have media replaced religion? What is the relationship between religious authority and symbolic practice? What constitutes the relationship between religion and media? Do new understandings of this relationship require new epistemology? What is abundantly clear from Horsfield's introduction and the following essays is the need to move away from institutional understandings of the media as a tool. Media should be understood more culturally than institutionally. The first part of the volume, "The Cultural

Perspective," provides the theoretical framework to move beyond institutional models.

This cultural frame focuses on meaning-making in media and in religion and emphasizes practice. In her "Reconceptualising Religion and Media in a Post-National, Postmodern World," Lynn Schofield Clark provides a thorough and useful introduction to the study of religion and media and the challenges scholars face today. The other articles in the section from Horsfield, Robert S. Goizueta, and Juan Carlos Henríquez reflect on the importance of media and their relationship to theology. In "Because God is Near, God is Real," Goizueta explores the use of media in both medieval Christianity and Latino Catholicism in which media become loci of religious revelation. In the second part of the volume, "Mediated Christianity," the contributors present case studies of religion and media, including J. Kwabena Asamoah-Gyadu's work on Pentecostals in Sub-Saharan Africa, Germán Rey's examination of Latin American telenovas, David Morgan's study of icons and images in Ethiopian Protestantism, Jolyon Mitchell's discussion of horror films in West Africa, and Stewart M. Hoover and Jin Kyu Park's research on religion and the internet.

This is the strongest section of the work because it demonstrates the interplay of religion and media the most clearly. Each of the case studies is a compelling testament to the cultural studies approach that the volume prefers. For instance, Jolyon Mitchell explores the popularity of horror films in West Africa, showing that the horror films are actually morality tales that bolster Christianity while degrading indigenous African religions. Additionally, David Morgan explores the ambivalence toward icons in Ethiopian Protestantism by demonstrating that certain icons might be unwelcome but others are embraced. The third part, "Media Culture and Christian Institutions," explores the impact of media on Christian institutions. This part, of course, drives home the message that institutions can no longer view media as simply tools for institutional messages; rather, the fluidity of media must be taken into account.

Mary Hess examines the importance of popular culture and how Christian institutions might adapt to it. Both Adán Medrano and Siriwan Santisakultarm reflect on the use of media in their religious backgrounds, Latino and Thai Catholicism, respectively. Medrano's "Making Religious Media" demonstrates the difficulty of creating religious television programming, which resonates both with the institutional message and the lives of adherents. In "Changes in the Thai Catholic Way of Life," Santisakultarm traces the changing media that dominated Thai Catholic life from oral culture to the purported loss of religious communication with modernization. The final essay in this part explores the U.S. Catholic Church sexual abuse scandal, and Frances Forde Plude suggests that, with this scandal, it becomes clear that the Church and the news media have different and often contrasting views of media.

She, like Hess, argues that religious institutions should adapt to these new understandings of media and begin to accept the importance of media as communication. This section might be best put to use by religious practitioners hoping to adapt their institutions to our global media culture. The final part is an overview of the study of religion, media and culture. Robert A. White emphasizes the basic theme of the work: studies of religion and media need to move away from institutional emphases to a more cultural framework. White's essay is the clearest articulations of the importance of the cultural framework to present the importance of social actors who are affected by historical forces but also create cultural meaning. White describes how media are often used by individuals to create religious identity, and how media foster religious systems, and how important the popular media are, among other themes.

Moreover, White believes that this book would argue that the religious and the popular are sites where we are building our cultures, including our religious cultures. We need to ask what kind of culture we are creating in these experiences, whether these are the kinds of cultures we want to create, and who is involved in the creation process." In the New Era of Religious Communication, Pierre Babin offers a striking contrast of world-views which helps to indicate the potential which TV and other media may have to affect our religiousness.

To begin with Babin introduces us to the practice among some Indian tribes living in the Canadian wilderness, of plugging their children's nostrils and covering their eyes after birth, the better to atune them to the noises of the forest in which they will have to survive. Then, in stark contrast to these 'hyperauditory' individuals, made alert to the subtlest natural sounds, Babin invites us to consider the modern American adolescent, reared amidst the clamour of competing mass media (such an individual will have logged some 20,000 hours of viewing by the age of sixteen). Is it possible that individuals with such different degrees of media exposure would have similar ideas about God and the transcendent? Could their sense of the holy be thought to follow even remotely similar contours?"

"Religion and Media" is a vast theme. References mainly will focus on television which has come to be the dominant medium. At the same time religion is spoken of in a very broad sense, which includes a feeling of transcendence, a cosmovision, an ethical evaluation, an emotive element and a certain personal commitment.

Society and Media

There are at least three considerations to take into account in dealing with the theme. First of all the pluralist character of modern society. Social mobility and geography give rise to conglomerates of cultural, ethnic and religious diversity. This happened in several countries in Europe, which mostly after WW II opened their borders to receive immigrants from Eastern European countries and from some Asian countries because they were short of labour. This plurality is closely related to a secularist development that need not necessarily be understood in a negative way. As David Bosch reminds us: "One now distinguished carefully between 'secularism' one rejected and 'secularization' which one welcomed and propagated." In other words, the world has reached a certain point of autonomy - human beings have now come of age [D. Bonhoeffer] - which affects, for example, the religious sphere. Thus, its relationship with the churches has become more critical, less submissive, and more individualist.

The influence of the Enlightenment, which among other things proclaimed that everyone was an autonomous individual, has an immediate effect on Christianity and on Protestantism in particular. The church lost its central role, the individual had the right and the ability to know God's will, and the individual could decide what to believe. Second, the place of media in modern societies. The source of information and value training is more and more often the media. A wellknown theologian used to say that we have to read the Bible and the newspaper together. But what newspaper? Which newspapers tell the truth, bring the information of what really is happening in the world? Who decides what the news and its contents are to be?

The process of privatising the media offers a particular model of communication that, undoubtedly, will affect all religious expressions, in public service the supreme criterion is the presence of society and its institutions and respect for religious and cultural traditions. In private service the objective is to reach the largest audience in order to obtain the greatest profit. What chance do we have of knowing ourselves and others' problems, needs and dreams, if our voices and theirs are forced to pass through filters that hold back all that affects the interests of the owners of the media? Today these filters are located in a handful of large centers that dominate the information and communication in our world.

Third, the nature of the media. The audio-visual media (cinema, television, etc.) populate their hours with an immense number of people in an endless attempt to excite our senses. Very deep areas of the human being are reached by the senses. The media invade our privacy, and we still do not know the effects that such a multiplicity of stimuli has on us. Religion and affectivity are closely related and all religious expression in the media is stamped by its affective impact. The mass media have shown signs of producing, above all, the destruction of the human being. The fragmentation of the image, of information, the manipulation involved in 'montage', creates a kind of partial 'truth', which prevents authentic communication. Mina Ramirez, a sociologist from the Philippines, reminds us: "The most subtle form of dominance is that of the mind. The most detestable sort of dependence is not material but spiritual: people have lost the power to think critically for themselves. The moment people lose this power, they are not able to communicate. They can only ape."

From Uncritical Acceptance to Total Resection

The attitudes of people of religion towards the media are extremely varied from uncritical acceptance to total rejection of media's presence in the life of society. The advent of the mass media was well received by the churches, although they expressed certain fears. For this reason, firstly, they tried to reduce the media to being instruments at their service. Secondly, they considered themselves the only ones fit to teach their correct use. Thirdly, they had a marked distrust of the audience, which had to be protected, directed and controlled. Generally, paternalism leads to domestication. Today, the biggest criticism levelled by people of religion is that media are usurping religion's place in society. That is to give shape to a value system and to express the essence of a culture. For some people, for example, television has come to be a kind of religion. As if its secret role were to tell us how the world- ip, how it works and what it means.

Therefore they think that the technological cosmovision offers at least three threats to religion. Firstly, it is derailing the greater part of interests, motivations, satisfactions and energies that are the purpose of religion. Religious people have feared the media especially because the media threaten traditional religious values and beliefs. They see how, as one result, the churches are emptying. Secondly, religious language is being appropriated. New symbols, images and rites are being created. "The mass media - especially television - have taken command of the power of myth... One role of myth is to situate us, to define the world and our place in it." Thirdly, religious themes that have no connection with organised religion are being developed. This is welcomed by some independent evangelistic groups shaped by a remarkably uncritical faith in the media.

Religion and Media: Three Responses

What can we say about the use of mass media for religious ends? There are multiple replies, but here are at least three. First, Malcom Muggeridge, a veteran English communicator with a long career in the world of radio and television, thought that one should do without television because it is a medium that traffics in fantasy that creates images and ideas that are not true and does not have and cannot have any relationship with truth. For him, the medium is an autonomous element capable of creating its own dynamic and, therefore, its own communication structure. Yet faith can be lived, received and shared outside society's structure and, so, the media are not only unnecessary but harmful. Muggeridge saw using mass media as a "fourth temptation" which Jesus would have rejected because in reality "this medium, because of its very nature, does not lend itself to constructive purposes."

On the contrary, media "are giving to Christian society something which is dangerously destructive." This position is based on a conception of faiths considered as timeless in order to maintain its purity and integrity. Without overlooking the manipulative and deceptive purposes of the mass media, it should not be forgotten that this same temporal concept is used by those who make use of the fantasy of the media to communicate very effectively the fantasy of their own "gospel". Second, according to Neil Postman, any religious celebration in the media requires an environment invested with certain sacrality. To do this certain rules of behaviour are needed which are denied by the circumstances in which a religious programme is watched. People eat or talk or distract themselves with other activities and the way of behaving required by the religious celebration is lacking.

But there is more - for Postman, the screen is saturated with profane happenings, associated with the world of commercialism and entertainment. In a way it supposes that religion can be successful on television only if it offers what people want, which presumes the trivialisation and emptying out of content. In this respect, we should accept a certain kind of warning against mass media because their manipulative intentions are more obvious. But this complex reality must not lead us to believe that a retreat to more traditional forms will simply provide us with the possibility of avoiding all contamination in communication. Has the Christian community always been unpolluted? Since when have only angels preached from pulpits?

Third, Giorgio Giradet, an Italian Waldensian pastor, believes that one can find an alternative to extreme positions like the total rejection of Muggeridge, or the marked optimism he finds in the "electronic church" and in Pope John Paul 11. For him, that alternative has to take five things into account: (a) the importance of the media in a context that includes technical, financial, political and cultural aspects; (b) that using an electronic medium, like it or not, is a political act; (c) doing everything possible not to isolate the medium from reality; (d) preventing technical questions from alienating the medium from reality (problems of quality, montage, etc.); (e) encouraging public participation, forestalling passivity.

He concludes: "The struggle for and insistence on possible and sensible use of the media of mass communication centers in the end on reflection about the church." We have to accept that in our world today mass media are more and more becoming the most important source of information and entertainment for us. We also need to recognise that they can play a significant role in encouraging participation in the search for a more just and peaceful world. We live in a pluralist society in which the relationship of people to organised religion has been weakened. And yet spiritual needs appear more evident. Is it possible and desirable to use the media as new channels for manifestations of the spirit? No simple answer can be given to this question.

Many different considerations have to be taken into account: media ownership, legislation, professional rivalry, economic interests, social and cultural mores, the media as supermarket of religion, guidelines for commercial advertising as a communication criterion and many more. What must not be forgotten is that communication is not offered to mass audiences. People receive, select and interpret the messages sent to them from their own social and cultural viewpoints and, on the basis of that interpretation, draw their own conclusions. For this reason, a genuine encounter between media and religion carries with it an attitude of respect for the dignity of people.

Religion played a much more significant role in the media coverage of President-elect Barack Obama than it did in the press treatment of Republican nominee John McCain during the 2008 presidential campaign, but much of the coverage related to false yet persistent rumors that Obama is a Muslim. Meanwhile, there was little attempt by the news media during the campaign to compre-hensively examine the role of faith in the political values and policies of the candidates, save for those of Republican vice presidential nominee Sarah Palin. And when religion-focused campaign stories were covered by the mainstream press, often the context was negative, controversial or focused on a perceived political problem.

In all, religion was a significant but not overriding storyline in the media coverage of the 2008 campaign. But in a campaign in which an Obama victory would give the U.S. its first black president, religion received as much coverage in the media as race. These are some of the findings of a new study of the coverage of religion in the campaign conducted by the Pew Research Center's Project for Excellence in Journalism and Pew Forum on Religion & Public Life. The study examined religion-focused election coverage in 48 different news outlets between June 1 and Oct. 15, 2008.

The "culture war" issues that have been prominent in past elections, such as abortion and gay marriage, received minimal attention in 2008. The coverage they did receive tended to come in the form of reaction to statements by the candidates and quickly receded without generating any sustained narrative. When Palin was introduced to the nation as McCain's running mate, her parenting choices raised the issue of abortion, but only momentarily. In one of the more episodic narratives – evangelical mega church pastor Rick Warren's presidential forum held at his church – the candidates' answers on a question about abortion gained attention in the press the week of the event. But the religious electorate – including evangelical voters – received relatively scant attention from the press during the general election, despite the Obama campaigns aggressive outreach efforts and the subsequent gains made among these religious groups on Election Day.

Among the Key Findings:

- Press narratives tied to religion accounted for 4% of the general election campaign's "newshole" – the time or space available in an outlet for news content. While this was less than coverage of the Iraq war (6%) or the economic crisis (9%), it was more prominent than coverage of energy issues (2%) and the environment (less than 1%), and equal to coverage of the Republican National Convention (4%). During the general election, storylines related to religion received as much attention by the press as those that focused on race (4%).
- Far more of the religion storylines involved Obama, and most of these involved controversy or had an unfavourable cast. In all, Obama was the lead news-maker in more than half (53%) of the religion-focused campaign stories. By contrast, McCain was the focus of just 9%. Palin (19%) was more tied to religion than her running mate, though less so than Obama. Examination of Palin's family values, church background and related issues made up one-fourth of the newshole devoted to religion in the campaign.
- The single biggest religion storyline in the general election phase of the campaign centered on rumors that the Democratic nominee, who is a mainline Protestant Christian, is a Muslim (30%). An additional 5% of the

religion-focused coverage dealt with evangelical broadcaster James Dobson's criticism of Obama's positions. But despite the largely negative focus of the Obama religion coverage, a Pew Forum analysis of exit polls shows nearly every religious group measured supported him in greater numbers than they supported Democratic nominee John Kerry four years ago.

- The notion of "pastor problems," or candidates' associations with controversial religious figures, was a clear narrative in campaign coverage. All four candidates faced coverage focusing on religious figures. Attention to clerics Jeremiah Wright, Michael Pfleger and John Hagee alone made up 11% of religion coverage in the general election. A feature of much of this coverage was replaying of the inflammatory recorded words and video images of these ministers. Circulated on cable news, talk radio and the Internet, these recordings were used to scrutinize the candidates' judgment in associating with such figures.
- The Aug. 16 Saddleback Civil Forum on the Presidency, moderated by Warren at his California megachurch, drew brief but intense media coverage. It made up 10% of all campaign coverage the week it occurred but quickly dropped to 5% the following week. By the end of August, it was no longer a major press topic at all. Still, that was enough to have that one event account for 11% of religion-focused campaign coverage in the general election.
- Culture war issues were not a driving narrative of this election cycle. The extent to which they were present, they emerged late in the campaign and were largely tied to the nomination of Palin. Together, social issues - including abortion, gay marriage and stem cell research —composed 9% of religion-focused campaign news but less than 1% of campaign news overall.

3

Religion in the Public Sphere

Conflicts about the public presence of religion are not confined to Western societies, but occur in many settings across the world in which the modern secular state has been taken as the norm, as for instance in Turkey or India. At stake here is the set up of the modern public sphere as a secular environment, in which religion is subordinate to the state and regarded as a private matter. Around the globe, this modern idea about the public sphere is contested by the articulate manifestation of religious groups and individuals, many of which, paradoxically, are able to voice their concerns due to processes of democratisation, media liberalisation and religious freedom.

Far from featuring as the norm, in the context of religious pluralism, secular positions are up against religious ones. This often means that conflicts about public religion are framed in terms of opposition between 'freedom of expression' and 'freedom of religion'. This part of the research programme invites comparative research that investigates struggles resulting from the public presence of religion by combining detailed empirical studies of all parties involved, the genesis and antecedents of such conflicts in a historical perspective as well as reflecting on the ways in which these conflicts are being framed. The following issues may be of particular interest in research on conflicts evolving around the public presence of religion.

One concerns the articulation of religious identities via dress styles and body techniques. In many settings, the wearing of a headscarf, niqab, or burka in public spaces is subject to heated debate, as are issues such as the question of (female) circumcision. By contrast, religiously grounded resistance to immunisation against particular diseases (as is the case in some areas in the so-called Dutch Bible belt), albeit less contested today, may also be subject to misgivings from a secular perspective.

Often, critiques of the practices mentioned are articulated via discourses that mobilise modern norms and values, such as female emancipation, education, hygiene or health. Discarding such practices as outmoded places them in a temporary scheme that opposes religion and modernity in terms of backwardness and enlightenment. And yet, for the people concerned, wearing a particular kind of religious dress or engaging in certain bodily techniques usually forms the bedrock of a—often newly found—religious identity. A second issue concerns the presence of religious buildings in public space.

With the rise of religiously and culturally plural populations, many societies witness severe conflicts about the construction and location of mosques and other purposely built religious constructions and the soundscapes associated with them. Examples concern not only struggles about mosques in Western societies, but also conflicts about the establishment of churches near traditional holy spaces, as is the case in many parts of, for instance, Africa, where Pentecostal-charismatic churches engage in a 'spiritual war' against indigenous religious traditions. Religious structures, it appears, seem to evoke a strong sense of presence by their sheer materiality that, in turn, accentuates their symbolic value.

For this reason, such structures may be hailed by religious practitioners for asserting their identity and, for the same reasons, being fiercely contested by opponents. A third issue concerns contests leveled from a religious position against mainstream secular practices and opinions. Examples are the rejection of homosexual marriage on the ground of a religious (Christian, Muslim or Jewish) conviction, campaigns against cursing and against allegedly indecent advertisements on TV or in public spaces (such as the recent protest on the part of the Dutch political party, the Christian Union, against a billboard showing a sparsely dressed woman advertising lingerie) and blasphemy. Concerning the issue of blasphemy, we should not only think about the worldwide protests against the publication of Rushdie's Satanic Verses and the recent upheaval around the so-called Muhammad cartoons published in Jylland's Posten, but also about campaigns, made in the name of Christianity, against allegedly offensive popular art, such as Madonna's crucifixion tour.

This part of the programme invites research that investigates the different positions that are being mobilised in conflicts about the public presence of religion from insiders' perspectives, as well as the representation of religion in public outlets (including newspapers, songs, adverts and films). A comparative perspective that is able to unravel similarities between different manifestations of religious assertiveness launched from the standpoint of different religious traditions is pertinent. How do personal affairs, grounded as they are on a religious or secular conviction, become heavily debated, public issues?

What is so vexing about certain religious practices regarding modes of dress and bodily techniques, and the presence of religious buildings from a secular perspective, whereas they appear as inalienable elements of religious and personal identity from the perspective of believers? Conversely, why are certain instances of secular modernity so much critiqued from religious standpoints? How are both religious and secular positions framed in relation to each other? How to balance 'freedom of religion' and 'freedom of expression' in religiously plural, multicultural societies? And, most importantly, what can a detailed investigation of the positions of all sides involved contribute to a better understanding of underlying causes and conflict resolution?

Religion in a National Public Sphere

Recent work on Islamism and the history of Muslim reform in Egypt reminds us that mass media, from the press that flourished in the late nineteenth century to the television of the late twentieth century, is part of a distinct public sphere in which public intellectuals could debate and discuss norms, policies, and the future of the community and civilization. Scholars have been concerned about what the outlines of this public sphere are and how the changing terms of debate and discussion are set. The Egyptian intelligentsia who produce television, film, theatre, and literature must be understood as having a certain independence from the state and labouring to a large extent in their own cultural fields.

Yet there are significant points of collaboration and convergence between intellectuals and the state today. Nasserism had contributed to the doctrine of a demarcation of separate spheres of religion and state, even if Islamic ideals were never completely purged from morality, pious practices continued in all classes, and various accommodations were forged between state and religious institutions. What seems to be one of the outcomes of the debates in which television programs of the 1990s participated, is that religion has become once more an ideological hub of the public sphere, but now with a certain form of the modern nation-state so entrenched and established that "the nation," and what is good for the nation, forms the only legitimate ground for debates about religion.

This is even so when viewers explicitly disagree with or criticize the representations of Islamists, or religiosity, that they watch. The airing of these serials ends up, in a variety of ways, revealing and exacerbating social cleavages, perhaps undermining the government's and some secular intellectuals' intentions of creating national community by trying to discredit Islamists. This is mostly because television's enthusiasm for circumscribing religious sensibilities in its serials rubs up against widespread convictions. However, one should not infer from these failures that television does not foster national community through its treatments of religious extremism. It does so indirectly, though, by appropriating for itself the role of a charged and popular arena for public discussion of and debate about Islam.

The arena is national and in this way contributes to an ongoing sense of the nation as the critical frame for all aspects of life, including the religious. Even Egyptian television's negative stereotyping of Islamists, however accepted or refused by the public, operates within and reinforces the frame of the nation. It never places the Muslim outside the frame; instead it makes and sustains distinctions between good and bad Muslims. It also reflects on what place religious identity and observance should have in daily life and asks what role Islam should have in society at large. Even though some of the negative imagery used to represent Islamists in Egyptian television may be eerily similar to that which is becoming numbingly familiar in the West, the contexts of reception and the import of this imagery give it a fundamentally different meaning.

Mediated Religion and Rights Claims

At one level, this essay on religious broadcasting in South Africa addresses the heightened relevance of the media sphere in today's global network society for the identity and survival of religious collectivities. But it is perhaps more concerned with the growing significance of the local and global media in shaping attitudes of religious tolerance or intolerance, and in managing religious diversity. Recent scholarship on religious discrimination and persecution more generally demonstrates the particular vulnerability of new religious movements and minority religious groups in this respect.

In fact British legal scholar Malcolm Evans goes so far as to claim that "the origins of contemporary forms of human rights protection flow from attempts to protect the religious freedoms of certain identified and vulnerable religious communities". Hent de Vries frames these interconnections well when he argues that "the relationship between religion and media sheds light on the question of how cultural identity and difference are constituted, as well as on how they relate to the aims of socio-political integration".

Because of its paradoxical universalizing and particularizing tendencies "religion... forms the condition of possibility and impossibility for the political." Rightly chiding Casanova for his neglect of the media sphere, he suggests that "the mediatized return of the religious" illustrates "an increasingly complicated negotiation between the private and public spheres". This accounts for some of the new forms of regulation of expression of religious communities being developed by both state and non-state actors. Studies of Africa's rapidly expanding and diversifying media sector, notably of the cultural and religious dimensions of media production, distribution, reception, and consumption, are growing apace. However, insufficient attention has been paid to the ways in which media institutions and representations may constitute an important site of conflict between religions and the state, and among religious groups.

So recognizing with Debra Spitulnik that "the mass media are extremely potent areas of political struggle" the present essay examines the case of South Africa and the various negotiations—at times acrimonious—over public religious broadcasting at the South African Broadcasting Corporation (SABC). These debates came to a head as South Africa moved into its post-apartheid phase in the 1990s. The literature on the role of religious organizations, predominantly the Christian churches, in this political process is extensive. The education sector as a politically strategic location for religious representation is well documented also. So too is the significance of the media sector in facilitating the new political dispensation. Less well analyzed is the religious dimension of public broadcasting; for example, the emerging policy questions surrounds religious programming, and issues of control and representation.

The chapter thus seeks to document and explore this neglected interrelationship of religion and media in the South African context, not just because of the light it throws on the role of public religion in a nation-state in political transition, but also because it provides an important insight into the mechanics of religious representation in the mediated public sphere. This "production and management of meaning" occurs not just at the formal, institutional level but also as the result of internal (and, in the case of South Africa, external) debates and conflicts.

Discussions will be primarily limited to public broadcasting, and the medium of television, in particular, for reasons of space. As Graham Mytton observes, most broadcasting in Africa is still "centralized, national and state-dominated". This is especially the case for television. So despite current scholarly trends to link the electronic mass media with global scapes and flows, and to favour "conceptualizing the world as a whole," I have chosen to focus on a nationally constituted society as a unit of analysis. Transnational and translocal forces are clearly active in South Africa, through the agency of religious and media institutions, which can serve to deterritorialise the process of imagining communities. Michael Herzfeld comes to the rescue by arguing that "the various kinds of media, ethnographically studied in context, can provide a very close look at the interaction of the local, the national and the international" and that anthropology's "subversive localism" can unmask globalization for the "realist fiction" it has become.

Broader Contextual Issues

Religious conflict and violence in Africa more generally, and in Nigeria specifically, notably in connection with the imposition of Shari'a by northern states, clearly indicates the instrumentality of the media sphere in relations between religions and the state, between religions, and between religious organizations and their followers. Conflict between religious groups is commonly linked to rights of access to the national media. Because of the asymmetry of resources, capacity and influence, some religious organizations find themselves at the head of the media table while others may not even enjoy the crumbs from underneath it.

These patterns of exclusion and inclusion, coupled with issues of fair representation, have been exacerbated by the processes of democratization and liberalization. Bias and misinformation affect whether air-time is accorded to minority groups. It is popular to oppose the "cult menace". We should not underestimate the influence of globalizing discourses of Satanism and anticultism which emanate principally from U.S. courts and the media, as well as religious and Parareligious organizations.

Currently, several European countries, notably France, have jumped on the anticult bandwagon. In most post-colonial African states the stakes of religious coexistence have changed. Mainstream religious organizations which enjoyed the patrimony of colonial and independence governments now find themselves threatened by newer religious formations, notably of the revivalist type. These minority groups are often acutely aware of their rights to freedom of religion and freedom of expression. They claim these rights in the new spirit of communal self-determination, constitutionalism and the global lingua franca of international human rights that is sweeping the African continent. In post-apartheid South Africa, this is commonly referred to as the new "rights culture" or the new "human rights dispensation."

Furthermore, the liberalization of the media sector has opened up all sorts of new outlets for expression, many of which escape government control in relation to balancing and nondiscrimination. With the growing dominance of the market paradigm, air time is frequently bought rather than meted out. In other words, ownership and commercial interests of media institutions increasingly trump respect for national diversity. This causes frustration to many religious organisations that maintain a state-centric mentality; but savvy religious leaders, usually of the younger and more entrepreneurial variety, know that a good media presence is proselytizing writ large in a competitive religious environment and are prepared to foot the bill.

The right to disseminate one's religion easily surpasses the freedom to believe and to practice one's religion as the most controversial aspect of religious freedom. African constitutions may not accord the same primacy to free speech as is the case in the United States, where the judicial protection of free speech has increasingly guided the protection of related constitutional principles. However, the structural connections between free speech and religious freedom or liberty can be noted. Almost all African states have included in their constitutions a bill of rights. Religious freedom features prominently in one form or another in those constitutions, although it is often subject to various conditions. The media sphere constitutes a critical "test site" where the interpretation and implementation of these "new" rights can be publicly evaluated by all concerned.

Contestation and Consultation

South Africa offers an illuminating case for considering the relation between religion, media and the public sphere. Since the first universal franchise election in 1994, there has been a widespread effort at every level of society "to introduce new and better, more democratic, more demographically equitable, more politically and gender sensitive ways of doing things". There has been an accompanying debate about how to manage cultural diversity in a way that reflects constitutional ideals ("united in... diversity") and does not evoke negative historical memory. The reform of the media has been central to these socio-political changes in the "new South Africa," for, in the words of leading media analysts, Ruth Teer-Tomaselli and Keyan Tomaselli, "newspapers, magazines, television and radio are both the sites and the instruments of transformation".

As "sites" of transformation, the structures, management, ownership, and workforce of the media industries have been subject to debate and reform. As "instruments" of transformation, the media provide the platforms for debate, the stories, the images and visions of personal and national identity, both real and ideal. Within the contested power relations of the mass mediated public sphere, religious broadcasting policy and practice constitute a significant microsphere. Given the former close ties between the apartheid regime and the Dutch Reformed Church, the reapportioning of airtime for the country's diverse religious groups has been a key element in the refashioning of the South African state.

David Chidester highlights the transformation in state broadcasting as offering not just "new possibilities for broadening the representation of South African religious communities in public media" but also as a "growth area for the future of the study of religion in South Africa" with its critical potential for "analyzing symbols, myths, and rituals that generate powerful moods and motivations" and engaging structures of power. Under apartheid, the SABC, as a tool of the state, offered only Christian programming. Despite the political constraints of the time, several religious broadcasters objected to the juxtaposition of news and religious programs as a strategy for displacing "the actual context of conditions".

The very conservative orientation of the programming and restrictions on preaching with political content drove a number of English-language churches in 1979 to challenge the racism and narrowness of the SABC. They, the South African Council of Churches (SACC), even appealed to the churches to boycott the SABC and to consider alternative broadcasting facilities. While they failed to counter the intolerance and extreme right-wing views of the organizer of religious television programs, they took advantage of the greater flexibility of radio with its live broadcasts. Some preachers were able to address socially relevant and politically sensitive issues through such rhetorical devices as allegory and analogy.

In one of the few published analyses of religious broadcasting policy in South Africa, Russell Baker, a research associate at the main hub of media studies in South Africa, the Centre for Cultural and Media Studies at the University of KwaZulu-Natal, Durban, directed by Keyan Tomaselli, aptly describes it as characterized by "contestation and consultation" as well as "progressive developments". He traces these developments through various policy documents specifically oriented to the coverage of religion, devoting particular attention to the more recent phase of religious broadcasting policy. He notes the role played by the South African Council of Churches (SACC) in establishing a discussion forum—the Independent Forum for Religious Broadcasting (IFRB)—aimed at addressing the problems associated with religious broadcasting and SABC's consultative process.

This resulted in the production of the IFRB's Charter for Religious Broadcasting in 1984. The forum consisted of members representing the various Christian churches (Afrikaans, English, and African Independent), as well as the Hindu, Muslim and Jewish communities. They advocated "fundamental changes in the relationships between religions and churches and the SABC" and "both equitable distribution of broadcasting time and greater theological control over the content of religious programmes". In response to these public concerns and the new democratic dispensation, SABC circulated a Working Draft Policy on Religious Broadcasting to religious organizations in October 1994 and established the Religious Broadcasting Panel (RBP) in the same year.

The RBP met several times between 1995 and 1998, serving as interface between the SABC and religious communities. It set up committees to address concerns of individual communities, such as traditional African religious groups, who complained about being included in the category of African independent churches, or as nothing else but culture. Steps were taken to cultivate interfaith programming, and to improve training and development for staff from previously disadvantaged communities. The head of Religion from the British Broadcasting Corporation conducted workshops at the major centers. Dangor notes that one of the most heated debates in the RBP was over time allocation.

Public Storm and Independent Criticism

A particularly revealing source regarding the contentious exchanges between SABC and the religious communities is the retiring chairman's report to the annual forum of the IFRB delivered on November 16, 1998. In this report Bishop Peter Lee refers to the mandate of the IFRB, namely "to make religious representation on behalf of the religious community into the broad process of broadcast policy revision in South Africa." He alludes to the "considerable public controversy" related to religious broadcasting between 1996 and 1998.

He attributes this controversy to two reasons: first, by SABC's unilateral decision "to breach the agreement solemnly made with the religious community regarding religious broadcasting" and second, the "drastic" reduction in amounts of time available for religious programs. He blames this decision for raising a "public storm" about the place of religion generally on the airwaves not just of the public broadcaster but also those of commercial and community license holders. The Chairman also talks of the "bad faith" created by SABC's reneging on its earlier commitment to the religious community, its public lies, and its poor treatment of the RBP. This panel, according to him, "suffered huge frustration and eventually found itself sidelined within the SABC"—a situation which he claims was ongoing.

He also criticizes the lack of transparency regarding some of the later elections to the panel. Furthermore, he strongly bemoans the lack of reference to religious broadcasting in a government White Paper, despite representations by the IFRB at various broadcasting policy colloquia and the earlier "furore" over religious programming. Bishop Lee vehemently criticizes the "secularizing tendency of the present management" for ignoring the grassroots influence of religious organizations and for "overriding the spirit of the Constitution." He goes on to cite section 31 of the Bill of Rights in the Constitution which guarantees the rights of cultural, linguistic and religious groups. Despite this provision, the broadcasting White Paper still ominously omits the category of "religious" groups, while referring to cultural and linguistic ones.

Lee also regrets the lack of serious treatment of religious issues in a published discussion paper on a code of conduct for broadcasters, limiting consideration to "blasphemy and possible offence to religious sensitivities." He ends the report by pledging to lobby the government on these issues and by urging the respective religious groupings to challenge this ongoing "process of being sidelined by public policy." When SABC announced cutbacks to cultural and religious programming in 1997 (75% reduction to 106 minutes per week or 0.5% of its total output), and informed the public that in the future all magazine programs would be sourced from outside the Corporation, an "enraged public and religious community" joined the fray of confused and upset staffers and independents.

Rev. Martin Frische, chairperson of the Association of Christian Broadcasters, graphically accused the SABC of cutting the tree on which it sat by ignoring the (moral) importance of religion in society. Dr. Ed McCain, acting president of United Christian Action, spoke of the "high-handed, dictatorial attitude" of the SABC in failing to consult with religious bodies over the cutbacks. The outraged response was not just limited to the Christian constituency, Abie Dawjee, a spokesman for Jamiatul Ulama (KwaZulu-Natal) (a council of Muslim theologians) and a member of IFRB, stated: "[w]e are appalled at this cut. The religious majority, a vast share of the population, will be deprived of broadcasting..." He went on to bemoan the loss of the small gains that the Muslim community had made in the face of Christian-dominated broadcasting.

Mediating State and Religious Interests

From 1998 onwards, following the revision and approval of the RBP, SABC, in its annual report (for 1997-1998), described its (new) role with regard to religious programs as follows. The SABC, in its role as a public service broadcaster, has an obligation to reflect all faiths in an unbiased and appropriately representative manner. This, therefore, sees the presence of dedicated religious broadcasts on both radio and television. These cover the various formats of devotional, worship service, magazine, panel discussion, phone-in and music programmes catering for a wide spectrum of ages and preferences, and in all 11 of the official languages.

Referring to the RBP, "which tries to ensure respect for all religions and equitable representation for the expression of each faith within the total amount of religious broadcasting air time", the SABC report further states that "the total amount of time allocated to religious broadcasting should be such that those religions with the smallest ratio of air time enjoy meaningful and sufficient programming on a faith-specific basis". The report also indicates the adjustment in guidelines for the allocation of airtime for the various religions:

- Christianity 70% (as previously)
- Hinduism 7.5% (increased from 5%)
- Islam 7.5% (increased from 5%)
- ATR 10% (increased from 5%)
- Judaism 5% (increased from 3%)

By the following year, the 1998-99 annual report had dropped the reference to the goal of reflecting "all faiths in an unbiased and appropriately representative manner" and, significantly, it did not feature in any of the subsequent reports. In the report of 2000-2001, the mention of "respect for all religions and equitable representation" has disappeared, yet the report describes the "positive impact on television audiences" of religious programs as they "continued to educate and inform viewers about the various religions and the life of their communities."

It vaunts the fact that the program, "Crux," on the life of the Church, was one of the first magazine programs in South Africa to avail itself of virtual reality technology, and that the program, "Crossing the Divide," brought together a pagan and an occultist on air. The highlighting of this particular encounter seems to trivialize an otherwise important and innovative program. The noticeably slicker website in the 2000-01 report was clearly seeking to reflect the diverse South African religious scene, and one could see images of black Zionist Christians, with a woman drumming in the foreground, and the Torah.

On the page outlining plans for the future, there was a composite graphic with images of a multitude of religious leaders and practitioners. Apart from the Pope, the majority of faces were non-white, with Hindus and Zulu traditional worshipers in the foreground. The 2003 report has less complex images, but there is a stunning full-page image of a female Zionist worshipper. SABC programming reflects a mix of South Africa's major religions—Christianity, African Religion, Islam, Hinduism and Judaism.

A number of tradition-specific programs were developed for television in the post-1994 period, but these were consolidated under the rubric of the popular and award-winning multifaith documentary, "Issues of Faith," or featured as documentaries. Some Christian programs retained their separate status—an option preferable to the more conservative end of the Christian spectrum. A new development is the Sunday morning breakfast show ("Spirit Sundae") which aims to be "inclusive of the full spectrum of religion in South Africa." With its more creative and flexible approach, it covers topics "ranging from current affairs to the arts, religious festivals, cooking and holistic healing." In addition, there are worship programs and evening devotions for each of the main religious traditions (e.g. the Jewish Voice, Aum, Izwi Labantu, Reflections on Faith), as well as and morning devotions in various languages (Afrikaans, Sotho, Nguni) which reflect the variety of expressions of Christianity around the country.

These devotional programs continue to claim the highest audience ratings. In terms of "multifaith" programs (and "faith" is clearly the SABC term of preference nowadays), there are the "Issues of Faith" documentaries on SABC2, which discuss topics such as liberation, caste, ubuntu, and human rights in relation to different religious communities. On SABC1, which aims to reach more youthful audiences, there is "Tapestries of Faith." Along these lines, SABC1 broadcasts "You Gotta Have Faith" every Friday morning. This is billed as a "life orientation program" which discusses the way religion affects the choices people make in life.

A 2001 program series, "Paul and the Menu: Cooking with Spirit," explored and celebrated religious multiculturalism through food under the aegis of a zany Anglican priest. The popular "Free Spirit," a program trendily described as "less about religion and more about spirituality," and destined "to enhance the lives of spiritually open South Africans" is the brainchild of Religion Commissioning Editor Yashika Singh. It is not only repeated midweek, but also has a related website. Music programs tend to have a Christian emphasis, such as the award-winning "Gospel Gold." Gospel Gold: Among the top performing religious programmes on television, it provides a platform for South Africa's gospel music industry.

A gospel talent show, "Gospel Star" has also been added to the "Crux" (the Christian magazine program) slot on SABC1. Wanting to be seen as promoting national harmony and integration, rather than division and conflict, producers may opt for a pastiche of viewpoints, rather than allowing direct confrontation. The current (global) trend toward framing news and issues in a much more entertainment, human interest guise may also mitigate conflictual differences between religious positions, and neutralize any "prophetic" critique of the state by religious leaders. Although, to SABC's credit, they air some hardhitting documentaries, such as the one (in 2001) on the controversial Nigerian Pentecostal miracle-worker, T.B. Joshua, who has been attracting supplicants from southern Africa.

Current Challenges

In addition to trying to balance the (devotional and informational) needs of South Africa's diverse religious constituencies and promote (inter)religious understanding and tolerance in the interests of nation-building, two of the most contentious issues that SABC has had to face on the religious broadcasting front have been outside funding, and "the neglect of African culture in the public media."

The question of funding became critical in the late 1990s with drastic cutbacks, forcing creative measures on the part of the religious broadcasting staff. For a time American

Christian programming took up the slack (as it has in many other African countries), but this was eventually seen as compromising the democratization process in the country. Moreover, there was reluctance to allow religious groups to use independent funding as a means of securing additional broadcast time. However, due to financial considerations, a decision was taken to allow selective sales of air-time, sponsorships and classical advertising as long as "profits from such endeavours enable SABC to fund more of its own local religious productions" and "such contracts do not in one way or another compromise either the editorial independence or integrity of the SABC or its Policy on Religious Broadcasts"

The second challenge for religious broadcasting in South Africa has been to contextualize and reflect African reality. The SABC Policy on Religious Broadcasting (revised and approved by the SABC Board in 1998) alludes to some of the battles fought over the place of traditional African religion: "In order to correct further neglect of African culture in the public media, special attention should be given to African Traditional Religion (ATR) and traditional cultures." This needs to be seen against the background of the African Renaissance movement launched by President Thabo Mbeki in the late 1990s. For several analysts, the capacity of the media to serve as facilitators of democracy and African cultural selfdetermination is closely linked to both structures of ownership and diversification of production.

One of the strongest voices on behalf of traditional African religions and fiercest critics of discriminatory practices by political and religious authorities has been Nokuzola Mndende. A former parliamentarian and freelance presenter turned educational consultant, and armed with higher degrees in religious studies to boot, she has campaigned forcefully to expose the racism "now clothed in religious attire". Because of their failure to include ATR in educational policies, civic events, and the Truth Commission, Mndende refers to the present government as "nothing else but Christianity at prayer." She vehemently criticizes the SABC for referring to indigenous African religions as "minority religions" and for not censoring the negative portrayals of these religions in their programming.

Mndende strategically resorts to rights talk when criticizing the then chair of the Human Rights Commission for disbelieving that there are Africans who can practice African religion without Christianity: "how can we speak of human rights when my right to believe and my freedom to practice my religion is still controlled and despised?"

In the same vein, she opines that "to define African Religion from a Christian perspective violates the rights of its followers to have complete freedom of religion: when a particular way of seeing the truth is imposed on others it violates their freedom to seek the truth". The RBP has also had to deal with complaints from several religious groups about the scheduling of many religious programs on Sunday– to which SABC replied that weekday evenings were reserved for prime-time programming into which religious programs did not fit.

In addition, the panel has received requests from various groups to be treated as separate entities, as in the case of the Mormon Church. While the RBP feels that it achieved some success in transforming religious programming in the SABC, they made less headway with radio broadcasting which is traditionally more decentralized and predominantly Christian. While Muslim groups in South Africa have made advances in the political and media spheres, in March 2000 concern was still being voiced about negative representations and reporting.

A Muslim media group, Media Review Network, reported to the South African Human Rights Commission in Johannesburg that the South African media were generating "Islamophobia" through their demonizing and stereo-typing, notably in connection with the bombings in Cape Town and South Africa. This is an ongoing problem, as evidenced by their comments to the SABC on its Draft Editorial Policies in 2003, notably regarding the "special vocabulary list" ("fundamentalist," "extremist," "fanatic," "terrorist,") used by the media almost exclusively in reference to Muslims. The

Muslim community has also complained to the RPB about documentaries portraying Islam in a bad light.

Rainbow Nation

From the above discussion one can see that the negotiations over the public, mediated presence of religion in a culturally and religiously pluralistic democracy such as South Africa are increasingly informed by appeal to the globalizing discourse of rights. Yet some critics, such as South African scholar of religion Ebrahim Moosa, are skeptical of the constitutional arrangements for freedom of religion in the South African context (and one could extend the argument to other African states also). Moosa claims that expectations of freedom are never realized because religion is reduced to the status of "junior partner" with the state.

He attributes the "fiction of the sovereignty of religion" to the framing of religious rights in binary terms (public/private, secular/profane, belief/practice, etc.) which reflect imported liberal and modernist constitutional values rather than the consensus values of the majority community. Other analysts point to the precarious nature of both the rights to freedom of religion and freedom of expression in the face of new strategies by state and non-state actors in many parts of the world, not least some European countries, to curtail these freedoms.

Moves to reregulate the media in terms of access, licensing, and censorship may be interpreted as a consequence of the loss of control by states over religious pluralisation and diversification, or as an effort by politicians to diminish the influence of the religious sector. Some governments see media censorship as a more feasible option for co-opting or excluding unpopular or subversive religious ideologies. In some cases this can be affected by encouraging the market forces which are reconfiguring religious power relations across Africa. Keyan Tomaselli, who has written extensively on the political economy of the South African media, has warned of the vulnerability of the electronic and print media in South Africa's public sphere in the face of globalization of capital, media and markets.

He has underscored the need to pursue critical media education, and the adoption of civil charters such as The People's Communication Charter. The Windhoek Charter on Broadcasting 2001 among other things calls on states to transfer regulatory powers on the airwaves and telecommunication structures to publicly constituted bodies under a three-tier system composed of public service, commercial and community operators. An important landmark in this connection for South Africa is the Media Development and Diversity Agency Act of July 8, 2002, which provides for a statutorily recognized body, to be funded by government and the media industry, for the development of community and independent media.

For religious broadcasting policy in particular, Baker argues that, in the age of (post) modern technologies and ideas, "simple objectivity," based on "dubious membership figures," is seriously challenged by the "emerging multi-channel, multimedia environment". He rightly considers that the "goal of impartiality will have to be addressed more in terms of the satisfaction of the needs of the full spectrum of the South African audience". In this regard, he underscores the need to incorporate those on the "fringe of formal religions" and advises against excessive normative limitations being placed on religious programs.

While such constraints (such as on proselytizing and discrimination) obtain in other locations, he considers the South African religious scene to be too diverse to enforce such restraints and the resultant "bland uniform programming" to be undesirable. Instead, he favours the democratic "right to reply" system, while acknowledging that such responsibility may conflict with the racist and sexist teachings still propounded by some religious groups. This concurs with efforts by the Africa Region of the World Association for Christian Communication (WACC) to encourage churches to work toward more "democratic communication" and to treat their constituencies as "active participants in articulating social/spiritual problems".

Because of the intimate relationship between the country's political and economic history and the ongoing divisions and differences of the South African religious landscape, Baker argues that SABC's religion department should proactively target economically disadvantaged groups, such as the African independent churches, previously marginalized by the mainstream media. This problematic heritage of religious conservatism and exclusion came up at a series of seminars on "Religion, Liberation and Transformation through the South African Experience" held at the Parliament of the World's Religions, Cape Town, in December 1999.

Under discussion was research conducted at the University of Stellenbosch in 1990 and 1996/7 which has shown that people with religious affiliations (except for Jews) were more likely to be politically intolerant (in terms of according civil rights to groups they did not support or agree with) than those who did not profess to be religious. So seminar participants called for religious leaders and communities to develop new attitudes of tolerance, given their power to socialize communities. They were enjoined to promote the African concept of community or ubuntu (one can only be human through relationships) and rediscover the emancipatory ecumenism that brought down the apartheid regime.

The South African case demonstrates that the fields of identity and action for religious groups are increasingly located in, and defined by, the interface of modern media, both local and global. It also further confirms Bourdieu's observation that the "journalistic field," most notably. Television profoundly modifies power relations in other fields of cultural production. There have been, and still are, great hopes for the modern media to help realize the African Renaissance, in whatever modality that is imagined–cultural pride, academic recognition, spiritual rediscovery, moral renewal, informational accuracy, political freedom, economic growth or social harmony.

In that regard, the particular focus in this essay on religious broadcasting demonstrates the strategic role that the state can, and should, play in transitional democracies such as South Africa, in promoting religious tolerance. It has further provided a revealing, yet salutary, window onto the entanglements of religion, democracy, and capitalism in one of the world's most strategic nation-states. Yet the story of this "rainbow nation," to use Archbishop Tutu's enduring symbol, and its quest to balance democratic nationalism with cultural and religious pluralism, and what Achille Mbembe calls "struggles over autochthony," is clearly far from over.

Reconfiguring the Public Sphere of Islam

For well over a generation, the public sphere of Islam has been an arena of contest in which activists and militants brought forth challenges to traditional interpretative practices and authority to speak for Islam, especially to articulate its social interests and political agendas. Patrick Gaffney has astutely noted that their claims draw on social and political experience as alternatives both to expertise in textual hermeneutics associated with the learned men of Islam and to more illuminationist priorities exemplified in Sufi and generally mystical ways. Opening the social field to new spokespeople and new discursive practices not only challenges authority long since thought settled to interpret what religion requires, but also blurs boundaries between public and private discourse and fosters new habits of production and consumption tied to media and particularly to new media.

Ideas and issues circulated in intellectuals' books a generation ago are now found in popular chapbooks and on street-corner newsstands ; audiocassettes that carried sermons of then-exiled Ayatouah Ruhouah Khomeini into pre-Revolutionary Iran likewise by the 1990s carried sermons by popular preachers into taxicabs and shops, altering listening habits as much as ulema delivering/atoas (religious opinions) on calling radio and television shows have transformed a highly interactive format for personalized answers into one more resembling publication, however ephemeral. This is an expanding social field characterized by more than contested authority and by more than proliferating voices or blurred boundaries; central to this expanding public sphere of Islam are new media and interest profiles they advance.

Media figure in this process in several crucial respects. First, they devolve access to consumption by more people on more occasions. Passage into media conveys previously "private" or highly situated discourses from interactive contexts to public display, where they are reattached to a public world and return as information conveyed through new media technologies with different habits of reception. Detached from traditional modes of production, they become messages in a world of messages. But more important, media are themselves complex social fields and activities. Analyses of print note an officialisation of discourse that moves into print; programs to Islamize knowledge, science, and politics generally pursue entextualisation strategies to recast those subjects in Islamic vocabularies with modern arguments.

Entextualisation puts discourse before authorities whose stock in trade is texts and textual methods from grammar and techniques of reading to portable testaments of authorization (jawaz) to interpret. And entextualisation lays claims to participate in the spaces in which discourse is so conducted. Twentieth-century Islamists not only—in some cases, not even—sermonized; they wrote, often prolifically, as in the cases of Mohammed Rashid Ridah and Maulana Maududdi, whose roots were in journalism but whose goals were to recast religious discourse. Increasingly, electronic communication is also moving Islamic discourse into the marketplace and aligning its practices, range of choice, and alternatives both metaphorically and literally with additional means to service those demands. Local media have been joined by satellite broadcasters, cassettes by the Internet, each enabling new voices to gather new audiences.

Like print before it, forms of electronic communication move Islamic discourse beyond the classical language of texts into contemporary vernaculars and involve new actors, sites of production, and consumption where audiocassettes are also a medium for folk music and poetry, much of it religious; satellite television not only for entertainment but, together with the Internet, for the transnational press. While the media-savy and militants capture attention, particularly of analysts, a quieter drama is unfolding. Pious middle classes are extending patterns of religious expression, seeking, and piety into new channels, whose production as well as consumption is accessible and increasingly developed around their specific needs and resources.

These range from sermons that circulate beyond the pulpit on audio and videocassettes to religious instruction material for children that parents can use where there are no religious schools or as alternatives to them; from "media iBuftis" dispensing theologically based religious advice on radio and television call-in or write-in shows to more psychological and social advice on Internet sites, whose offerings range from foundational religious texts through hagiographies and handbooks to selections of news and views of current events focused on how to lead a Muslim life in a modern, increasingly middle-class world not denominated primarily in Muslim terms. These developments render problematic the distinction of public and private domains and forms of expression that became apodictic for a generation of research on Muslim and Middle Eastern societies.

Introduced by Hanna Papanek and Cynthia Nelson to place a sociological ground under discussions of honour and shame in traditional settings, the public/private distinction opened up the private world of sentiment and expression, particularly women's, but to the relative neglect of the public sphere that new media make increasingly permeable to the circulation of messages from more restricted realms, diluting and in some cases challenging the authority to represent. Today, satellite television is everywhere, with Al-Jazeera's signature discussion shows and dedication to airing opposing points of view its current poster child. To conventions of the press and transnational broadcasting, these add interpretive and discursive forms from more restricted realms, much as the audiocassette earlier allowed sermons to circulate outside both their occasions and official approval.

Passing messages out of conventional channels is a feature of new media. They blur boundaries not only between genres of expression but also between their social spaces. Within days of the Arab States Broadcasting Union rejecting the application of Al- Jazeera TV in December 1998, the story was spread internationally on the Internet by Arabia online, then experimenting with a mix of entertainment and regional news. At the time, only a handful of transnational Arabic language newspapers targeting regional elites were on the Internet; now every major daily, all state news services, and many magazines from the region have versions online, where they compete not just with each other but with other—notably with religious purveyors of news, interpretation, and other information previously circulating in more limited realms. Increasingly, many are multilingual and invite interaction with their users, both for market research and as the practices of the profiles they project OB to the Internet.

This is the scene of energetic, experimental, and intensely creative activity; but what is new can be problematic. It attracts new people, albeit primarily from younger and subaltern segments of existing elites. Globally, the Internet is barely 30 years old, with a public career outside the research precincts that spawned it spanning little more than a decade and half that in the Middle East. Early enthusiasms for cyber democracy, which frequently replayed hopes invested in mass media a generation earlier, have given way to pessimism about digital divides; but in the realm of media, the Internet unites separate features of other new media: lower barriers to entry for producers, a more symmetrical relation between producers and consumers, and higher degrees of interactivity between them than older media from print to state monopoly broadcasting.

How it is public is also problematic. Conceptions of "publics" are very much tied to media and the state. From media come their specifications as audiences, from politics their specification as opinion, with both as features of modern mass society. But mass media provides a poor model, for it is precisely their features such as few senders and many receivers, social distance between them, gaps between production and consumption of messages, and between the activity of production and the passivity' of consumption—that new media most clearly contravene. They multiply rather than reduce the number and range of message producers and are far more interactive, not only in the minimal sense of an increased range of choice, than mass media. The technology for producing and modifying them is far more at-hand.

For the Internet now as for audiocassettes earlier, it takes little more technical skill and resources to produce than to consume in this medium. What sort of public is this, if it cannot be thought of as an audience or as mass opinion? How might we think about a public marked instead by interactivity, convergence of producers and consumers, fragmentation that ultimately blurs that distinction and barriers to entry? Two bodies of theory are useful for thinking through these issues and how they play out in the Middle East and Muslim worlds. One is Habermas's theory of the public sphere as a form, locus, and activity of communication relatively unfettered by demands of status and the ritual representation of formal authority. Such communication has to succeed on its own merits, carried not by the authority (social, religious, political) of the speaker but by well-formed words.

While Habermas was primarily interested in "rational-critical" communication as the ideal standard of modernity, he identified its practical emergence with the intermediate space of coffeehouses and salons, where private citizens could assemble as a public, between the private space and personalized authority of kin and the public realm marked by the theatre of royal and religious ritual. It was set apart from those by communication that had to be convincing without the external support of the authority of the speaker. This view has been roundly critiqued, mostly for narrowness as sexist, classist, Eurocentric, and illiberal by modern standards. These critiques pertain more to how Habermas tied this conception of a public sphere so tightly and specifically to modernization, and that to rationality, than to the essential identification of the emergence of new public spheres around communications relatively freed from demands of ritual representation, particularly of mystical authority.

The notion is comprehensible without the duty to narrate European modernization. In broader comparative terms, Habermas draws attention to communication freed from status and its ritual representation; his key insight was that this is not limited to private spheres of conscience, the market, or intimacy but can take on a public life characteristic of a bourgeois public sphere. Except as channels, media play a secondary role in this theory, but a more central one in Benedict Anderson's alternative focus on "imagined community". Employing a more robust conception of communication modelled less on the systemic properties of language than on the actual practice of speech communities, Anderson located the modern imagination of community along ethno-linguistic lines in the Diasporas of early modern empires.

There language became the basis for more extensive community than religion or dynastic states through the shared experiences of "Creole journeys" and then of "reading together" fostered by early print capitalism. While this emphasis on imagination seems distant from Habermas' on rationality, both point to practical links between community and communication, particularly outside of institutional boundaries, and to the more material basis of their reification in new forms for representation of that experience from newspapers to novels spawned by that new media at the same time that they fostered an enormous market. Both focus on margins, but Anderson's is the more open and flexible conception of communication that includes more of mediated communication than only what it shares with interpersonal communication and so is applicable to a broader range of media than its typesite of print. Also, his notion of "Creole journeys" foregrounds developments outside Europe and the European priorities in Habermas's theory.

Like Habermas, Anderson can be criticized for what he leaves out or leaves flattened as objects rather than as constituting subjects. This includes women, indigenous peoples, and lower classes. While this matters to the story of modernization, removing that story leaves the fundamental insight that links creolization to new media and locates their stations in Diaspora journeys. Drawing on these perspectives is not to imply that new media mark some onset of modernity in the Muslim world, but to suggest more global frames of comparison than modernization, modernity modelled on European experience, or drawn from mass media. Globally, today's new media, particularly the Internet and particularly as it is unfolding in the Muslim world, have more in common with the print revolution of early modernity than with the mass media of late modernity, and a public sphere more comparable to the salons and coffeehouses of early modernity than to mediated-saturated mass society that Habermas came to see as later modernity.

As recently as 20 years ago there was little or no Islam online, and the Internet was barely visible even in the universities to which it was spreading from research labs where it was developed. Twenty years ago the Internet had essentially the form that it has today: a distributed, decentralized, network-structured rather than hierarchical open communication space into which users brought interests, placed content, and thereby structured it around those interests, which quickly came to include a vocational as well as professional interests of its users at every stage of its development and extension. In this permissive context, Islam initially came online through the agency of what I have called "technological adepts" who had the access and skills to bring interests they had as Muslims into this new medium.

They included students who went or were sent abroad to study in institutes of engineering and applied science that spawned the Internet and, like their counterparts there, used the Internet to place their interests online and to engage others like themselves. These students, together with émigré professionals, political exiles, and labour migrants, form part of the contemporary Muslim Diaspora. It is a mobile population, not just of settlers but with ties and the material means to maintain links with homelands in a world shrunken by advances in transportation and communication available to ever more people. Students in particular seized on the early Internet and were in time followed by others as the Internet spread.

What these technological adepts brought online was, first, texts of the Holy Qur'an and collected traditions of the prophet, much as others in hightech centers also created file archives for hobbies as well as technical databases. Second were electronic discussion forums on Islam and related subjects that particularly engaged by Muslims who were overseas for longer or shorter periods as students, émigré professionals, exiles, and others with continuing ties to and interests in their homelands and in leading a Muslim life in the modern world that was not configured primarily in Muslim terms. Why texts and debates about leading a Muslim life? Only part of the reason is that the technology of the early Internet was built around archives and message forums. For over a hundred years, Islamic responses to modernity had reified Sharia—"law" in the sense of behavioural prescriptions, as opposed to piety—as the public face of Islam, or its socio-political engagement with the world.

This construction emphasized the texts of revelation and record of prophetic practice as the religion's sources, while deemphasizing various living carriers of tradition from Sufi masters to descendants of the prophet to the ulema of Islam as guides to or mediators of tradition. Within this long cycle is a shorter one that Eickelman has identified with the spread of mass public education in the independence period of Muslim-majority countries after World War II. To ever increasing numbers was conveyed a new "intellectual technology" associated with science and "objective" study, whose principal difference with traditional religious education was that it was analytic where the latter was hermeaeutic. These two trends come together in the technological adepts, who were often tracked into science from an early age and approached religion in their 20s and 30s without much training in the hermeneutic practices of traditional religious interpretation. Instead, they used the alternative intellectual technology of modern education, and in settings of Diaspora life among others similarly situated.

Their approach was more objectifying and analytic and consonant with efforts going back for a century to treat Islam as a system in a modern idiom. Its archetype was Mohammed Rashid Ridah, a Syrian-born journalist whose initial religious education was complemented with training in modern science and who set out to cast Islam in the new idiom. He operated in Cairo, then a new-media hothouse of hundreds of journals spawned by the advent of mechanical print in Arabic. Eschewing the demonstrative formats and deep contextualization of ulema discourse, Ridah employed the more self-contained forms of journalism and the journalists' collected-article book format. Ridah was a thoroughly intermediate figure, on the one hand compatriot of Islamic reform thinkers, whom he sought to engage and to influence, and on the other a source and model for the subsequent creators of Islamic political parties.

Three-quarters of a century later, in this context and with this model, technological adepts first brought Islamic core texts and discussion of them to the Internet. The texts were translations, scanned from university libraries, and placed online with discussions largely in English, sometimes in French, that came to include others as the Internet spread beyond universities to the professionals those trained. In this context they were followed by activists after the invention of the World Wide Web in the early 1990s made the Internet more accessible to the non-technically trained. Attracted by the technology but more focused on religion, a range of activists stepped up to provide missing contexts for the texts. Both oppositional and official spokespersons typically claimed to restore what those trained in science and technology left out: to some, that was 14 centuries of scholarly exegesis and to others contemporary political and social critiques.

Others took advantage of web technology that made the Internet accessible to wider publics and created web pages for traditional schools and modern universities, transnational Sufi networks and national religious movements, traditional missionary organizations, and for nationwide organizations of Muslims in Western countries. This ushered in a phase of professional spokespeople, diversities of opinion, social capital, and networks. It began with the more transnational, who were drawn to the medium, including the already transnational segment of Arab press and extended to others who were already organized offline. What emerges in this widening arena is not just contest, challenges to authority and responses. Rather, it is the real diversity of the Muslim world and Muslim opinion.

Sufi orders, traditional Madrasa (religious schools), particularly those with outreach missions, as well as modern-form schools and seminaries from Qom to Al-Azhar, movements from the Muslim Brotherhood and its multiple descendants, the Front Islamique du Salut in North Africa, the Taliban and their opponents in Afghanistan and Al Qaeda sympathizers, plus a range of religious publishers from the pious to the revolutionary, and more from individual efforts to those of long-established *da'wa* (mission) organizations all established websites. But there is more. By itself, web technology is more a publication medium than its predecessor formats, its distinctive feature being "hypertext" or links a user could follow, but not create. Initial versions were accessible without much technological training that, as much as their "userfriendliness," facilitated explosive growth of websites.

This growth increases not only overall diversity but also social distance between producers and consumers: in the Internet's preweb phase, users shared a high level of expertise in the technology, but few shared professional expertise or interests in Islam. The advent of the web lowered the technical bar and opened the Internet to the latter and to alternative expertise generally, which brought their underlying social order as well as overlying priorities onto the Internet. To this initially limited interactivity, further development of Web technology in the latter half of the 1990s added search tools and "portals," which give users capability not just to sample but to configure an information profile. Portals are the first native format of the web; they both aggregate material on the Internet and provide tools, such as searchable databases, and configurable interfaces that enable users to find more of the same and to reaggregate information. They also require higher and more sustained technical skill to create than earlier websites.

In this context, Islamic portals have emerged, tied not so much to existing institutions, as were the initial Islamic websites, although those still exist, as to mediating interests and material more modulated to the lives of those familiar with the Internet through work and as an information seeking tool. This enhanced interactivity and depth resets the Internet baseline and has been exploited by a new generation. A diagnostic example is the islamonline.net site produced in Qatar with content created in Cairo and featuring perhaps the most internationally famous Sunni preacher today, Shaykh Yusuf al- Qaradawi. Al-Qaradawi is a member of coterie that Malika Zeghal has called "young Azhari," wholly orthodox in theology but expressing it in a more modern idiom that attracts a transnational audience among professional middle classes.

Islamonline.net addresses this population both through conventional fatwa in response to queries and through more psychological kinds of advice, news from and about the Muslim world, religious lessons, including sermons but also instructional material for children, and various services, all of which provide interaction either directly with shaykhs or with databases of fatwa, other advice, religious lessons, sermons, hajj guides, health information, entertainment, personal testimonials and interviews with public figures, as well as texts of the Qur'an, Hadith, and Sunnah collections. In a broad sense, theirs is a post radical Islam for pious middle classes focused on issues and techniques of modern life. While other Islamic sites present clearly partisan lines, Shaykh Yusuf is widely regarded in the region as a moderate and draws an audience interested in a more modulated Islam, often nearer interests and lifestyles than those coming to islamonline.net can find closer to home. It is very much a transnational audience.

The site is formally similar to Islamic sites in Western countries that provide gathering points and information for Diaspora populations; but it is also especially directed at homeland populations that could be said to constitute a sort of "internal" Diaspora. Who is this internal Diaspora? Their numbers are as difficult to identify as the external Diaspora, with which they overlap. They belong to an increasingly transnational population of professionals, identifying with and by professional interests and practices that increasingly include the Internet as one of their work tools. They include in addition to Internet professionals (developers, designers) others for whom the Internet is a tool or where they turn for information, as a means of communication, and for networking—the practices that are the precursors of community.

They may or may not include alienated youth and a proletariat, although they do include some of the more traditional labour migrants who make use of the Internet; but their principal characteristic is to share characteristics of the external Diaspora, except emigration to non-Muslim-majority countries. For parts of this population moving between Muslim countries instead of from them, the Internet is one of the ways they are "at home" in transnational social spheres of its technological, arts, and other professions and other no local identity groups, including special interests as Muslims not available where they live. Developmentally, regional builders of the Internet fit this profile and have moved into the niche pioneered by the early technological adepts, some of whom scale up earlier individual efforts into Internet-building services of site hosting and web design. In this, some find in religious patronage a steadier, longer-term source for developing these businesses in a market where commercial customers are few and usually part of conglomerates that sponsor their own.

The largest Arabic-language software house developed its technology first on religious texts. The company that put islamionline.net on the web also designed and maintains the website of aljazeera.net and can point to cointerprets almost literally down the street that do the same for more conservative Salafi websites. In other words, religious patrons provide long-term support for developing a "soft infrastructure" of programmers and content providers who are parts of a scattered, mobile population that includes people very much like them at the consuming end and joined with them practically in a transnational space, if not quite a community of mutual recognition. The practices of this space extend personal, local, special, and sometimes class-tied interests and practices into an emerging public sphere, which gathers them up in an intermediate space between the discursive space of Islamic textual traditions, where divergent opinions are confronted systematically around a common base of learning, and divergent authority that remains embedded in personal experience and personal relations with masters.

In another time or place, or for other people, Sufism or a political Islam might have provided an alternative or complementary path to the official one of Sharia authorities. Another range of options emerges with the Internet and the sphere of interaction it provides for expression, gathering, and examination in a mediated public. Just how this is public is partly tied to specific media from Al-Jazeera's signature discussion shows and policy of presenting opposing points of view to playing taped sermons in cafes and taxis to the Internet? On the Internet, a lawyer in Jordan explained, he can find Yusuf Al-Qaradawi and other shaykhs who speak to his situation and provide an Islamic expression not available at his neighborhood mosque or from local shaykhs; so can his counterparts in the suburbs of northern Virginia, Hamburg, or Cairo's Mohandisseen. Their religion does not become private, but transferred to another public and style of interaction. On the Internet, the latest web technology not only provides choice in the form of searchable databases and user-configurable interfaces.

It also reflects back choices through continuous online polling and display of the results, membership areas, and chat that present to users and visitors their public opinion. Islam online net, some other Islamic portals, and many press portals provide these reflexive features for people who otherwise never meet that Benedict Anderson singled out for imagined community. It would be too strong to call this a cyber community, such as imagined by tech pioneers, but not too strong to see it as an emerging public sphere of discourse relatively freed from ritual representation to live on its own, and at least partly to address that condition. The Internet in particular is a sphere of Creole discourse and Creol journeys, an intermediate sphere between more private worlds and those of public rituals; it is part of a continuum between those along which social actors can move.

Viewed statically, as languages, Creoles appear mixed; but viewed dynamically, as speech communities, they look more like intermediate points on a continuum of activities and encounters that people enter and leave. The Internet has featured such intermediate speech communities in the initial appearance of online Islam, in presentations and explorations by technological adepts, followed by activists with perspectives to represent, and now in the modulations of Islam by and for a growing population that seeks and finds an Islamic public sphere, or continuum of public spheres, through its own practices. This is very much a diasporic sphere and one that brings practices of a transnational community back home to an internal Diaspora distinguished primarily in not having emigrated very far.

A Society of Enclaves

Israel is a society of enclaves, and of profound cultural divisions. They emerged in the way in which the country was settled, first in the quasi-legal status of early Zionist settlement, and in the leading role played in that settlement by highly centralized political parties parcelling out power and space among themselves, and later in the peculiar relationship (for a modern democracy) between religion and the state. The pattern is graphically described by Swirski, who uses the term 'microsocieties'. Since the boundaries are relatively porous, and their substance - political, doctrinal, ethnic, territorial, liturgical, vestimental, linguistic, educational, and of course socio-economic – extremely diverse, the word 'ethnicity' does not properly account for this phenomenon. The word enclave describes spaces delimited in these many different ways.

The notion of enclaves is both territorial and analytical: it describes distinct territorial enclaves inhabited by the highly observant ultra-Orthodox Jews, the secular, and even the fairly observant – and the settlements in occupied territories are an extension of the same principle; it also describes the parcelling out of state bureaucracies or departments as fiefdoms to particular parties or factions. It can even be seen in the way governing coalitions are formed: once a party has a Minister in place that Minister is in effect the owner of his Ministry and does not seem to be bound by collective Cabinet responsibility. Beyond these tangible enclaves are the less tangible ones: people signal their religious or political allegiance in how they dress, in whether they speak Yiddish, in what they eat and where they shop, even in how they walk on the street. Given that religious life is deeply marked by concepts of pollution and the proliferating taboos arising there from, it is hardly surprising that the social and territorial space of the country is criss-crossed by infinity of additional boundaries.

Institutional enclaves are seen in rabbinical control over family law, and indeed over nationality law, but also in the influence of rabbinic authorities over vast areas of public life, from the El-Al flight timetable to the subsidies accorded to hundreds of thousands of full-time young and adult Torah students (who neither work nor serve in the army) and their vast families, and to the institutions in which they study. Enclaves mean muscle, and the ultra-orthodox exercise their muscle in issues of Sabbath observance just as West Bank settlers exercise theirs territorially and politically. Likewise, state-funded education is divided, for the Jewish population, into a mainstream secular system and a 'national religious' system, both directly funded and operated by the state, and an ultra- Orthodox system, as well as a separate state-run system for the Arab population. The ultra-orthodox educational system is in turn divided into two separate systems, one controlled by the Ashkenazi authorities of the Eastern European tradition and the other, recently created and predominantly Sephardi, is controlled by the leadership of Shas, the party of religious renewal and Sephardi identity, founded in 1982.

The discourse and actions of the Shas leadership and their most active followers have tended towards the superimposition of disagreement and conflict across several different faultlines at once: the 'eternal' secular-religious conflict, the ethnic divisions between Ashkenazim - people of European descent - and Sephardim – migrants from North Africa and the Middle East and their descendants, and the division between elite and popular culture. Shas is different from the Ashkenazi ultra orthodox parties because of its emphasis on t'shuva – the process whereby large numbers of people are brought 'back' to religious observance. Shas attracts people who are either 'traditional' (masorati), in that they preserve some customs but are not punctiliously observant, or else from a highly secularized lifestyle. Shas is also recognized as the party of the Sephardim.

The word Sephardi refers strictly speaking to the Judeo-Spanish (or ladino) speaking people of the Northern Mediterranean and Northern Morocco, but in recent decades it has come to refer to all Jews of North African, Middle Eastern and Persian descent, most of whom are by now second and third generation immigrants, and many of whom are married to non-Sephardim. Taking into account the resulting impossibility of giving precise numbers, it is generally accepted that they constitute slightly less than half of Israel's Jewish population. In political campaigns the party capitalizes deftly on the symbols and accoutrements of Sephardi identity – accent, popular language and culture, Oriental music, popular religion such as healing and the veneration of saints – but in more formal statements of policy the leadership emphasizes t'shuva above everything else.

The fact that different authors emphasize in different ways the ethnic and religious elements in Shas's appeal, demonstrates the impossibility of separating the two. In the long run, as some have also said, Shas is transcending these alternatives, and forging an Orthodox Israeli Judaism which, if its influence continues to grow, will become the dominant form, replacing the Ashkenazi-Sephardi divide inherited from Jewish history and deepening the divide between Israeli religious culture and that the Diaspora. Like the Pentecostals in Latin America, Shas and the t'shuva movement in which it is the leading force, can be understood as a revolt against the hegemony of a cultural elite, and it is also reshaping the religious sphere.

The genius or good fortune of Shas's founders was to link ethnic and religious renewal, so that now it is hard to choose between a description of Shas as embedded within a broader t'shuva movement, or of t'shuva as embedded within the ethnic renewal, which Shas has led. In common with social movements generally, the t'shuva movement uses multifarious means of communication and organization – adopting a capillary approach to social mobilization as opposed to the hierarchical methods used by conventional political parties or trade unions, or the Ashkenazi haredim – whose communal activity is much more subject to rabbinical control and therefore leaves less space for initiative and entrepreneurship.

This t'shuva movement lives by trusting its emissaries, and by drawing them from its 'target population'. A movement spreads by capitalizing on points of commonality with a range of constituencies as much as by broadcasting a message. Thus the emissaries or activists of Shas have a language in common with the second and third generation Sephardim, but they also have a common taste in Oriental popular music with some, and a common taste in Oriental liturgical music with others; with some they may share a hostility to the secular establishment, with others to the haredi establishment; they develop characteristic ways of dressing, characteristic headgear (black velvet skullcaps), and, as Nissim Leon explains, a characteristic language, so that gradually people find multiple ways of joining, of being part of the flow.

In all these niches of social life the movement's activists introduce an unfamiliar innovative set of signs, symbols, emblems, and markers, by joining a haredi motif with elements of secular Israeli culture which have been kept at arm's length by the Ashkenazi haredim: they bring in Army slang, they bring in the jargon of t'shuva (with, for example, special terms to describe newcomers, the ones who 'need strengthening', the ones whose strength 'is confirmed'), they adopt slight but significant variations in speech, accentuating Sephardi, or conceivably pseudo- Sephardi, pronunciation. The pattern can be described as the conformation of a movement's identity by the creation of unaccustomed, innovative symbolic and behavioural allusions across previously or otherwise watertight boundaries. The role of the broadcast media in promoting the movement, arises not only, perhaps not principally, from the size of their audience, especially in this case where television is excluded for reasons of principle and where the radios are mostly shoestring operations which rely heavily on phone-in programs and have a limited range.

Rather the media provide more markers for the movement and its followers: the regularity of programs, the consistent tone or content of programs broadcast at certain times of day on certain frequencies, the differentiation of the audience into t'shuva-defined segments, and perhaps above all the bridge provided by these media between public and private spheres, all make of the radios and the cassettes integral parts of the movement of ethnic and religious renewal. Stated more simply the use of media characteristic of popular culture, namely radio and cassette tapes, of itself provides an interface between religion and the ethnic group most identified with 'the popular' in Israel. In appealing to Sephardim, and among them often to young people whom they regard as mired in the frivolities – or worse - of consumer culture, the broadcasters could not but adopt a language and a style unfamiliar to traditional ultra-Orthodoxy, more streetwise, less hidebound, less weighed down by the somniferous tones of traditional yeshivas, a trend reinforced by the intervention of freebooting social and religious entrepreneurs in media previously unused by ultraorthodoxy.

All this does not mean that the core of Shas is not deeply rooted in yeshiva life. But social movements are like concentric circles, with a hard center (the 'cadres') and eversofter peripheries, and they conform social spaces linked not by organizational structures but by inferential symbols embodied as we have indicated, in language, posters, iconic figures and much more besides pirate radios in the broadcasting system. Until 1999 the Israeli state had direct legal control of all nationwide radio and TV stations through the Israel Broadcasting Authority. Only in 1995 were private commercial radio stations permitted, and exclusively at the local level operated under a franchise arrangement with the Israel Broadcasting Authority. The state monopoly had been challenged long before, though more for political reasons, by unofficial 'pirate' broadcasting, which began in 1973 when dissident political groups, first against the country's occupation of the West Bank, later in favour of settlers in the selfsame West Bank, began transmitting from ships offshore.

By 1995, 'more than 50' active pirate stations were identified, and in the late 1990s Caspı, the leading authority on the subject, could still safely say that they were mainly broadcasting music and entertainment. After some resistance from their senior leader Rav Schach, the Ashkenazi haredi community began to use radio stations, though they remain controversial in this prickly constituency, and today there seems to be only one pirate station broadcasting specifically in the idiom of the Ashkenazi haredim – Kol Simcha '(The Voice of Celebration'). However, radio transmission enables people to cross boundaries without doing so too publicly, and there is no reason to believe that Ashkenazim do not listen to other, stations of a more Sephardi complexion.

The stations' broadcasts, despite their Sephardi tinge reflected in accent, style and music, do not give any space to material expressing some of the resentment against Ashkenazim which we have heard in interviews. Although the Sephardi 'tinge' is not explicitly promoted, it is a very important feature of these radios' broadcasting and of their appeal, expressed in broadcasters' accents, in much accompanying music, even in the streetwise language they use. This appeal is most straightforwardly explained by the limited presence of Oriental music and culture in the official stations. Those stations only broadcast one hour of Oriental content until a few years ago, but even now, though the amount has increased, the content is not in tune with Israeli popular taste, let alone with the religious tastes of the t'shuva movement or of Shas followers.

Official radio in Israel is heavily oriented to high culture and educational themes, plus an endless diet of news, and this narrowness opens a space for more popular – and therefore more Sephardi – modes of communication and entertainment. The entertainment stations on official radio certainly lack any appeal to a public at once popular and interested in religious themes and traditions. From another point of view, it could be said that by their use of Oriental-style music the stations are joining the Israeli mainstream, just as by promoting a Sephardi religiosity Shas is trying to create an Israeli mainstream Orthodoxy in the religious field. Israeli popular music is distinguished by continual mixing of styles, combining either the 'indigenous' tradition originating with the formative period of Israeli Jewish culture with rock and other cosmopolitan forms, or the Oriental style with those forms and with the indigenous ones.

Although there was for a time a prejudice against both cosmopolitan and quasi-Arab music, this has now given way to post-modern syncretism which are acceptable if they catch on. The pirate radios, then, which to some might appear as beyond the mainstream, may be fitting very nicely into this post-modern mainstream. Today, at least in the Jerusalem area, many, if not most, of the pirate stations are religious, and although they sometimes like to call themselves 'Holiness channels' (arutsei kodesh), they are happy to be known as piratim. There are also pirate stations devoted to popular music, and serving the West Bank settlers and the million-strong Arab population. But the religious stations, whose central theme is t'shuva, are now so numerous that people find themselves listening almost by accident as they turn the knobs on their car radios or in their kitchens, and as a welcome alternative to the official stations. During 2002 it has been noticeable that they are going beyond their core audience and penetrating the secular world, and they are also becoming the Subject of debates on the mainstream channels' chat shows and political discussions. Their number and proportion are matters for speculation.

In a Knesset debate on 20 October 1999, a Shas member (MK) stated that there were 150 between 1996 and 1999 of which only 14 were religious. Yet he also said that in 1999 the authorities closed down 90 stations, of which 48 were religious, and that in the two months prior to the debate 21 out of the 28 stations closed down were religious. Any conclusions drawn from these numbers should keep in mind that stations routinely reopen after being 'closed down' – a blatantly illegal procedure which has never been followed by a prosecution or conviction (which could in theory carry a sentence of three years' imprisonment or a fine of up to US$330,000).

The pirate stations play a game of cat-and-mouse with the government, operating under the constant threat of having their equipment confiscated. They do not like to give out their address, and they say that not infrequently they have to bundle their equipment out of a location in the face of a possible police raid. Although insiders mention links between particular stations and religious organizations or prominent Rabbis, they do not publicize these links. The degree of indulgence or repression by the authorities varies with the colour of the government of the day – the more right wing, the more tolerant. But the received wisdom among the haredim is that they suffer relentless persecution, and they make the point with the customary hyperbole of Israeli political debate.

The Shas MK quoted above declared that the persecution of the pirate radios reminded him of when the authorities in his native Georgia sent tractors to steamroller their synagogues in 1953, and the people lay down on the ground to stop them. The unwillingness of successive governments and parliaments to legalize their radio stations is also taken as proof of the discrimination they suffer at the hands of what they see as a secular dictatorship: the same MK, referring unashamedly to the pirate stations' support for his party, said that it was clear that 'they' want to 'silence millions who have no other station', and that the Prime Minister 'wants to destroy Shas' (which was a member of his coalition). A broadcaster in Netania spoke to us bitterly of their treatment by the Rabin government. Haredim, of course, would never accept space in what they regard as a godless state broadcasting station, but this does not stand in the way of routine pointscoring: thus, the Shas MK did not miss the opportunity to make the further point that, although the religious population were 20 per cent of the population, religious broadcasting accounted only for 0.5 per cent of broadcasting time on legal channels.

In recent years debates on this subject have been held on 12 March and 28 May 1997, 18 February 1998, 20 October 1999, 20 June and 23 July 2001, and they convey both the tenor of debate in Israel on and with haredim, as well as the unwillingness of the political class to regularize the situation. All have a vested interest in the status quo whereby the pirate radios – mostly religious as far as the MKs is concerned – are de facto tolerated. Caspi and Limor confirm the same point, though writing at a time when the religious stations had not become major players in pirate broadcasting, saying that they preserve an 'illusion of media pluralism', and are 'not perceived as threatening'. Today, they are perceived as a threat, along with the t'shuva movement as a whole, by secular Israel, but in practice almost the entire political class has a vested interest in turning a blind eye.

All the Knesset debates have a tone of polemical banter, and end inconclusively as the participants disingenuously fail to decide to which committee the issue should be referred. On one occasion the Chair asks how many pirate radios there are in Jerusalem, and a Shas MK responds 'one – the state radio!' In March 1997 the Shas Minister of Transport said that when the only pirate radios were those of the Peace Movement and the settlers they were left alone, but as soon as religious groups started to broadcast they were persecuted. In May that year a Shas MK said that the stations might not be 'very legal', but they do express the views of a 'hated and persecuted' section of the population. On another occasion a member complained that the police leave the Christian evangelical radios, 'which propagate a mistaken interpretation of the sources', undisturbed, leading gullible Jewish listeners to fall into a trap, while harassing the religious radios which broadcast 'love for Israel and the truth'. Secular parties, namely Meretz (the Centre Party), and Labour, intervene little, and when they do it is to complain that the law is not being implemented – a complaint which cuts little ice with Shas, nor with any government in this connection.

The views of the Shas MKs quoted above are echoed by the pirate station operators. The director of the Mikol Ḥalev station also says that there are hundreds of pirate stations in the country, but that only the religious ones are troubled by the police. Asked whether there might may be advantages to illegality, he responds guardedly: he does not see benefits from legalization 'in all situations', especially because legal stations are watched by the authorities and he does not want any authority looking over his shoulder or, as he put it, 'telling him what to say'. A newspaper journalist explained to us also that becoming legal involves bidding for a wave band, which would be far beyond the means of any of these stations – because of the heavy competition for the few legally available bands. Legality would also impose all sorts of time-consuming paperwork. On the other hand, legal status would allow the stations to earn revenues from advertising. In short, while radio 'piracy' is tolerated by the authorities, the attitude of the radios themselves is neatly summed up in a broadcaster's comment that 'no revolution is ever made in legality'. Outside the officially recognized media sector cash is scarce.

It can be raised from donors, and collections for the radios are often made at open-air public meetings in support of the t'shuva movement. At Mikol Halev, the broadcasters and workers, even the website designer, are volunteers, yeshiva students or people who have returned to religion full time. The station receives many offers – or approaches – from people who want to broadcast, but the director only accepts those recommended by trusted individuals. For someone who wants to build a reputation as a preacher the radio is a good opportunity, as in the case of Rav Shalom Arush who heads a network of several yeshivas and broadcasts on Kol HaChesed ('The Voice of Charity'). There are also degrees of professionalisation, exemplified by Rav Gilles, an experienced broadcaster in several different idioms on several stations, sometimes answering phoneins, sometimes delivering learned commentaries, sometimes interviewing a guest - always adept at switching his accent and style of speech between different audiences. Stations are now taking to recruiting media professionals who have made t'shuva or are at least sympathetic to their cause. Rav Gilles' ethnic/community identity is of no concern to the stations, which are eager to put this well known and experienced voice on their own wavelengths.

The radios do not stand still. Mikol Halev, which looks and sounds like a shoestring operation, has a website which permits listeners to hear native-speaking Rabbis expounding in Hebrew, Spanish, French and English. The size of their audience is of course impossible to judge, and many wavering listeners, responding to an audience survey, might not admit they do listen until 'they have crossed a certain line'. Rav Gilles reckons he can tell by the number of callers – on some stations he has long queues of callers while on others there are very few. All arrange for a few callers in advance to get the show going. On this basis he reckons that Mikol Halev is a small station, whereas its director says it is one of the biggest.

Pirate Radios and the T'Shuva Movement

The pirate religious stations are linked with a range of grassroots and street-level activities. We have seen the links with evangelists, but the case of Kol HaChesed shows that these links can spread much further, and that their multimedia capacity has the effect of shifting established social boundaries. This is a nationwide broadcaster run out of Netania by a group who resemble a social rescue brigade. Asked about their mission the first word they say is 'family' – their vocation is to spread a message of love, of reconciliation within families, and to do so in a language which is readily understandable to people unfamiliar with Judaism. Their radio is at the hub of a range of activities: they distribute didactic cassettes by giving a person 100 to sell as a good deed (mitzvah), they respond to requests for help and advice, on family and education matters especially; they provide a marriage guidance service whereby listeners can consult a Rabbi personally or by telephone, off the air. And, as so often, there are miracles: when a lady rang in saying she was having difficulty finding a husband, the Rabbi on the air told her she should sell 100 cassettes – three weeks later she was married!

The station operates within the framework of a NGO which is itself involved in many other activities – indeed our interlocutors say that they could not operate without that framework. The NGO is in the early stages of setting up a school for yeshiva dropouts who, having never served in the army, fall between these two poles of Israeli society and find themselves unequipped for making their own lives. Volunteers provide their services as teachers, and the students serve a type of apprenticeship, but there is an important condition for their participation: they must study Torah for two hours per day. Another project takes in 120 school dropouts – in premises which are rented out for private gatherings to fund the operation. Together with other organizations, they provide food boxes to 1000 needy families, train orphans for their bar mitzvah, and help young women who might be thinking of having an abortion – if necessary and possible by arranging marriages for them.

Through the organization 15 doctors provide weekly free medical attention – and though this is unpaid they benefit from the advertising of their work on the radio station. Their radio also advertises seminars – often residential and sometimes unpaid - run by Arachim ('Values') an organization devoted to the cause of t'shuva and also to training activists and professionals in propagating the message of t'shuva. Thus we can see how radios are linked with other activities and organizations, crossing boundaries which in the routine of everyday life would be much thicker. The non-sectarian quality of the Kol HaChesed operation is seen in the lack of interest in emphasizing Sephardi or Ashkenazi traditions and in the use of Rabbis from different traditions and tendencies. The wider impact of such an approach should not, however, be exaggerated. Sectarian attitudes to secular Jews are definitely not softened, as witness the barely concealed fury at the persecution the Netania radio activists say they suffered from the Rabin government. Also, our conversations in the one Ashkenazi haredi station revealed Ashkenazi indifference to reaching out to the Sephardi population or to potential returnees, jointly dismissed with the quip: 'T'shuva. That is for Sephardim'.

The consequence of such attitudes is that the t'shuva movement does not have an Ashkenazi voice, but rather a distinctively Israeli (not just Sephardi) voice. Partly because of its doubtful legal status, pirate broadcasting creates an intimacy with its audience: callers are not all that numerous, so they have time to chat, they are invited to make their needs known, and the speakers follow up through their religious or political networks to satisfy urgent personal needs. Most programming consists of homilies or phoneins, with musical interludes of varying length. Mikol Halev is hosted every morning by a former ice-cream seller known as Ovadia Mehaglida, for whom nothing is too much trouble. While we were there, someone rang in with a request for thirty items of religious apparel for a group of students who want to begin adopting religious dress. They sounded like candidates for t'shuva and the radio's prompt call brought immediate offers of money or donations in kind and once a week there is a program to match buyers and sellers of anything from household goods to real estate.

Many stations reserve extensive airtime for requests from individuals for help in emergencies. They also broadcast on health issues and (not surprisingly in this connection) alternative medicine. Whereas previously the stations tended to shy away from explicit political statements, in the increasingly polarized context of the second Intifada (from late 2000) some stations have become more vociferous and partisan on the subject of Jewish relations with Arabs and Palestinians. Sephardim may express occasional nostalgia for an the North Africa of their ancestors where Jews and Arabs coexisted in peace, and 'everyone was religious', but they do not transpose that into the context of contemporary Israel.

The radios, therefore, fit into the dense undergrowth of the t'shuva movement. The Sephardi element is not explicitly played up, but is an implicit presence through references to Shas or to Ovadia Yosef, through the accent of broadcasters and their chatty style which stands in contrast to the formalism of the state channels, characteristic of the Ashkenazi (secular) elite. Boundaries are redrawn by bringing listeners into new networks, which at first may be only virtual; but, if the radios achieve their aims, they eventually will reshape social lives as people put children into religious school, start attending synagogue, and become ever more involved in religious life. The content of the broadcasts, like the videos and tapes directed to the popular, less educated sectors, could be described as 'folksy'. They make a point of using images, proverbs and examples from everyday life, and these produce conclusions in the manner of folk wisdom.

There is a similarity with Pentecostal preaching, and a contrast with the heavily text-centered disquisitions of fundamentalist Christians and of the more erudite, especially Ashkenazi, haredim. Indeed, it is a trademark of Ovadia Yosef himself that he peppers his addresses though not his writings – with popular language and anecdotes. It is clear that women are an important section of the audience, and that stations pay a great deal of attention to their needs and problems. Although managers are uneasy about allowing them to speak on air, the emphasis given to family problems – and family solutions – reflects women's presence in the audience. Some speakers allow women on the air (but only 'so long as they keep to the point') while others only allow them to leave messages - questions which are read out and answered, and which listeners can then follow up with requests for further clarification. In response to frequent requests for advice in overcoming family conflicts, speakers tend to recommend patience, long-term commitment, and love in the family.

For these broadcasters, even major political problems have their solution in the rebuilding of the family, helped by a more observant lifestyle. This reflects the much-discussed collapse of family values and parental authority among Israel's Sephardi population. A man wants more children but cannot convince his wife; a woman wants to convince her household to adopt more strict observance, but encounters resistance among her men folk; men and women call to ask advice in resolving family conflicts. The responses tend to focus on 'peace-building' in the home, especially by advising women not to respond to their husbands' inconsiderate or offensive behaviour. Thus a woman calls to complain that her husband shouts at her constantly. In response the speaker (somewhat counter-intuitively) tells a story about a Rabbi who gave a woman an amulet to put in her mouth and keep it there. As a result she could not speak of course, but each day her husband came with more and more generous presents – flowers, a diamond ring, and so on. Eventually the Rabbi tells her that the 'amulet' is nothing but an empty card... Independently of the content of such advice, the allusion to an amulet provides a ready referent to the world of Israeli Sephardim.

Listeners identify quite readily with 'their' station, to the point that, when asked to place themselves on a religious spectrum, they may use the name of their preferred station as a shorthand response. The format makes of the station an extension of the home, helped in this by the unofficial status of the station, and the friendly, helpful, 'can-do' responses of the speakers. Some daytime programmes are for children, often using cautionary tales to convey a message. Thus we see a range of mechanisms whereby the activities of radios, when combined with other organizations and of course with politics, are redrawing some of the boundaries which separate – though, by emphasizing religious belonging and encouraging religious and political activism, they also integrate - the multiple ethnic, religious and cultural enclaves of Israeli society. Listeners can find a radio which uses a particular style of speech, uses a certain type of music, emphasizes certain themes, and enables them to combine religious observance with an engagement with the media – something quite uncommon in the haredi world until the t'shuva movement took hold.

The intimacy of the radio – both in the sense that it can be heard in private and in the home, and also that its style is designed to make listeners feel at home among an audience with whom they have a strong social and implicitly ethnic affinity – redraws boundaries in a society where these are unusually important in daily life. The airwaves are used to form networks of solidarity which feed in to Israel's enclave system. Politically, the organizations which the radios promote rely directly or indirectly on government funding, and thus Shas' strongholds in the apparatuses of Ministries of Social Affairs, Labour, the Interior, and Religious Affairs are strengthened. This fits in with the pattern of Shas activism, and indeed of nationalist and religious activism in Israel generally, which advances by creating 'facts on the ground', enclaves which begin as territorial entities – settlements, ultraorthodox neighbourhoods–and then become institutionalized in political parties or factions, and may eventually gain control of Ministries or ministerial departments.

T'shuva and the tension between high and low culture

For those whose knowledge or experience of Judaism is limited to the Diaspora it is hard to imagine the adoption of strict religious observance as a dissidence directed against high culture, or that the propagation of an observant lifestyle might be wrapped in symbols and motifs drawn from the sphere of popular culture. Ultra Orthodoxy, after all, seems so austere, so bound up with the written word and canonical texts, that it is hard to think of it as anything but high culture. In Israel, the ultraorthodox communities could for a long time be regarded as erudite, austere and self-isolated, relating to the rest of society only through their leaders' indefatigable political pressure and occasional direct action against violations of their bodily inhibitions and Sabbath observance.

Drawing the line between high and popular culture turns out to be a complex issue, requiring account to be taken of the diversity of the ultra-orthodox world itself and the difficulties of setting the secular-religious contrast against that between high culture and its popular counterpart. For the time being, therefore, it is enough to say that the powerful Chassidic strand in ultra- Orthodoxy, with its anti-intellectual elements of mysticism and physical expressions of devotion and identity (through chanting and dance), is clearly self-identified as popular culture; that the text-centered character of the life of ultra-orthodox men (including the Chassidim, for they too learn) does not in itself detach them from the popular; and finally that even in nineteenth century Eastern Europe, ultra-Orthodox identity developed as a reaction against the sophistication of secularized and modernized Jews who wanted to join an overwhelmingly nonJewish elite, and was also powerfully enhanced by the struggles over intellectualism within highly observant circles, which witnessed ferocious denunciations by extremely learned Rabbis of the Chassidim for their corporal effusion and messianism.

To understand the popular cultural dimension of today's movement of return to religion, it must first be recalled how radically different circumstances in Israel are from those in preHolocaust Europe or indeed in today's diaspora, if only because as a state it constitutes a space in which the interaction of high and low culture is bound up with relations of power. In Israel also, high culture is not a matter of religion – rather it is the culture of the secular elite, English-speaking, sophisticated, cosmopolitan and enamoured of the canon of Western civilization, and many indications tell us that the t'shuva movement is a cultural dissidence against that culture and its secularism. The Rabbinic erudition of the haredi communities stands in sharp contrast to the secular erudition of the university: where academics bring modern sciences such as archaeology and linguistics to bear on canonic texts, and place them in a historical context, while in the yeshivas the Rabbis do not accept the treatment of those texts as historical documents.

Although they cultivate an extraordinary command of the texts, as far as they are concerned, Rashi -05 in France, Maimonides in Cordoba and Cairo, and the authors and editors of the Talmud in Babylon and Jerusalem, might as well all have lived at the same time in the same place. The Ashkenazi Rabbinical world has imparted to their Sephardi pupils its hostility to the secular elite. The broader Sephardi population, for their part, are themselves marked out from the secular elite by a range of linguistic, educational and socio-economic markers, and they repeatedly charge that elite with making them feel inferior in culture and social status. So the t'shuva movement has been able to mobilize popular culture and strict religion against the secular elite and its cosmopolitan (European-Ashkenazi) practices, building on the affinity of the ethnic Sephardi theme with return to religion.

The streetwise tinge to the movement – evidenced in Ovadia Yosef's asides, the chatty style of some cassette tapes, the religious music on tape, and the fabulous imagery (mixed with an abundance of wit) of Amnon Yitzchak's apocalyptic discourses – is the vehicle for its openness to the broader society, and demarcates t'shuva from the haredi obsession with practices denoting taboo, pollution and thus closure, introspection and exclusion. The circle of dissidence is finally closed by the identification in Israel of the popular sectors with the Judaeo-Arab heritage, rather than with the Yiddish-speaking Eastern European culture, because the Sephardim are disadvantaged, because theirs is the language of the street, of the criminal underworld, and even because the pronunciation of modern Hebrew itself derives from the Hebrew of the Northern and Southern Mediterranean shores and of historic Palestine itself.

Similarly, Israeli popular music also derives from the North African and Middle Eastern musical modes, not from those of Eastern Europe. Some might remind us that outside Israel other t'shuva movements also use modern media and also conduct extensive t'shuva campaigns. This is true especially of Chabad, also known as the Lubavitch Chassidim, the one Ashkenazi sect which regards t'shuva as its primary commitment, which uses cassettes, co-opts popular music, and also New Age themes and motifs into its activities. Chabad has outreach programmes in the Jewish community, on many university campuses especially in the USA, and is well known for its missionary activities in peripheral Jewish communities, for example in Madrid, Rio de Janeiro, São Paulo, Santiago, Caracas and Buenos Aires. But these are directed inevitably at middle class people, and operate in a parochial Jewish cultural field in the Diaspora, not in a national cultural space as is possible in Israel.

Indeed it is striking that Chabad, though it has extensive operations in Israel, including an entire settlement known as Kfar Chabad, and although its methods have been borrowed by sections of the t'shuva movement (especially the Or HaChayyim educational network which is closely identified with Shas), does not have a high profile there – for example in radio or other media. The Israeli t'shuva movement, in contrast, with Shas as its vanguard, has developed not just as a 'conversion' (or 'reversion') movement, but also as a form of cultural dissidence vis-à-vis the Ashkenazi secular elite, and with Shas as its political wing has been able to marshal an ethnically based electorate and large scale state finance to fuel its advance. The confluence of popular culture, religious renewal and multimedia intervention is well represented in the figure of Amnon Yizchak. Yitzchak is a one man road show: his cassettes are distributed for free at street intersections, he makes CDs of his appearances in Israel, England and the US, and his personal appearances in Israel seem calculated to challenge or offend the country's cultural elite. Like evangelists in other religious traditions and other places, he uses shock tactics in a symbolic antielitist crusade, for example by hiring venues usually occupied by symphony orchestras and international theatre groups.

When he hired Tel-Aviv's Hichal Hatarbut ('Temple of Culture') legal challenges were (unsuccessfully) taken right up to the Supreme Court to stop his appearance there, and the audience at his – by now unchallenged – appearance in the equally highbrow Jerusalem Theatre auditorium in November 2001 were gleefully treated to a video of those very protests. To support his campaign against television, another symbol of Israeli secular culture, Yitzchak promises that anyone who throws theirs out will receive a free copy of the Babylonian Talmud, and to demonstrate the success of his evangelizing campaign, he exhibits a box of earrings and ponytails discarded by women and men (respectively) who have converted at his public meetings. ('Throwing the television out' is a metaphor, or at least a rhetorical device: ultra-orthodox people still watch approved videos, for example in community centers. Yitzchak's target audience, though, are people who have still a long way to go before their 'conversion' has reached the point of literally throwing out the television.)

Yitzchak's Yemeni origin is central to his mediatic persona: his accent identifies him with that underprivileged and Oriental sector of society, and he wears a djellaba with unique accoutrements, including a skull–cap which he jokingly refers to as his 'antenna'. He litters his addresses with wordplay, talking of the 'temblevisia' instead of the 'televisia' – an allusion to the mind-numbing effects of television and likening (George W.) Bush's name to the Hebrew word for embarrassment – busha. Yitzchak manages to soften stark choices and thick boundaries, presenting t'shuva as a gradual purification of social relations, with an emphasis on joining a new community rather than on breaking bonds with the old, as a solution to everyday problems of love, family, and finding a spouse, and as a gradual process rather than a painful radical break.

Yitzchak's road show is also a business operation with some characteristics of a NGO, since it relies in part on the cooperation of volunteers and on donations. His Shofar organization claims to have distributed a million videos for free in its first year, and to have sold a further million after 1996. The free distributions of videos and cassette tapes are made in the expectation that a certain number of the recipients will then become buyers and sellers. At meetings he invites his audience to 'win' (i.e. buy) 1000 cassettes by making ten monthly payments of 100 shekels. If, as in one instance, he persuades a mere 20 people out of 500 at one neighbourhood meeting to sign up, that makes 20,000 tapes in a small area.

The mischievous millenarian: the use of parables and myths to subvert official discourse. His Judaism apart, Amnon Yitzchak has many, if not all, of the attributes of a Christian evangelist. His Shofar organization claims to have distributed a million videos in one year for free, to have sold a million a year since 1996, and to have brought 100,000 returnees per year back to religion. As illustrated in the previous paragraph, blanket coverage trawls a small number of committed activists, who then become collectors and distributors of cassettes and propagandists for the cause. His Hayyim Keflayim ('Living Twice') program follows up people who give their names at meetings, and gives them cassettes. Thus the organization builds up a database of people with whom it comes into contact, who might become more involved or donate funds.

Like the radio stations, it encourages people to put their children into religious schools and encourages returnees on their road back to religious observance, but Yitzchak and his people have gone much further than the radio stations in creating a public of their own, in the application of business principles, and in adopting the content of American millenarian fundamentalism. His rhetoric also goes further than (almost) any Israeli politician would dare. At the Jerusalem Theatre Yitzchak made constant reference to his cassettes: The cassettes seem to be the emblem of his operation, to own and listen to them is to belong, and to distribute them among one's friends and relations is to draw even closer to his campaign of t'shuva. Dressed in his distinctive attire, Yitzchak is his own trade mark.

The format of his meetings includes an address by him followed by questions from the floor. Many people want their personal problems resolved – one needs a husband, the other a wife, a young boy wants to attend religious school but his mother will not let him, and so on. Almost all the questioners – some of whom may be 'planted'– speak with ease and eloquence, and Yitzchak responds in a down-to-earth sort of way. Those who have specific needs are asked to hand in a piece of paper and he blesses them all at the end of the meeting. Anti-establishment rhetoric is fuelled by wordplay and judicious use of accent and turns of phrase. In one videocassette, filmed live, he defends the privileges enjoyed by haredim in Israel, on the analogy of a watermelon.

This is a reference to a remark by Ezer Weizman, Israel's recent Head of State and, for the preacher's audience, an archetypal representative of the European, educated, secular elite, who had picked out the development of the seedless watermelon as a source of great national pride. For religious people, for whom Israel is above all the Promised Land, the notion that the country should take pride in such mundane achievements is itself laughable. But Yitzchak builds his retort around the metaphor of 'black' as the colour of strict religious observance. For him, Weizman, like all secular Israelis, wants an Israel without the black seeds – without the haredim.

For Yitzchak, in contrast, the haredim are not only black seeds, they are also the seeds of continuity of Judaism, while the red flesh represents communism and dictatorship – i.e. the godless Zionist secular regime – and the green outer skin represents fertile pasture, an image of a fertile Israel. The kibbutz, secular and emblematically Zionist, took the juice of state subsidies first, and so the haredim then had to come and extort their due: if the haredim had staked their claim first, they would not have had to exercise so much pressure later on. He then attacks a towering icon of Zionism, namely David Ben-Gurion. Ben-Gurion, he claims, had said that Israel had to make the Jews into a 'people with a culture' – thus ignoring 5300 years of Jewish culture - and introduced a German culture – that is, anti-semitism.

What, Yitzhak asks, of charity, of Sabbath observance, of respect for the sages – are these not also culture? We had occasion to appreciate the effectiveness of Yitchak's use of these devices in his address, entitled 'Before the End', more or less word for word the same as a cassette he issued the day after the 11 September attacks –which offered a golden opportunity to merchants of biblical millenarianism. He recalled his prediction at the time of the 1993 Oslo agreements that 'there is no peace with terrorists'. Two years before he had predicted that 'the great America would shrink': no one would have predicted it, not even in their worst nightmares.... 1,000,000 Interpol agents... millions of recorded telephone conversations... all these 'sources' are of no use because those without 'spiritual sources' are unprotected. Only those who had the Jewish 'sources' knew it would happen. The discourse then discusses the biblical origins of claims to the land of Israel, and quotes the Zohar, a Kabbalistic text which, having been compiled in thirteenth century Spain, is claimed as their own by Sephardim: 'there will come a time when their right to the Holy Land will expire.

Then the sons of Ishmael will wage war on the whole world – on sea, on land and near Jerusalem, and other peoples will participate in the struggle, but there will be no victor – there will be three months of war in a far-off place – and in the end only Israel will remain and the whole world will recognize the one God and his name is One...No one believed these or other prophecies, yet "the sons of Ishmael" have made us – the sixth power in the world – and the Americans, look like circus performers, like dwarfs: they took away the King's crown and slapped him in the face'. Yitzchak ridicules the Americans – branded by implication as the global champions of the consumer society - and indeed the Israeli state itself, which trusts too much in military prowess. He predicts that two thirds of the world will perish in the war of Gog and Magog: 'in 9 months of catastrophe, there will be epidemics, and limbs will be cut from bodies. Two thirds of the world will die.

It is all written down – there is nothing to be done. The American attempt to impose globalization, democracy and liberalism, ignoring all religions, has come to this.' But there is a chance of salvation for Israel if the people make t'shuva and return to God. The history of the Jewish people is an endless alternation between abandonment of God and t'shuva–but 'maybe this is the last t'shuva, maybe we can be saved as in the Exodus from Egypt. Maybe now we have finally understood and the Messiah will return in our times'. Apart from the violence of the language and the message, it is worth remarking on the constant inversion of official language in the discourse, with the use of wordplay and caricature: the Twin Towers and the tower of Babel; Bush juxtaposed with the Hebrew word 'busha', the 'intelligence sources' juxtaposed with 'spiritual sources', and the ridiculing of a great power humiliated, an image of the 'world upside down'.

Written black on white, the speech seems extremely threatening, but in the auditorium, delivered in a low-key measured tone, mischievously peppered with jokes and ridicule of the great and powerful, including all Israeli political factions – save Shas - the audience did not respond with abnormal emotion or enthusiasm, as they might have done to fiery political rhetoric in a less genteel location. The t'shuva movement in a comparative perspective and as occasional remarks have indicated, there is much in the t'shuva movement which we have already encountered in Latin American Pentecostalism, and, although of course there are differences, it is the similarities which deserve close attention, simply because similarities across the boundaries established by religious tradition – and of course by the interests of religious bureaucracies - are more counterintuitive, as are differences within the boundaries. Both Pentecostals and the t'shuva movement propagate a change of life, a strengthening of the family by infusing their discourse on family relationships with a halo of happiness and positive feelings, together with a strengthening of parental control over children and of husbands' authority over their wives.

There are variations within as much as between: some churches insist more than others on the authority of husbands, as do some Rabbis; some Rabbis and preachers direct a message towards women and focus on the misfortunes of family life – unruly children, cruel husbands, lack of self-esteem – and both movements have in common a focus on changing one's life by changing one's attitudes or outlook, through return to Christ or trust in God. Occasionally a New Age tinge is added, as when people are called upon to 'listen' to one another, to stay calm, to find an inner peace, but for the most part the solution offered is t'shuva in one case, and accepting Jesus' in the other. In both cases we observe much attention to fundraising from the public, fronted by mediatic entrepreneurs of varying wealth, effectiveness and influence.

These entrepreneur/preachers who combine proselytizing, managerial and communications skills have become a standard feature of religious campaigning worldwide. The example of the Brazilian – but now international - Universal Church of the Kingdom of God, which has developed a vast centralized bureaucratic and commercial apparatus out of this combination, is exceptional, but emblematic: for the most part such ventures are one-man shows which operate in conjunction with other religious organizations on the ground, as Amnon Yitzchak does. There is a straightforward explanation for the preference for radio over television and for local stations over national networks. Radio is cheaper and allows the broadcaster to target a niche audience. Local stations have technical and commercial advantages: their phonein programs have low startup costs, they probably avoid liability for copyright fees, operate with volunteers, and do not need to sustain uninterrupted programming – their audience quickly becomes accustomed to tuning in, so long as broadcasts keep to a regular timetable.

In Latin America Pentecostalism has evolved a subtle and complex relationship with popular culture, and with the complex of relationships which bind the popular to the erudite in both religious and secular spheres. Pentecostals attack the culture of Catholicism and it's intertwined institutional and popular expressions, yet manage to do so while apparently deepening their penetration of popular culture. The institutional Catholic Church is depicted as luxurious and self satisfied, cosseted in its finery and arrogant in its elaborate architecture. As in Israel, the intertwined secular cultures of the elite and the people are also targeted, using the media to present a counter-culture against the rational secularism of the intellectual elite, and against the political elite. Popular culture exists in interdependence with the culture of the erudite and the elite – it is not a relationship of dependence, nor is the popular a mere artefact of elite manipulation.

Rather in these contexts the cultural struggle is not only for the control of popular culture, but also for the power to state with authority what that culture consists of. The paradox is that, despite their often-dramatic rejection of the culture of the popular sectors Pentecostals also successfully portray themselves as closer to the language and daily concerns of those same popular sectors. This is achieved by a refashioning of the imaginary of popular culture and by operating transformations in the popular-elite relationship. Pentecostals benefit from the contrast between the social distance separating highly trained priests, educated in seminaries and sometimes abroad, and the style of their own pastors who are close to 'the people', speak a direct, jargon-free language, and confront the day-to-day problems of their followers. But the pastors retain a distance, though a different sort of distance: they do not adopt a humble persona of 'men of the people'. Instead, they present to their followers a role model of prosperity and petty bourgeois respectability.

If in Israel we have observed the affinity of t'shuva with the renaissance of the Sephardi ethnicity, in Latin America we find that Pentecostals are particularly successful among indigenous people, and that in Brazil Pentecostals have appropriated and refashioned the symbolic apparatus associated with the African heritage, while claiming to discredit them. The t'shuva movement's Sephardi leaders have inverted symbolic structures of exclusion and low status by invoking them as emblems of a grand tradition which, they say, remained unbroken while the Ashkenazi tradition was interrupted and weakened by the Enlightenment and the Holocaust. Like the Pentecostals they have also mounted a two-pronged attack on the religious establishment of the Ashkenazi ultra-Orthodox – whose parties Shas outnumbers by 17 to 5 Knesset seats – and on the secular elite.

They have adapted the music of popular culture to their religious crusade by keeping the tunes but exchanging secular lyrics for liturgical verses; their radio broadcasts are a permanent thorn in the side of the regulators of broadcasting; they transform talmudic debate by their use of street language and their evocation of the stresses and strains of daily life – sprinkled with abundant Rabbinic allusions and stories. T'shuva Israelistyle does not explicitly confront the religious establishment in the same way as Pentecostals confront Catholic hegemony. But in these matters content counts for less than form – and by form is meant the rearrangement and appropriation of symbols and ethnic identifiers, and the concomitant redrawing of public spaces. In this chapter we have shown how, for all the use of modern communications media, the time-honored formal accoutrements of religion – ritual, taboo, the delineation of space, style, language, dress and more besides – are more than equal to the challenge of reclaiming public space from a secular intelligentsia to whom these arms are quite foreign. They are hardly likely to reclaim the whole of public space, as no doubt they would like, but they are certainly redrawing its boundaries.

4

The Politics of Difference and Diversity Management

"Diversity stands for a comprehensive approach in understanding the differences between employees as an opportunity not only for the employees themselves, but also for the company as a whole Ford is becoming an "employer of choice"... for whom one gladly works or would like to work in the future." Diversity management is not so much a question of social justice, but an instrument to gain a highly qualified, creative, and loyal workforce, which identifies happily with its employer. Economists argue that acknowledging demographic development diversity management even becomes a necessity, because in the field of highly qualified personnel there is sharp competition to get hold of the best people on the labour market. A workforce with a wide range of cultural knowledge also promises advantages in marketing strategies, since the specificities of customer groups are represented in the company. Last but not least, people who feel acknowledged, self-assured, and part of a supportive social group can be expected to produce a higher work-output than those who are/feel devalued or discriminated against.

Therefore from an employees' point of view quite a few reasons speak in favour of diversity management. It is not surprising that up to now self-employment has been a fairly attractive form of work for lesbians and gays, and even more so for transgender and transsexuals. The workforce of public and private employers might change significantly if they decided to install measures and practices to end discrimination – as well as the more subtle normativities of a naturalized heterosexuality, whiteness, able-bodiedness, Christianity. There is something very interesting about the way diversity management conceptualizes difference. It not only problematizes the stigmatizing effects of categorizations (as 'other' or 'minority' if not 'deviant'), but it also avoids the kind of individualization, which understands difference as any one's private business and any one's personal responsibility to cope with discrimination. Rather, diversity management explicitly takes up the task of understanding (the construction, regulation, management of) difference as a communal task.

By translating it into diversity, that is, from problem into promise, it even challenges dominant norms. Ideally, it includes anybody in his or her specificity in the field of diversity. But this is, indeed, the way diversity management forecloses questions of how socio-historical relations of power constitute differences. In referring to a liberal model of individual freedom, diversity management depoliticizes difference. Though difference is not privatized, it is personalized and understood as a trait of individuality. It is captured as independent of the economic class relations and capitalist principles that organize the companies that promote diversity.

These capitalist principles imply that employees produce surplus value, which becomes profit of the company, and it also implies that global economic processes are fueled by exploitation of humans and resources. In other words, contradictory interests rule the socio-economic field, but these contradictions cannot be expressed or even politicized under a regime of diversity management, which suggest a common interest of employers and employees within "our rainbow company family". Therefore it is not very realistic to hope for unconditional acceptance. Certain normative standards, certain unspoken rules have to be fulfilled in order to gain acceptance or recognition. An extended integration and diversification at work, marketed under the label of diversity management does not guarantee that the newly integrated subjects gain the power to participate in organizing the field of integration.

Maybe, heterogeneous forms of gender and sexuality can be expressed openly – but what about expressing political differences and critique? Diversity management can be understood as a moment of precarisation, because it addresses people as individuals, and asks them to submit their individuality to the companies' interests, while they will gain individual recognition. Solidarity has to be limited within the company's walls. Still, one does not know whether this kind of depoliticizing and regulation of social relations succeeds. Is it really the case that employees do not question power dynamics and economic injustice? It would be interesting to analyze processes of communication and/or negotiation between employers/management and employees, and ask particularly how power relations are challenged and structures of economic exploitation addressed.

Effect of the Interplay

Many factors have contributed to the development of Malaysian public relations into what it is today. Efficient mass media infrastructure (e.g. availability of cable and satellite television) allows more radio and television channels to operate. Although private ownership of the media remains under government jurisdiction, there are now more private radio and television stations than ever, which create job opportunities. In Malaysia, the government uses the media to disseminate information to the general public in order to gain support for policies, such as the privatisation of organisations such as the *Tenaga Nasional* (electrical provider), *Pos Malaysia* (Malaysian Post) and *Telekom Malaysia* (Malaysian Telecommunications) in the 1980s.

After opposition parties and some members of the public mounted aggressive 'public opinion' challenges to large-scale government projects such as the Petronas Twin Towers, the

Sepang Formula One circuit and the Kuala Lumpur International Airport, the government became aware of the need to ensure that government policies were well-understood by the public. According to Idid, the strategies developed for conveying such information to the public were uniquely Malaysian, because of the need to change the general public's attitude towards these development projects by disseminating adequate information to the public in a timely and meaningful manner.

In this case, public relations benefited from the parliamentary system of government that relies on public opinion. Politicians and political campaigners must obtain public support for their election campaigns by disseminating information about their programmes and strategies. The government need for public relations tools has fuelled a demand for public relations graduates in the job market, which has in turn aided the growth of public relations education in Malaysia. Despite these advances, it is obvious that the public relations industry in Malaysia is still struggling to define itself as a profession. Although the number of consultancies, internal public relations departments and public relationsrelated personnel are on the increase, the services required are very much technically oriented (e.g. writing) in contrast to the services required in more developed countries. This indicates that the public relations profession in Malaysia is way behind the development of the public relations industry in the United States. Services in demand in Malaysia today, such as obtaining publicity in the press, are typical of what USA consultancies and corporations were concerned with in the 1980s.

As in Malaysia, the dependent relationship between public relations and the press in Singapore is especially significant as the number of print and broadcasting media outlets are limited. There is a great need for more public relations programmes in which practitioners have the opportunity to share their experiences of carrying out successful public relations manoeuvres with both their peers and aspiring entrants to the profession. The recent approval for accreditation status for public relations professionals by the Institute of Public Relations Malaysia (IPRM) indicates a strong desire for the development of better public relations education programs in the country. The ideal public relations practice serves the public interest by developing a mutual understanding between the organisation and its publics, contributing to informed debates about issues in society, and facilitating dialogue between all interested parties.

This assists complex and pluralistic societies in reaching decisions and helps them to function more effectively, often by bringing private and public policies into harmony. The role of public relations today is no longer to merely serve the organisation but to build bridges and alliances with publics to create an environment conducive to the smooth operation of businesses, government, voluntary agencies and other bodies. In order to achieve these goals, institutions need to develop effective relationships with different publics such as employees, members, customers, local communities, shareholders and the public at large.

However, it will be difficult to achieve these objectives in many Asian countries (particularly Malaysia) where the government has power over both the organisations and over the organisations' control of their strategic publics. In Malaysia, as well as in many other countries of Asia such as India, Korea, Indonesia, Thailand, the Philippines and Singapore, the media and the political, social and cultural environments vary from those of the West. Therefore, the practice of public relations in any country has to take into account the special circumstances of the various local environments.

The Implications of the Media for Public Relations Practitioners

No one can deny the power the media possesses to both disseminate and influence information. According to Nelson, "The media have the potential to exacerbate an issue, create much greater awareness than desired, and continuously find negatives in either neutral or positive news". It is not easy for organisations to secure media cooperation. Therefore, from a public relations standpoint, it is crucial for organisations to maintain good contacts with the media in order to get their message across to their publics and to succeed in their businesses. As a result, media relations has become one of the most important functions of public relations practitioners sees the relationship between the media and public relations as fundamental, as while they are mutually independent, the media relies on public relations sources for access to businesses and other organisations, and public relations needs the media to disseminate messages to publics (organisations, clients, government and shareholders).

This relationship is described by Pavlik as "symbiotic". He adds that tension between the media and public relations practitioners has a positive impact as it encourages each group to remain conscious of each other during the communication process. The media in Malaysia actively supports private organisations, which is why most government and large corporate success stories are given prominent coverage, while their failures are never revealed. The strong relationship between the government, large corporations and the media ensures this state of affairs. According to Khattab, the Malaysian media has purely mainstream, mechanical, and uniform modes of message transmission to an assumed passive public.

In theory, the amount of attention given to an issue (whether by media personnel, members of the public or policy makers) represents the power of those individuals or organisations to influence the decision making process. For a country such as Malaysia where interpersonal networking and contacts with influential people are important to a public relations professional, good media relations are important for an organisation wanting to disseminate its messages to the public and make them part of the media agenda. Rapid developments in information technology are making it vital for organisations to foster positive relations with media professionals. This helps organisations counter problems by releasing their versions of the story to the public during a crisis, as well as generally using the media as a vehicle to disseminate information to their target publics.

According to Khoo, because the mass media in Malaysia is controlled by the government, it is essential for organisations to have a good rapport with the government in order to maintain good relations with the media. Most medium-scale private organisations will have difficulty in dealing with the media in terms of favourable news coverage unless they know the relevant media staff well through personal contacts and networks. As a result, most organisations prefer to appoint former journalists to work in and manage their public relations departments. This state of affairs explains why Malaysia was ranked 154th out of 193 countries in a 2004 global survey of media independence. Malaysia fell below Iraq, Russia, Yemen, Bangladesh and Bhutan, and was only slightly better than China, Laos, Vietnam, Burma, North Korea, Afghanistan and Brunei. In addition, Malaysia was placed third in the category of *Not Free* nations.

The extent of the freedom of the media has an impact on the effectiveness of public relations. This is because public relations have different relationships with different media in different systems. McLuhan reveals that the media has a totally different role in different cultures, which indicates why the media's functions differ between countries. For example, the press in the US uses news, politics and personal entertainment to capture readers.

Citizenship, the Public Sphere, and Media

Historically, citizenship can be traced back to ancient Greek city–states. It is traditionally understood as a system whereby rights are granted to and duties put upon citizens. Citizenship can also be viewed as a way of structuring society, of enforcing boundaries that allowed the (city) state to include, but above all to exclude. From this perspective, citizens are the 'official' and registered inhabitants of a geographically delimited territory. They are allocated specific rights by the state, which 'others' – non-citizens, foreigners, denizens, deviants, prisoners, slaves, etc. – do not have. In return, certain duties are expected from the citizen. However, citizenship, as it is understood today, has evolved considerably since the Greek city–states or since the formation and consolidation of the nation states after the treaty of Westphalia in 1648.

Western Enlightenment, the struggle for universal suffrage and modernism, in close connection to the class struggles, as is shown in T. H. Marshall's seminal work Citizenship and Social Class, has considerably extended citizenship rights. The assumption of an intrinsic link between the notion of citizenship and the nation/welfare state remains predominant in most of these approaches. Citizenship is developed and conceptualized within the 'boundaries' of the modernist state, which remains the most important political space in which rights are voted, upheld and enforced through the rule of law (at least within democratic societies).

However, the increasing globalization of the world economy – characterized by post-Fordism and fuelled by the introduction of innovations in communication, distribution and mobility, ecological and demographic pressures, as well as ethnic and nationalistic forces – has considerably undermined the sovereignty and legitimacy of the nation state. Due to these social, economic and political transformations, it is fair to assert that the conceptualization of the Westphalian nation state, as a sovereign state linked to a geographical territory with relative material, economical, social, physical and psychological autonomy, has become very difficult to sustain.

Besides the effects on citizenship of the power shift from states to the market, from states to regions or to international organization/regimes, the linkage of citizenship and the nation state is also being challenged by culturalist and poststructuralist theories, which put cultural citizenship on the agenda. Cultural citizenship is 'understood as membership of an actual or virtual community based not on nation but on, for example, ethnicity, gender, sexual orientation, region, age, etc'. This form of citizenship implies the redefinition of citizenship as 'sets of different and sometimes overlapping communities that constitute individuals as competent members of sets of different and sometimes overlapping communities which should ideally constitute the national (political) culture'. From these perspectives, special attention is attributed to the relationship between global media (including the Internet) and cultural globalization, and to what this means for the notion of citizenship.

Both the post-Fordist global economic and the culturalist challenges to citizenship have given rise to a number of 'unbounded' citizenship notions such as ecological citizenship, net citizen(ship), transnational citizenship, cosmopolitan citizenship or denationalized citizenship. These citizenships transcend the personal and the individual and collective rights focus inherent to formalized legal citizenship. As Mouffe argued, citizenship thus becomes a 'form of identification, a type of political identity; something to be constructed, not empirically given'. These also reflects an ethical stance that sees the moral being inscribed into the political and a strong belief in change, agency and the capacity of democracy to constantly transform and adapt itself. It points to an idealized citizenship and – to a certain extent – to the impossibility of Full – complete and stable – citizenship.

Citizenship is thus constantly renegotiated and increasingly linked to sexual, cultural and/or ethnic identities and subcultures. It points to the distinctiveness, but also (possibly conflictuous) coexistence of, on the one hand the citizen as a legal subject, linked to communities of birth, the polis and welfare state rights, and on the other hand the citizen as a normative subject, linked to social, sexual or cultural identities and practices, to communities of interest. What binds both types of citizenship is that they simultaneously exclude and include; they set boundaries as to who is in or out, thereby constructing the identities of all involved.

Communication has always played an important mediating role regarding the facilitation of the debate on, the articulation of and the struggle for new citizenship rights. As Urry argued, 'citizenship has always necessitated symbolic resources distributed through various means of mass communication'. Citizenship thus refers to the process that leads to the articulation of certain rights, the forging of a societal consensus about the nature and extent of rights and obligations, about the balance between different often conflicting rights. The public sphere is a central – albeit contested – notion in this regard. From a liberal perspective, the public gathering is conceived as the marketplace of ideas. While pluralism is heralded as an important democratic value, at the same time, the personal autonomy of individuals is emphasized in determining which ideas prevail over others. Thus, from a liberal perspective a consensus is reached if a majority of individuals make the same or similar choices.

Making a Difference to Media Pluralism

In theorizing the relationship between media and democracy, citizens' access to a wide range of information in the public sphere is unarguably a key condition. Furthermore, notions of pluralism and diversity today seem to invoke a particularly affective resonance; to an extent that they permeate much of the argumentation in current European media policy debates. Yet opinions on the meaning and nature of these values are manifold, and they embody some of central conflicts in contemporary media policy. Based on the undisputed merits of social, political and cultural pluralism, diversity and variety in the media can even be seen as desirable ends in themselves. But as McLennan noted, the constitutive vagueness of pluralism as a social value gives it enough ideological flexibility so that it is capable of signifying reactionary tendencies in one phase of the debate and progressive values in the next.

From the perspective of democratic theory, it has, thus, been noted that 'pluralism is currently one of those values to which everybody refers but whose meaning is unclear and far from adequately theorized'. In media policy, the resonance of pluralistic discourses has been exploited accordingly in arguments for various and often incompatible objectives; for free market competition, as well as further public interventions and public service obligations. The aim of this chapter is to deconstruct some of the paradoxes involved in the use of diversity and pluralism as media policy objectives. The argument is mainly conceptual and rooted in theoretical debates on media and democracy, but the context of contemporary European media policy debates, within political decision-making processes, as well as in expert discourses of policy analysts, serves as an illustration of the conceptual frameworks being adopted by different actors.

In both political and analytical discourses, the concepts of media pluralism and media diversity are used more or less synonymously, raising some confusion regarding the difference, or a possible hierarchy, between the two concepts. Although the purpose here is not to offer any new systematic definitions, the notion of media diversity is generally used in a more empirical or tangible meaning, whereas pluralism refers to a more diffuse societal value or an underlying orientation. In the broadest sense, the concept of media diversity refers to the heterogeneity on the level of contents, outlets, ownership or any other aspect of the media deemed relevant. Respectively, different frameworks have been suggested to analyze its different subcomponents such as source, content and exposure diversity, as well as their mutual hierarchies and relations.

In any case, both function as umbrella terms or conceptual categories whose fundamental ambiguousness and indeterminacy is the very focus of this chapter. In this chapter, the focus lies on the definitional power involved in political uses of pluralism and diversity. Of course, the contestation over politically and ethically charged concepts is not limited to these, but is rather characteristic of the recent debates around media governance, on the national, European and global level. Similar observations could thus be made of struggles around a number of concepts such as freedom, access or any other concept that is central to the debates on communication rights and citizenship. As such, the contestation of normative concepts and the fact that they can easily be remoulded for various political purposes is not foreign, or undesirable, to any sector of politics. According to Rose and Miller, political discourse is by definition 'a domain for the formulation and justification of idealized schemata for representing reality, analyzing it and rectifying it'.

From this perspective, analyzing policy is not so much about what concepts or words, such as freedom, diversity or democracy, mean but rather of analyzing what they do, the way they function in connection with other elements, what they make possible, the sentiments they mobilize and regimes of truth they constitute. In accordance, the intention here is not to seek the foundations of concepts or to offer new definitions, but to find contradictions, ambiguities and instances of definitional power in their current use in politics. The purpose of this chapter is, thus, to argue for a more reflexive, open-ended understanding of pluralism as a media policy value. Equally, the contribution can be conceived as an attempt at scholarly self-reflection since academic research clearly is one of the main institutions of intellectual machinery that produce the conceptual schemata of political discourse.

Diversity and the Structure of Differences

Is more diversity always better? Based on any discussion of pluralism as a social or philosophical value, the belief that it can be unambiguously turned into a linear variable is easy enough to repudiate. While the notion of media diversity clearly denotes heterogeneity on some level, it can be defined in any number of ways and it can refer to any aspect of the media: sources, outlets, opinions as well as genres and representations. In debates on media policy, diversity can refer to the extent in which media contents reflect and serve various interests and opinions of the public, or it can refer to the general diffusion of media power in society on the level of ownership, economic structures, and political influence.

Considering the variety of possible definitions, empirical evidence on the relations of different aspects of diversity tends to be very ambiguous as well. The relationship between the number of media outlets, the diversity (however defined) of available content, and the actual content that is being provided is all but straight-forward, as is shown by a number of contradictory and ambiguous studies on the effects of competition and ownership structures on content. For instance, it is entirely possible that market competition would enhance the number and variety of program types and genres available to the public, while at the same time reducing the diversity of political views or cultural representation or even excluding some contentious issues altogether. Thus, it needs to be recognized that any act of constructing the differences against which diversity is analyzed or measured is itself an act of power.

Theoretically, this has especially been stressed by Mouffe who explicitly denies the type of extreme pluralism that valorizes all forms of difference and espouses heterogeneity without any limits, because for her, such pluralism crucially misses the dimension of the *political*. Differences need to be constructed before they can be measured, and because of its refusal to acknowledge the relations of power involved in all 'constructions of differences', such naive pluralism is actually compatible with the liberal evasion of politics, converging with the typical liberal illusion of pluralism without antagonisms.

It is clear that there are no absolute means to define or measure media diversity or pluralism, but rather they are only intelligible in relation to some criteria and definitions that are deemed more important than others. As Van Cuilenburg puts it, media diversity always has to be 'gauged' in some way to the variations in social reality. The question then arises, how to conceptualize this relationship. How are the differences – against which diversity is examined – constructed, institutionalized, and operationalised? Although often presented as an end in itself, speaking of pluralism and diversity in any political context always requires a frame of reference in which it makes (political) sense.

Most empirical studies usually follow or modify McQuail's conceptualization in which the media is seen to contribute to pluralism in three ways: (1) by reflecting proportionately existing differences in society, (2) by giving equal access to any different points of view, or (3) by offering a wide range of choice for individuals. Each of these frames implies a different interpretation of the meaning of media diversity and the standard by which it should be assessed. Most empirical approaches, however, are based solely on the third, liberal freedom of choice perspective, while political arguments would seem to rely equally on the broader conceptions of pluralism and reflection of social and cultural differences. Respectively, choice is usually discussed in terms of the market – as expressed through the metaphor 'the free marketplace of ideas', where the limits and criteria are set by free competition and consumer choice.

Social scientists, critical of these market oriented models, have instead privileged the neo-Habermasian perspective of the public sphere as a favourite frame of reference in which the need for plurality of political views and social perspectives is conceptualized as part of rational democratic public deliberation. The marketplace model and public sphere approach, thus, rely on very different political rationalities in interpreting diversity and pluralism as media policy goals. While the former is based on competition and freedom of choice, the latter emphasizes broader defence of 'principled pluralism', an attempt to serve the whole society with various political views and cultural values. Further challenges to the notion of media diversity are of course posed by technological developments and the complexity of the contemporary media landscape. In particular, the suggested shift from the mass broadcasting model to a more differentiated and individualized narrowcast model of communication only adds to the blurring of the 'old' dichotomy between public and private communication.

Although the technological development would seemingly diversify the uses of media, it has also brought about concerns over fragmentation, extreme individualism, loss of common public platforms, and their consequences for the public sphere. Van Cuilenburg has presented some of these problems in 'diversity paradoxes', contradictions between the aspects of diversity that cannot be reconciled. For instance, the aim of increasing proportionate representation of social interests might not be compatible with ideal openness to new ideas, and increased consumer choice does not necessarily increase the visibility of minorities. The explosion of information increases choice, but also leads to high degrees of information waste and to an overload of information. Even though the expansion of channels might lead to increased choice, there is no corresponding effect on the citizens' access to relevant information. On the contrary, increase in the diversity of supply may even reduce the actual consumption of diversity.

Besides this, another tension can be identified, namely between two basic functions of the media in a democratic society; pluralism, and integration. The media are often seen as a central tool for creating a common culture, constructing a national identity, or a shared arena for public debate, values that would seem to be in contradiction with the strong pluralist agenda. This relates to the idea in political theory that at some point, the emphasis on diversity and pluralism runs against the imaginary presuppositions of democracy itself and that there is an inherent tension between pluralism and 'publicness'.This in turn reflects what Mouffe calls 'the democratic paradox'; how to envisage a form of commonality strong enough to institute a 'demos', but nevertheless compatible with true religious, moral, cultural, and political pluralism?

In particular, with the media market increasingly being structured into smaller segments and citizens getting less and less exposed to competing views and unnoticed problems, there is a genuine fear that polarization of media consumption may lead to unwanted social fragmentation or 'balkanization' of the public, which contrasts with the traditional republican ideal of a large and heterogeneous public sphere. Based on these paradoxes, Sunstein claims that the public sphere requires 'appropriate heterogeneity', thereby acknowledging that while all arguments can never be heard, the public sphere is above all a domain in which multiple perspectives should openly engage. For Sunstein, such a system of engagement between differing views should rely on something other than unrestricted individual choices. Citizens should, therefore, not only fall back on a range of common experiences, but should also be exposed to materials and information that they would not have chosen in advance.

The New Cultural Politics of Difference

In the last few years of the twentieth century, there is emerging a significant shift in the sensibilities and outlooks of critics and artists. In fact, so far as to claim a new kind of cultural worker is in the making, associated with a new politics of difference. These new forms of intellectual consciousness advance new conceptions of the vocation of critic and artist, attempting to undermine the prevailing disciplinary divisions of labour in the academy, museum, mass media, and gallery networks while preserving modes of critique within the ubiquitous commodification of culture in the global village.

Distinctive features of the new cultural politics of difference are to trash the monolithic and homogeneous in the name of diversity, multiplicity, and heterogeneity; to reject the abstract, general, and universal in light of the concrete, specific, and particular; and to historicize, contextualize, and pluralize by highlighting the contingent, provisional, variable, tentative, shifting, and changing. Needless to say, these gestures are not new in the history of criticism or art, yet what makes them novel - along with the cultural politics they produce - is how and what constitutes difference, the weight and gravity it is given in representation, and the way in which highlighting issues like exterminism, empire, class, race, gender, sexual orientation, age, nation, nature, and region at this historical moment acknowledges some discontinuity and disruption from previous forms of cultural critique.

To put it bluntly, the new cultural politics of difference consists of creative responses to the precise circumstances of our present moment - especially those of marginalized First World agents who shun degraded self- representations, articulating instead their sense of the flow of history in light of the contemporary terrors, anxieties, and fears of highly commercialized North Atlantic capitalist cultures (with their escalating xenophobias against people of color, Jews, women, gays, lesbians, and the elderly). The thawing, yet still rigid Second World ex-communist cultures (with increasing nationalist revolts against the legacy of hegemonic party henchmen), and the diverse cultures of the majority of inhabitants on the globe smothered by international communication cartels and repressive postcolonial elites (sometimes in the name of communism, as in Ethiopia),or starved by austere World Bank and IMF policies that subordinate them to the North (as in free- market capitalism in Chile), also locate vital areas of analysis in this new cultural terrain.

The new cultural politics of difference are neither simply oppositional in contesting the mainstream (or *male* stream) for inclusion, nor transgressive in the avantgardist sense of shocking conventional bourgeois audiences. Rather, they are distinct articulations of talented (and usually privileged) contributors to culture who desire to align themselves with demoralized, demobilized, depoliticized, and disorganized people in order to empower and enable social action and, if possible, to enlist collective insurgency for the expansion of freedom, democracy, and individuality. This perspective impels these cultural critics and artists to reveal, as an integral component of their production, the very operations of power within their immediate work contexts (i.e., academy, museum, gallery, and mass media). This strategy, however, also puts them in an inescapable double bind - while linking their activities to the fundamental, structural overhaul of these institutions, they often remain financially dependent on them. (So much for "independent" creation.)

For these critics of culture, theirs is a gesture that is simultaneously progressive and co-opted. Yet, without social movement or political pressure from outside these institutions (extra-parliamentary and extra-curricular actions like the social movements of the recent past), transformation degenerates into mere accommodation or sheer stagnation, and the role of the "co-opted progressive" no matter how fervent one's subversive rhetoric - is rendered form of crisis in civilization - a crisis usually generated by organizations or collectivities that convince ordinary people to put their bodies and lives on the line. There is, of course, no guarantee that such pressure will yield the result one wants, but there is a guarantee that the status quo will remain or regress if no pressure is applied at all.

The new cultural politics of difference faces three basic challenges - intellectual, existential, and political. The intellectual challenge - usually cast as a methodological debate in these days in which academicist forms of expression have a monopoly on intellectual life – is how to think about representational practices in terms of history, culture, and society. How does one understand, analyze, and enact such practices today? An adequate answer to this question can be attempted only after one comes to terms with the insights and blindness of earlier attempts to grapple with the question in light of the evolving crisis in different histories, cultures, and societies. That shall sketch a brief genealogy - a history that highlights the contingent origins and often ignoble outcomes - of exemplary critical responses to the question.

The Intellectual Challenge

An appropriate starting point is the ambiguous legacy of the Age of Europe. Between 1492 and 1945, European breakthroughs in oceanic transportation, agricultural production, state consolidation, bureaucratization, industrialization, urbanization, and imperial dominion shaped the makings of the modern world. Precious ideals like the dignity of persons (individuality) or the popular accountability of institutions (democracy) were unleashed around the world. Powerful critiques of illegitimate authorities - of the Protestant Reformation against the Roman Catholic Church, the Enlightenment against state churches, liberal movements against absolutist states and feudal guild constraints, workers against managerial subordination, people of colour and Jews against white and gentile supremacist decrees, gays and lesbians against homophobic sanctions - were fanned and fuelled by these precious ideals refined within the crucible of the Age of Europe. Yet, the discrepancy between sterling rhetoric and lived reality, glowing principles and actual practices, loomed large.

By the last European century - the last epoch in which European domination of most of the globe was uncontested and unchallenged in a substantive way - a new world seemed to be stirring. At the height of England's reign as the major imperial European power, its exemplary cultural critic, Matthew Arnold, painfully observed in his "Stanzas from the Grand Chartreuse" that he felt some sense of "wandering between two worlds, one dead/the other powerless to be born." Following his Burkean sensibilities of cautious reform and fear of anarchy, Arnold acknowledged that the old glue - religion - that had tenuously and often unsuccessfully held together the ailing European regimes could not do so in the mid-nineteenth century. Like Alexis de Tocqueville in France, Arnold saw that the democratic temper was the wave of the future. So he proposed a new conception of culture - a secular, humanistic one - that could play an integrative role in cementing and stabilizing an emerging bourgeois civil society and imperial state.

His famous castigation of the immobilizing materialism of the declining aristocracy, the vulgar philistinism of the emerging middle classes, and the latent explosiveness of the working class majority was motivated by a desire to create new forms of cultural legitimacy, authority, and order in a rapidly changing moment in nineteenth-century Europe. The second historical coordinate of my genealogy is the emergence of the United States as the world power (in the words of Andre Malraux, the first nation to do so without trying to do so). The United States was unprepared for world power status. However, with the recovery of Stalin's Russia (after losing twenty million lives), the United States felt compelled to make its presence felt around the globe. Then, with the Marshall Plan to strengthen Europe, it seemed clear that there was no escape from world power obligations.

The first significant blow was dealt when assimilated Jewish Americans entered the higher echelons of the cultural apparatuses (academy, museums, galleries, mass media). Lionel Trilling is an emblematic figure. This Jewish entree into the anti-Semitic and patriarchal critical discourse of the exclusivistic institutions of American culture initiated the slow but sure undoing of the male WASP cultural hegemony and homogeneity. Trilling's project was to appropriate Matthew Arnold's for his own political and cultural purposes - thereby unravelling the old male WASP consensus while erecting a new post-World War II liberal academic consensus around cold war, anticommunist renditions of the values of complexity, difficulty, variousness, and modulation. This suspicion of the academicisation of knowledge is expressed in Trilling's well known essay, "On the Teaching of Modern Literature." Trilling laments the fact that university instruction often quiets and domesticates radical and subversive works of art, turning them into objects "of merely habitual regard."

This process of "the socialization of the anti social, or the acculturation of the anticultural, or the legitimization of the subversive" leads Trilling to "question whether in our culture the study of literature is any longer a suitable means for developing and refining the intelligence." He asks this question not in the spirit of denigrating and devaluing the academy, but rather in the spirit of highlighting the possible failure of an Arnoldian conception of culture to contain what he perceives as the philistine and anarchic alternatives becoming more and more available to students of the '60s - namely, mass culture and radical politics. This threat is partly associated with the third historical coordinate of my genealogy – the decolonization of the Third World.

It is crucial to recognize the importance of this world historical process if one wants to grasp the significance of the end of the Age of Europe and the emergence of the United States as a world power. With the first defeat of a western nation by a non-western nation - in Japan's victory over Russia (1905); revolutions in Persia (1905), Turkey (1908), Mexico (1911-12), China (1912); and much later the independence of India (1947), China (1948); and the triumph of Ghana (1957) - the actuality of a decolonized globe loomed large. Born of violent struggle, consciousness-raising, and the reconstruction of identities, decolonization simultaneously brings with it new perspectives on that long festering underside of the Age of Europe (of which colonial domination represents the costs of "progress," "order," and "culture"), as well as requiring new readings of the economic boom in the United States (wherein the Black, Brown, Yellow, Red, White, female, gay, lesbian, and elderly working class live the same costs as cheap labour at home as well as in U.S.-dominated Latin American and Pacific rim markets).

The impetuous ferocity and moral outrage that motors the decolonization process is best captured by Frantz Fanon in The Wretched of the Earth (1906): Decolonization, which sets out to change the order of the world, is obviously a program of complete disorder.... Decolonization is the meeting of two forces, opposed to each other by their very nature, which in fact owe their originality to that sort of substantification which results from and is nourished by the situation in the colonies. Their first encounter was marked by violence and their existence together - that is to say the exploitation of the native by the settler - was carried on by dint of a great array of bayonets and cannons. Fanon's strong words describe the feelings and thoughts between the occupying British Army and the colonized Irish in Northern Ireland, the occupying Israeli Army and the subjugated Palestinians on the West Bank and Gaza Strip, the South African Army and the oppressed Black South Africans in the townships, the Japanese police and the Koreans living in Japan, the Russian Army and subordinated Armenians, and others in southern and eastern Russia. His words also partly invoke the sense many Black Americans have toward police departments in urban centers.

In other words, Fanon is articulating century- long, heartfelt, human responses to being degraded and despised, hated and hunted, oppressed and exploited, and marginalized and dehumanized at the hands of powerful, xenophobic European, American, Russian, and Japanese imperial countries. During the late 1950s, '60s, and early '70s in the

United States, these decolonized sensibilities fanned and fuelled the Civil Rights and Black Power movements, as well as the student antiwar, feminist, grey, brown, gay, and lesbian movements. In this period we witnessed the shattering of male WASP cultural homogeneity and the collapse of the short-lived liberal consensus. The inclusion of African Americans, Latino/a Americans, Asian Americans, Native Americans, and American women in the culture of critical discourse yielded intense intellectual polemics and inescapable ideological polarization that focused principally on the exclusions, silences, and blindnesses of male WASP cultural homogeneity and its concomitant Arnoldian notions of the canon.

In addition, these critiques promoted three crucial processes that affected intellectual life in the country. First is the appropriation of the theories of post-war Europe - especially the work of the Frankfurt School (Marcuse, Adorno, Horkheimer), French/Italian Marxisms (Sartre, Althusser, Lefebvre, Gramsci), structuralisms (Levi-Strauss, Todorov), and post structuralisms (Deleuze, Derrida, Foucault). These diverse and disparate theories - all preoccupied with keeping alive radical projects after the end of the Age of Europe - tend to fuse versions of transgressive European modernisms with Marxist or post-Marxist left politics, and unanimously shun the term "postmodernism." Second, there is the recovery and revisioning of American history in light of the struggles of White male workers, African Americans, Native Americans, Latino/a Americans, gays and lesbians. Third is the impact of forms of popular culture such as television, film, music videos, and even sports on highbrow, literate culture.

The Black-based hip-hop culture of youth around the world is one grand example. After 1973, with the crisis in the international world economy, America's slump in productivity, the challenge of OPEC nations to the North Atlantic monopoly of oil production, the increasing competition in hitech sectors of the economy from Japan and West Germany, and the growing fragility of the international debt structure, the United States entered a period of waning self-confidence (compounded by Watergate), and a nearly contracted economy. As the standards of living for the middle classes declined - owing to runaway inflation and escalating unemployment, underemployment, and crime - the quality of living fell for most everyone, and religious and secular neoconservatism emerged with power and potency. This fusion of fervent neonationalism, traditional cultural values, and "free market" policies served as the ground work for the Reagan-Bush era.

The ambiguous legacies of the European Age, American preeminence, and decolonization continue to haunt our post-modern moment as we come to terms with the European, American, Japanese, Soviet, and Third World *crimes against and contributions to humanity*. The plight of Africans in the New World can be instructive in this regard. By 1914, European maritime empires had dominion over more than half of the land and a third of the peoples in the world - almost 72 million square kilometers of territory and more than 560 million people under colonial rule. Needless to say, this European control included brutal enslavement, institutional terrorism, and cultural degradation of Black Diaspora people. The death of roughly 75 million Africans during the centuries- long, transatlantic slave trade is but one reminder, among others, of the assault on Black humanity. The Black diaspora condition of New World servitude - in which they were viewed as mere commodities with production value, which had no proper legal status, social standing, or public worth - can be characterized as, following Orlando Patterson, natal alienation.

The state of perpetual and inheritable domination that Diaspora Africans had at birth *produced the modern Black Diaspora problematic of invisibility and namelessness*. White supremacist practices - enacted under the auspices of the prestigious cultural authorities of the churches, print media, and scientific academics – promoted Black inferiority and constituted the European background against which Black Diaspora struggles for identity, dignity (self-confidence, self-respect, self-esteem), and material resources took place. The modern Black Diaspora problematic of invisibility and namelessness can be understood as the condition of relative lack of Black power to present themselves to themselves and others as complex human beings, and thereby to contest the bombardment of negative, degrading stereotypes put forward by White supremacist ideologies. The initial Black response to being caught in this whirlwind of Europeanization was to resist the misrepresentation and caricature of the terms set by uncontested non-Black norms and models, and fight for self recognition.

Every modern Black person, especially cultural disseminators, encounters the problem of invisibility and namelessness. The initial Black Diaspora response was a mode of resistance that was *moralistic in content and communal in character*. That is, the fight for representation and recognition highlighted moral judgements regarding Black "positive" images over and against White supremacist stereotypes. These images "represented" monolithic and homogeneous Black communities in a way that could displace past misrepresentations of these communities. Stuart Hall has discussed these responses as attempts to change the "relations of representation." These courageous yet limited Black efforts to combat racist cultural practices uncritically accepted non-Black conventions and standards in two ways. First, they proceeded in an *assimilationist manner* that set out to show that Black people were really like white people -thereby eliding differences (in history and culture) between whites and Blacks.

Black specificity and particularity was thus banished in order to gain White acceptance and approval. Second, these Black responses rested upon a *homogenizing impulse* that assumed that all Black people were really alike - hence obliterating differences (class, gender, region, sexual orientation) between Black peoples. The insight in the first claim is that Blacks and Whites are in some important sense alike i.e., in their positive capacities for human sympathy, moral sacrifice, service to others, intelligence, and beauty; or negatively, in their capacity for cruelty. Yet, the common humanity they share is jettisoned when the claim is cast in an assimilationist manner that subordinates Black particularity to a false universalism, i.e., non-Black rubrics and prototypes. Similarly, the insight in the second claim is that all Blacks are in some significant sense 'in the same boat' – that is, subject to white supremacist abuse. Yet, this common condition is stretched too far when viewed in a *homogenizing* way that overlooks how racist treatment vastly differs owing to class, gender, sexual orientation, nation, region, hue, and age.

The moralistic and communal aspects of the initial Black Diaspora responses to social and psychic erasure were not simply cast into simplistic binary oppositions of positive/negative, good/bad images that privileged the first term in light of a White norm so that Black efforts remained inscribed within the very logic that dehumanized them. They were further complicated by the fact that these responses were also advanced principally by anxiety-ridden, middle-class Black intellectuals (predominantly male and heterosexual) grappling with their sense of double consciousness - namely their own crisis of identity, agency, audience - caught between a quest for White approval and acceptance and an endeavour to overcome the internalized association of Blackness with inferiority. And I suggest that these complex anxieties of modern Black Diaspora intellectuals partly motivate the two major arguments that ground the assimilationist moralism and homogeneous communalism just outlined. Kobena Mercer has talked about these two arguments as the *reflectionist* and the *social engineering* arguments.

The reflectionist argument holds that the fight for Black representation and recognition - against White racist stereotypes - must reflect or mirror the real Black community, not simply the negative and depressing representations of it. The social engineering argument claims that since any form of representation is constructed - i.e., selective in light of broader aims - Black representation (especially given the difficulty of Blacks gaining access to positions of power to produce any Black imagery) should offer positive images, thereby countering racist stereotypes. The hidden assumption of both arguments is that we have unmediated access to what the 'real Black community' is and what "positive images" are. In short, these arguments presuppose the very phenomena to be interrogated, and thereby foreclose the very issues that should serve as the subject matter to be investigated.

Any notions of "the real Black community" and "positive images" are value-laden, socially loaded, and ideologically charged. To pursue this discussion is to call into question the possibility of such an uncontested consensus regarding them. Hall has rightly called this encounter "the end of innocence or the end of the innocent notions of the essential Black subject... the recognition that 'Black' is essentially a politically and culturally *constructed* category." This recognition - more and more pervasive among the post-modern Black Diaspora intelligentsia - is facilitated in part by the slow but sure dissolution of the European Age's maritime empires, and the unleashing of new political possibilities and cultural articulations among excolonized peoples across the globe. One crucial lesson of this decolonization process remains the manner in which most Third World authoritarian bureaucratic elites deploy essentialist rhetoric about 'homogeneous national communities' and 'positive images' in order to repress and regiment their diverse and heterogeneous populations.

Yet in the Diaspora, especially among First World countries, this critique has emerged not so much from the Black male component of the left, but rather from the Black women's movement. The decisive push of post-modern Black intellectuals toward a new cultural politics of difference has been made by the powerful critiques and constructive explorations of Black Diaspora women (e.g., Toni Morrison). The coffin used to bury the innocent notion of the essential Black subject was nailed shut with the termination of the Black male monopoly on the construction of the Black subject. In this regard, the Black Diaspora womanist critique has had a greater impact than the critiques that highlight exclusively class, empire, age, sexual orientation, or nature.

This decisive push toward the end of Black innocence - though prefigured in various degrees in the best moments of

James Baldwin, Amiri Baraka, Anna Cooper, W. E. B. DuBois, Frantz Fanon, C. L. R. James, Claudia Jones, the later Malcolm X, and others - forces Black Diaspora cultural workers to encounter what Hall has called the "politics of representation." The main aim now is not simply access to representation in order to produce positive images of homogeneous communities - though broader access remains a practical and political problem. Nor is the primary goal here that of contesting stereotypes - though contestation remains a significant though limited venture. Following the model of the Black Diaspora traditions of music, athletics, and rhetoric, Black cultural workers must constitute and sustain discursive and institutional networks that deconstruct earlier modern Black strategies for identity formation, demystify power relations that incorporate class, patriarchal, and homophobic biases, and construct more multivalent and multidimensional responses that articulate the complexity and diversity of Black practices in the modern and post-modern world.

Furthermore, Black cultural workers must investigate and interrogate the other of Blackness/Whiteness. One cannot deconstruct the binary oppositional logic of images of Blackness without extending it to the contrary condition of Blackness/Whiteness itself. However, a mere dismantling will not do - for the very notion of a deconstructive social theory is oxymoronic. Yet, social theory is what is needed to examine and explain the historically specific ways in which "Whiteness" is a politically constructed category parasitic on "Blackness," and thereby to conceive of the profoundly hybrid character of what we mean by "race," "ethnicity," and "nationality." Needless to say, these enquiries must traverse those of "male/ female," colonizer/colonized," "heterosexual/ homosexual," et al., as well. Demystification is the most illuminating mode of theoretical enquiry for those who promote the new cultural politics of difference. Social structural analyses of empire, exterminism, class, race, gender, nature, age, sexual orientation, nation, and region are the springboards - though not landing grounds - for the most desirable forms of critical practice that take history (and her story) seriously.

Demystification tries to keep track of the complex dynamics of institutional and other related power structures in order to disclose options and alternatives for transformative praxis; it also attempts to grasp the way in which representational strategies are creative responses to novel circumstances and conditions. In this way, the central role of human agency (always enacted under circumstances not of one's choosing) - be it in the critic, artist, or constituency, and audience - is accented. It is partisan, partial, engaged, and crisis-centered, yet always keeps open a skeptical eye to avoid dogmatic traps, premature closures, formulaic formulations, or rigid conclusions. In addition to social structural analyses, moral and political judgments, and sheer critical consciousness, there indeed is evaluation. Yet the aim of this evaluation is neither to pit art-objects against one another like racehorses nor to create eternal canons that dull, discourage, or even dwarf contemporary achievements.

We listen to Laurie Anderson, Kathleen Battle, Ludwig Beethoven, Charlie Parker, Luciano Pavarotti, Sarah Vaughan, or Stevie Wonder; read Anton Chekhov, Ralph Ellison, Gabriel Garcia Marquez, Doris Lessing, Toni Morrison, Thomas Pynchon, William Shakespeare; or see the works of Ingmar Bergman, Le Corbusier, Frank Gehry, Barbara Kruger, Spike Lee, Martin Puryear, Pablo Picasso, or Howardena Pindell - not in order to undergird bureaucratic assents or enliven cocktail party conversations, but rather to be summoned by the styles they deploy for their profound insights, pleasures, and challenges. Yet, all evaluation - including a delight in Eliot's poetry despite his reactionary politics, or a love of Zora Neale Hurston's novels despite her Republican party affiliations - is inseparable, though not identical or reducible to social structural analyses, moral and political judgements, and the workings of a curious critical consciousness. The deadly traps of demystification - and any form of prophetic criticism - are those of reductionism, be it of the sociological, psychological, or historical sort.

The Existential Challenge

The existential challenge to the new cultural politics of difference can be stated simply: how does one acquire the resources to survive and the cultural capital to thrive as a critic or artist? By cultural capital, I mean not only the high-quality skills required to engage in critical practices, but more important, the self-confidence, discipline, and perseverance necessary for success without an undue reliance on the mainstream for approval and acceptance. This challenge holds for all prophetic critics, yet it is especially difficult for those of colour. The widespread modern European denial of the intelligence, ability, beauty, and character of people of colour puts a tremendous burden on critics and artists of colour to "prove " themselves in light of norms and models set by White elites whose own heritage devalued and dehumanized them. In short, in the court of criticism and art - or any matters regarding the life of the mind - people of colour are guilty (i.e., not expected to meet standards of intellectual achievement) until "proven" innocent (i.e., acceptable to "us").This is more a structural dilemma than a matter of personal attitudes.

The profoundly racist and sexist heritage of the European Age has bequeathed to us a set of deeply ingrained perceptions about people of colour including, of course, the selfperceptions that people of colour bring. It is not surprising that most intellectuals of colour in the past exerted much of their energies and efforts to gain acceptance and approval by "white normative gazes." The new cultural politics of difference advises critics and artists of colour to put aside this mode of mental bondage, thereby freeing themselves both to interrogate the ways in which they are bound by certain conventions and to learn from and build on these very norms and models. One hallmark of wisdom in the context of any struggle is to avoid knee-jerk rejection and uncritical acceptance. There are four basic options for people of colour interested in representation - if they are to survive and thrive as serious practitioners of their craft. First, there is the Booker T. Temptation, namely the individual preoccupation with the mainstream and its legitimizing power. Most critics and artists of colour try to bite this bait.

It is nearly unavoidable, yet few succeed in a substantive manner. It is no accident that the most creative and profound among them - especially those with staying power beyond mere flashes in the pan to satisfy faddish tokenism are usually marginal to the mainstream. Even the pervasive professionalisation of cultural practitioners of colour in the past few decades has not produced towering figures who reside within the established white patronage system that bestows the rewards and prestige for chosen contributions to American society. It certainly helps to have some trustworthy allies within this system, yet most of those who enter and remain tend to lose much of their creativity, diffuse their prophetic energy, and dilute their critiques. Still, it is unrealistic for creative people of colour to think they can sidestep the White patronage system. And though there are indeed some White allies conscious of the tremendous need to rethink identity politics, it is naive to think that being comfortably nested within this very same system - even if one can be a patron to others - does not affect one's work, one's outlook, and, most important, one's soul.

The second option is the Talented Tenth Seduction, namely, a move toward arrogant group insularity. This alternative has a limited function - to preserve one's sanity and sense of self as one copes with the mainstream. Yet, it is, at best, a transitional and transient activity. If it becomes a permanent option it is self-defeating in that it usually reinforces the very inferiority complexes promoted by the subtly racist mainstream. Hence it tends to revel in parochialism and encourage a narrow racialist and chauvinistic outlook. The third strategy is the Go-It-Alone option. This is an extreme rejectionist perspective that shuns the mainstream and group insularity. Almost every critic and artist of colour contemplates or enacts this option at some time in his or her pilgrimage. It is healthy in that it reflects the presence of independent, critical, and skeptical sensibilities toward perceived constraints on one's creativity. Yet, it is, in the end, difficult if not impossible to sustain if one is to grow, develop, and mature intellectually, as some semblance of dialogue with a community is necessary for almost any creative practice.

The most desirable option for people of colour who promotes the new cultural politics of difference is to be a Critical Organic Catalyst. By this I mean a person who stays attuned to the best of what the main stream has to offer - its paradigms, viewpoints, and methods – yet maintains a grounding in affirming and enabling subcultures of criticism. Prophetic critics and artists of colour should be exemplars of what it means to be intellectual freedom fighters, that is, cultural workers who simultaneously position themselves within (or alongside) the mainstream while clearly aligned with groups who vow to keep alive potent traditions of critique and resistance. In this regard, one can take clues from the great musicians or preachers of colour, who are open to the best of what other traditions offer, yet are rooted in nourishing subcultures that build on the grand achievements of a vital heritage.

Openness to others - including the mainstream - does not entail wholesale cooptation, and group autonomy is not group insularity. Louis Armstrong, Ella Baker, W. E. B. DuBois, Martin Luther King, Jr., Jose Carlos Mariatequi, Wynton Marsalis, M. M. Thomas, and Ronald Takaki have understood this well. The new cultural politics of difference can thrive only if there are communities, groups, organizations, institutions, subcultures, and networks of people of colour who cultivate critical sensibilities and personal accountability - without inhibiting individual expressions, curiosities, and idiosyncrasies. This is especially needed given the escalating racial hostility, violence, and polarization in the United States. Yet, this critical coming- together must not be a narrow closing of ranks. Rather, it is a strengthening and nurturing endeavour that can forge more solid alliances and coalitions. In this way, prophetic criticism - with its stress on historical specificity and artistic complexity - directly addresses the intellectual challenge. The cultural capital of people of colour - with its emphasis on self-confidence, discipline, perseverance, and subcultures of criticism - also tries to meet the existential requirement. Both are mutually reinforcing. Both are motivated by a deep commitment to individuality and democracy - the moral and political ideals that guide the creative response to the political challenge.

The Political Challenge

Adequate rejoinders to intellectual and existential challenges equip the practitioners of the new cultural politics of difference to meet the political ones. This challenge principally consists of forging solid and reliable alliances of people of color and White progressives guided by a moral and political vision of greater democracy and individual freedom in communities, states, and transnational enterprises - i.e., corporations, and information and communications conglomerates. Jesse Jackson's Rainbow coalition is a gallant, yet flawed effort in this regard -gallant due to the tremendous energy, vision, and courage of its leader and followers; flawed because of its failure to take seriously critical and democratic sensibilities within its own operations.

The time has come for critics and artists of the new cultural politics of difference to cast their nets widely, flex their muscles broadly, and thereby refuse to limit their visions, analyses, and praxis to their particular terrains. The aim is to dare to recast, redefine, and revise the very notions of "modernity," "mainstream," "margins," "difference," "otherness." We have now reached a new stage in the perennial struggle for freedom and dignity. And while much of the First World intelligentsia adopts retrospective and conservative outlooks that defend the crisis ridden present, we promote a prospective and prophetic vision with a sense of possibility and potential, especially for those who bear the social costs of the present. We look to the past for strength, not solace; we look at the present and see people perishing, not profits mounting; we look toward the future and vow to make it different and better.

5

Public Truths vs Private Truths

Many people believe that such a use of religion ultimately results in violations of the separation of church state, and thus other people's religious liberty. Many religious believers, however, argue that it is wrong to exclude religion from public debates and that such a policy effectively constitutes discrimination against religion and religious believers. Who is right? In a way, both perspectives are "right" — it would be a mistake to assume that only one is valid and that the other must be wrong. Nevertheless, it must also be pointed out that former position is ultimately stronger. So long as it is not taken too far, it is the position which must serve as guiding principle. There are a number of reasons why this is so, but perhaps the most fundamental and important is the fact that there is no one single religious perspective on the world or on questions of public policy. No matter what issue you might consider, even the existence of gods, there are a variety of religious positions on it.

What this means, then, is that it simply isn't possible for the government to "take the religious perspective" into consideration — there is no one "religious perspective." The government also can't take every religious perspective into consideration because there are simply too many for that. For the government to adopt any particular religious position as a basis for laws or policies, though, would mean treating the religious beliefs in question as true — or at least as more true than the religious beliefs that have been excluded. All other religious beliefs that have something to say on the matter are treated as if they were false, or at the very least as worthy of less consideration. This is a genuine example of religious discrimination which cannot be tolerated in a democratic, tolerant society.

To understand how this might be so, we can look at any number of examples from the headlines today: capital punishment, abortion, cloning, war, etc. What is the "religious position" on such issues? There are some especially vocal religious perspectives involved, but in no case is there a single religious perspective that we can consult. If those vocal religious views obtain a prominent role in the shaping of public policy when it comes to something as contentious as abortion, other religious views must be ignored — and that isn't fair. But why isn't this case any time the government adopts one basis for laws rather than other?

The difference is that religion is based on what might be called "private truths" — ideas, beliefs, and "truths" that rely upon divine revelation. Such "truths" are a personal, private conviction which cannot claim as creating obligations for others. Nonreligious arguments, however, can be based upon what might be called "public truths" — ideas, beliefs, and "truths" that rely upon public arguments and publicly accessible perspectives available to everyone, regardless of their religion. When public policy is based upon such public truths, then everyone is a part of the debate; but when private truths are used, then a great many people who do not recognize that particular divine revelation are automatically excluded.

The Politics of Public Religion

An example of a private truth would be the idea that murder is wrong because God commands it. This may be a true statement — but it has no normative force in terms of public policy because even those who believe it cannot reasonably expect the public assent of their fellow citizens who have not experienced this revelation, who do not share a religion which teaches it, and who are unwilling or unable to accept such religious teachings on faith.

An example of a public truth would be the idea that murder is wrong because it causes suffering in other human beings. Even if such an argument were wrong, it would be "public" because no one has to experience a personal revelation from a god in order to understand or believe it. It is "publicly accessible" in that regardless of one's religious beliefs, the terms, inferences, and conclusions can be comprehended, critiqued, and accepted by anyone at all.

Of particular importance is the fact that the idea that murder causes suffering can actually be demonstrated (or, at least in theory, refuted) empirically. This is a major difference from either the existence of a god or the idea that a god actually wants us to do anything. Does this mean that people shouldn't personally believe that murder is wrong because God commands it? No, this isn't an argument about what individuals should themselves believe. Rather, this is an argument about what grounds may be legitimately used to coerce other citizens to avoid certain behaviors and engage in other behaviors.

In a theocracy, it would be expected to base public policy and public laws on religious doctrines and divine revelation — that is, after all, what makes a political system theocratic. If a theocracy is what someone wants a nation to be, then they should by all means advocate that position openly and be forthright with their goals. In a liberal democracy, however, where freedom generally and freedom of conscience in particular are valued, neither religious doctrines nor divine revelation are legitimate sources of public policy. It is, after all, public policy that we are talking about — and in such a context, only public arguments are legitimate.

Whatever private reasons a person might have for following a certain course of action, they cannot expect others to necessarily share those reasons unless they are publicly accessible. Most of the time, this means that the arguments will be secular rather than religious — pure appeals to religious tradition or divine laws must be rejected. Sometimes religious arguments may be employed, but in such a case "religious" will be descriptive more of the origin of the position rather than the structure of the argument itself. Thus, a person might believe for religious reasons that every human being has an essential dignity and, from that, argue that abortion or capital punishment is wrong.

Such an argument could be legitimate because it doesn't necessarily matter (for the terms of public discourse) why each human has an essential dignity or even why a particular person believes it — what matter is how well the premise can be sustained and what conclusions might be derived from it outside of purely private revelation. We might then be able to make a case for the idea that insofar as a religious position can serve as a basis for public policy that may only happen if the position does not require a particular theological support structure. Believers may not personally choose to disentangle their theological beliefs from their arguments — and there is nothing wrong with that when it comes to what they believe privately. Yet if such disentanglement is possible for the purpose of public policy debates, then their arguments may be legitimate.

Religion, Politics, and the State

Twenty years ago, most social scientists tended to see religion as a vestige of a bygone age, an increasingly irrelevant remnant from a prior epoch of superstition and miseducation. But about 1979 things began to change. Astonishingly enough, religion took on a new political importance as phrases like "liberation theology," "fundamentalism," "solidarity," and "moral majority" were shouted from the political ramparts in countries as diverse as Nicaragua, Iran, Poland, and the United States. Suddenly the topic of religion and politics was less boring, and like the scholar whose scoffed-at laboratory work finds an indispensable application, we found people actually cared. But, of course, we had not been alone in chronicling religion's new political urgency. In the last several years, several other scholars have written important works that deal with religion and politics in different countries. We commend especially the recent works of Martin Riesebrodt (1990), Mark Juergensmeyer (1993), Jose Casanova (1994), Lester Kurtz (1995) and the magisterial five volumes on fundamentalisms edited by Martin Marty and R. Scott Appleby (1991-95).

Meanwhile, over the last ten years or so, in search of key sources of violence, vacuity, vulnerability, and vitality, Demerath has been examining the present and tending relations between religion, politics, and the state in some fifteen countries around the world. He has visited Guatemala and Brazil in Latin America, Northern Ireland, Poland, and Sweden in Europe, Egypt, Israel, and Turkey in the Middle East, Pakistan, India, Indonesia, and Thailand in South Asia, and China and Japan in the Far East. Of course, our own country, the United States, always lurks in the background as a comparative anchor point. Moreover, the project spans various forms of Christianity, Islam, Hinduism, and Buddhism, as well as political systems that range between dynamic democracies and strict one-party states. One common finding within this variety involves the very different relations between religion and politics, on the one hand, and religion and the state, on the other. Few will be surprised to learn that campaigning politicians everywhere tend to invoke local religious themes and symbols as sources of legitimacy and what Demerath and Rhys Williams have called "cultural power".

What may be more surprising is the frequent tendency for governmental regimes and their officials to try to keep religion at arm's length. While religion is often an ally in the pursuit of power, once power has been secured, religion can become an unwelcome constraint in the quite different processes of state administration. Demerath developed this point in an earlier article (1991), arguing that, while few countries have the kind of formal, legal "separation of church and state" that characterizes the U.S., an informal de facto separation is almost a commonplace. The most conspicuous exceptions here are not "religious states" but rather "state religions" in which the government seeks to control religion. Strangely enough, this often involves state support for religion in an effort to co-opt and nullify it as an independent power-base. Here we want to continue in a similar vein but with somewhat wider scope.

Specifically, we want to sketch four types of situation implied at the intersection of two basic distinctions, one between the religious and the secular (ambiguously straddling the nonreligious and the religiously neutral, as we shall see), and the other between politics and the state. Thus, one can imagine religious politics with a religious state; secular politics and a secular state; secular politics and a religious state, and finally religious politics with a secular state. We shall comment on each of these four combinations momentarily. But a few preliminary cautions are in order. First, typologies for their own sake and in their own terms can be stultifying as mere scholastic exercises. However, each of the four combinations here has empirical standing, and the differences between them amount to more than a conceptual conceit. In many situations, life itself hangs in the balance, since levels of religiously implicated violence vary greatly among the types in question. Second, these distinctions are not as clear as the bold dichotomy suggests. For present purposes, the "religiousness" of a government or a political party is more a matter of consensual perception than formal acknowledgment or even legal documentation.

In virtually every country, as we shall see, one can identify tendencies towards combinations other than the one assigned. Then too, every state administration involves some degree of politics as well; politics only become religious in response to broader religious tensions within the society at large; and the distinction between religion and the secular is itself artificial, especially if religion is defined more sociologically than theologically in terms of the sacred. Third, although each of these types deserves detailed exploration, we shall devote disproportionate attention to the last combination of a secular state with religious politics. If it is not a panacea, it at least offers hope in an area too often suffused with hopelessness.

Religious States and Religious Politics

From both a simple conceptual point of view and a simplistic historical perspective, this would appear the purest of the four cases, and perhaps the most common stereotype of non-Western, hence nonsecular, societies around the world. Because religion in one sphere is matched symmetrically by religion in the other, a religious state would seem to go hand in hand with religious politics. In fact, the combination is more the exception than the rule, and this is because it is so volatile and potentially violent. When a religious state is faced with religious politics, there is a religious conflict at issue. Under such circumstances, the state's very legitimacy is called into question, and violence may reflect preemptive actions of state control as well as the clash among contending religious parties. If there is a single pattern that lends itself to the most widespread religious and cultural violence, it is surely this one.

And, alas, while the category is rare, it is hardly nonexistent. Within our "sample" of countries, several cases invite inclusion here - at least at various points in their histories. Like most other Latin American countries, both Brazil and Guatemala were once officially Catholic states in a religious political system that involved the subjugation and suppression of indigenous religious alternatives. Formally, both countries had severed these state religious ties by the end of the nineteenth century; informally, ties have persisted in varying forms. In Brazil, the Catholic ecclesiastical hierarchy is now seeking to reappropriate and renegotiate its seat at the right hand of the state, while at the same time both church and state are engaged in a new religious politics animated by persistent strains of liberation theology on the one hand and a surging Pentecostal Protestantism on the other.

In Guatemala, the dominant military state has shifted its ostensible religious affiliation from Catholic to Protestant in the last decade, and there is no question that its ongoing guerilla opposition is in part a movement of Mayan religious revitalization. Or consider the case of Israel. Many Israelis would protest its categorization as a religious state, arguing that Zionism itself can be seen as a secular movement, and that the state makes ample provision for both secular practices and various non-Judaic faiths, especially Islamic and Christian. At the same time, there is no question that the Israeli state is perceived as Jewish by most Jews and non-Jews alike.

Even if this were not the case, Zionism itself may be a sufficiently sacred commitment to qualify as religious in its own terms. Certainly there is no question that Israeli politics often take religious forms. This not only applies to the participation of Muslim Palestinians, including the Hamas, but also to the struggles among various Jewish groups - whether secularists on the left or contesting movements on the right, such as the Gush Emunim and the ultra-orthodox Haredi. As Yitzhak Rabin's assassination makes clear, the stakes are large and the rates of violence are correspondingly high. But perhaps the clearest combination of a religious state with religious politics is found in Northern Ireland. There is no question that the state is perceived in Protestant terms, whether de jure as a result of its inclusion within Anglican Britain, or de facto because of the three-hundred-year political dominance of local Protestants. Certainly there is no doubt that politics are driven with religion - at least insofar as they have involved extreme civil religious blocs that are "culturally" if not always "religiously" Protestant and Catholic respectively.

The recent truce and possible signs of a negotiated settlement signal a change in the religious politics, but by no means its end. What was once a small Catholic minority may well become an effective political majority early in the next century, and Catholics have already begun to make gains through the ballot rather than the bullets of the IRA? Such a development is hastened by the increased out-migration of Protestants with resources, who read the new writing on the graffitiemblazoned walls; it is compounded by the frustrations of those less advantaged Protestants remaining behind. As all of the above examples attest, the combination of a religious state and religious politics has occasioned some of the most deeply rooted and tragic violence of the modern era. This makes it especially important to consider the alternatives, even though it is one thing to point out the dangers of this combination in the abstract and quite another to prevent countries from sliding towards it in reality. Then too, some of the alternatives have warts of their own.

Secular States and Secular Politics

If the first combination is stereotypically non-Western, this one is commonly associated with the West. In one sense, it represents a realization of the Enlightenment vision through what Bryan Wilson called the "secularization of public religion" and what Rodney Stark and Laurence Iannaccone call the "desacralization of the state." However much these authors are thought to disagree on other matters, they are in basic concurrence here. There is no question that the secular-state secular-politics combination is often associated with Western Europe in particular. Despite the continued existence of "Christian" Democratic parties in Germany and France, both countries fall into this category, as does Italy in the wake of its recent revocation of its long-standing concordat with the Vatican. Much the same is true if one looks functionally rather than formally at Anglican England or Lutheran Scandinavia.

In fact, there are active movements on behalf of religious disestablishment in all of these symbolically religious nations. In part, these are efforts to revitalize religion as an autonomous political force, since many church folk now regard the relationship as inhibiting their prophetic roles. Indeed, the establishments that survive are often defended principally on nonreligious grounds. In Sweden, the church has functioned somewhat like an unofficial census bureau and is subvented for the purpose. However, Sweden has recently voted to disestablish religion by the year 2000. Many politicians see these establishments as cases of the sublime-gone-ridiculous and the purely symbolic source of vestigial charm and occasional humor.

Although Europe does not exhaust the secular-secular category, its influence is apparent in two additional cases: Turkey and China. Turkey had been tilting toward the West throughout the latter days of the Ottoman Empire in the nineteenth century, where there was a special fascination with the secular theology of French positivism.

In a sense, Kemal Ataturk both had and ate the Ottoman cake when he seized power in 1921 and carried through one of the most far-reaching and enduring politico-cultural revolutions in the twentieth century. Ataturk was familiar with sociologist Emile Durkheim's argument that an ethical society and effective political culture could be sacred without being religious. Partly as a result, Ataturk banned religion from both government and politics, just as he banned irregular verbs and Roman numerals from everyday discourse. For the most part, the reforms have remained. Although there have been several instances in which the military has stepped in to preserve secularity, it is characteristic of Turkey that even some members of the Islamic Refah ("Welfare") Party describe it as "fundamentalism-lite." However, Muslim political interests have begun to mobilize, and after winning a plurality of more than 20 percent in the 1996 election, Refah is now sharing power with the previously dominant "True Path" Party. China also qualifies as a doubly secular case, again partly on the basis of an imported Western ideology - in this case, of course, Marxist socialism.

Actually, the regime's opposition to religion has softened of late, and there is even waggish talk of a "Third Opium War," in this case an intraparty dispute concerning whether Marx was correct in dismissing religion as the "opiate of the masses." Of course, there are many respects in which Marxism itself resembles a religion, including its recent secularization. Indeed, one of the reasons why some Chinese leaders are more accepting of traditional Christian, Buddhist, and Islamic religious communities (as long as they operate on the state's own terms) is a much-lamented void at the core of Chinese society where only money has currency. While some would argue that this is a cue for the reintroduction of Confucianism, this is less preferable than imported faiths because party cadres see it as a feudal and anti-revolutionary anachronism, despite its considerable informal persistence.

This is a time of transition in China, but not one that threatens a serious religionizing of either the state or politics in familiar terms. Clearly, the combination of a secular state and secular politics has some empirical standing, and it is in some measure correctly associated with Western post-Enlightenment developments. But this does not mean that all cases are confined to the West, or that religion is entirely absent in any instance. Indeed, the combination in pure form runs the risk of cultural lassitude, if not sterility.

Many of the above cases reveal persisting strains toward some form of religious or "sacred" alternative that must often be officially, if not coercively, dampened. While these pressures rarely operate as major trends in their own right, they are also seldom dismissable as idle epiphenomena. So far, then, we have dealt with the two opposing polar combinations: the doubly religious associated with violence and the doubly secular tending toward vacuity. Of course, there are many anomalies within each. But the most instructive disjunctions involve the two combinations off the main diagonal. In most typologies these bear the most succulent fruit of the conceptual labour.

Religious States and Secular Politics

There are basically three scenarios for the combination of a religious state and secular politics. The first involves instances in which the religiousness of the state is an empty symbol rather than a compelling commitment - more a case of anachronistic form than contemporary function. In fact, I noted several such countries under the secular-secular rubric. Lutheran Sweden is a case in point. While the state is formally religious, it actually reflects a culture and a political scene that is highly secular; the occasional religious movements and issues which compel attention are very much the exception. If this first model suggests a certain ritualized indifference to religion, a second version involves a far more active and pointed religious presence.

Here, religion is an important source of state legitimacy, and no alternative religious views are tolerated. Religion is banned from politics precisely because it is potentially as upsetting as an emotionally charged component of the culture at large. Often politics of any real substance is frowned upon, and religious grievances against the state are suppressed along with all others. Here are the true theocracies represented by some traditionally Catholic Latin American states as well as a number of Islamic hegemonies in the Middle East, including Pakistan at various points in its history. It also applies to several countries in South East Asia such as Buddhist Thailand. Here the state controls the political world very tightly and embraces religion more to control it than to submit to it. In some ways these first two models of religious states with secular politics are opposites of each other.

The first represents religious tokenism in the midst of apathy, while the second reveals a religious order imposed to quell potential religious disorder, meanwhile, a third qualifies as a perverse variant of the second: states that carefully construct their own religion to frustrate the political mobilization of a genuine religious alternative. Indonesia offers a case in point. Here the state has used "pancasila" as an imposed civil religion seeking to bind syncretically the loyalties of Christians, Hindus, Buddhists, and animists - not to mention the 90 percent of the population who are formally Muslims.

Strict electoral rules make it virtually impossible for any one religious group to raise up against the regime, and the state's administrative apparatus ("golkar") also functions as a controlling political structure. In all of this, the object is to stifle the development of the so-called "Islamic fundamentalists," some of whose actual agendas are more secular than religious. Thus, the combination of a religious state with secular politics produces strange partnerships. All three of its model scenarios are somewhat procrustean, and the latter two shares a sense of unstable vulnerability as a sort of way station for cases caught in transition between the other three basic combinations.

Secular States and Religious Politics

At first blush, this seems another strained and uneasy combination with squirming inclusions. After all, if a society is able to sustain a government that is basically secular, isn't this because there is too little religious action to animate its politics significantly? Put oppositely, when any society's politics become religiously infected, how can its state structures be sufficiently inoculated to resist the virus? There is merit in both these queries; yet the logic behind a secularly neutral state with a free-ranging religious polity is that each complements and constrains the other. There need be no limits to the free exercise of religion in politics as long as there is a strict prohibition of any religious establishment within the state. Politicians, as politicians, may not campaign on - and even vote - their religious consciences; nor is there anything to prevent them from bowing to the bidding of their religious organizations. But state officials and state administrations have a different responsibility.

They must remain formally and functionally neutral, and not only in the pluralistic fray between religions but also in the larger struggle between religion, on the one hand, and secularism, on the other. The overall result should be a necessarily contested but vital politics framed by an equitable state that rises above the fray to guarantee fairness to all. This at least describes the constitutional theory and founding enthusiasm behind two countries that constitute the world's largest and oldest democracies respectively; namely, India and the United States. When India obtained independence in 1947, it took three years to develop a constitution. The result reflected a number of Western models, including the U.S. itself. But while the Indian form of government enjoyed a successful run of almost thirty years with its stability and legitimacy intact, this began to unravel in the 1980s. A growing complaint within India today is that its Independence leaders were too quick to apply Western secular forms of government to an Eastern cultural reality that required a unique state response.

The argument as articulated by such leading intellectuals as T. N. Madan and Ashish Nandy holds that a secular state may work well enough in a country like the U.S., but it is discordant within an Indian society that remains intransigently non-secular at its core. Indeed, the very imposition of Western secularism has served perversely to fan the flames of religious politics by forcing religious advocates to adopt increasingly more extreme measures to make their case - measures that even include communal violence. Some go so far as to suggest that India is not just a deeply religious country but a basically Hindu society that can only be led by a Hindu government. As Hinduism finds its natural expression in state control, it will revert back to its natural historical tolerance of the minority religions in its domain. And yet this is only one reading of the Indian case. By no means all Indian intellectuals have thrown in the secular towel. Scholars such as Andre Beteille, Dipankar Gupta, and T. K. Oooman continue to defend and a religious rather than antireligious reading of the Indian constitution.

From this perspective, the cause of communal violence is not that the state is too secular but rather that it is not secular enough, not that the state should use its influence to curb or end religion, but rather that the state should be neutral among contesting religious groups and concerning the larger question of religion versus non religion as a cultural desideratum. Alas, from the very beginning, the Indian constitution included controversial religious allowances such as a state exemption for Muslim personal law; it also mandated liberal religious reforms within Hinduism concerning such matters as temple administration and a continuation of the British "reservations policy" designed to provide a form of occupational affirmative action for Hindu "untouchables." These exceptions in secular state policy have festered and exacerbated over the years.

From a neutral vantage point, religious personal obligations are fine as long as they do not contradict the minimal (not maximal) rights and responsibilities of the citizenry at large. Rather than use religious status as a basis for reserving jobs, some argue that this should be based on more general socio-economic disadvantagement (and with an educational rather than occupational compensation). In any event, it is clear that India's recently increasing "communal violence" (Hindus vs. Muslims in Ayodhya, Bombay, and

Kashmir; Sikhs vs. Hindus in the Punjab; Tamil rebels in the South) reflects the tendency for state leaders and state structures to become embroiled in religious conflicts. As concessions made to one group require concessions made to its rival, constructing state policy has come to resemble shortening a chair one leg at a time: the results are never quite even, and the seat of power becomes increasingly unstable.

The assassinations of both Indira and Rajiv Gandhi offer tragic reminders of the possible consequences. But in a strange way, one's reading of India depends upon one's reading of the United States, and here too there are opposing options. On the one hand, the U.S. has also been construed as among the most religious nations in the world. It ranks high in virtually every measure of religiosity, with some 95 percent of Americans claiming a "belief in God," and more than 40 percent claiming to attend religious services on any given Sunday. And amongst the profusion of active religious movements, today one hears a good deal about America's "culture wars" as storm clouds gather on the religious right. On the other hand, the U.S. can be portrayed as the secular nation par excellence, especially given its widely heralded "separation of church and state."

This image has provoked both positive and negative assessments, the latter including Richard Neuhaus's critique of the "naked public square" (1984) and Stephen Carter's more recent concern over a "culture of disbelief" (1992). James Hunter's portrayal of hostility between "orthodox and progressive" religious forces (1991) can be seen as illustrating a democracy at work rather the kind of culture wars that are tragically waged elsewhere (cf. Demerath, 1991). And as for those high estimates of religious belief and participation - both have come under close recent scrutiny. For example, Hadaway, Marler and Chaves (1993) have shown that actual religious attendance is probably less than half of what is claimed. If Asians tend to minimize their involvement in religion, Americans tend to maximize theirs. It is not hard to produce corrected estimates that are quite similar for both. As Demerath and Williams have argued (1992), however, these two images of the United States are not as contradictory as one might suppose.

Like the earlier account of a secular state and a religious polity, they are contingently compatible in the sense that each depends upon the other. Thus, we can have highly vocal and widely mobilized religious politics precisely because there is a separation of church and state where the actual affairs of government are concerned. At the same time, that same separation would be intolerable if there were not ample opportunity elsewhere in the society to exercise and express one's religious preference - or lack of one. Overall, the United States may be the exception that commends the rule concerning the virtues of a secular state and a religious polity. It would be naive and unseemly to assume that the same combination would work identically for all other nations. Nor is India the only cautionary case. In Egypt (as in neighboring Algeria), the nation as a whole seems a battleground between a coercive and antireligious (as opposed to neutral) state "secularism," on the one hand, and a small group of religious extremists (led by the Islamic Group and other legatees of the Muslim Brotherhood).

The scenario is not uncommon and has surfaced in a variety of other states that are unsuccessful in their efforts to suppress religious opposition - e.g., as previously described, Indonesia, Turkey, and Thailand. Of course, a variety of factors are involved, and "democracy" itself is not always a panacea or even always interpreted the same way. Thus, democratic elections are one thing, but a democratic state is often quite another. In addition to regimes that constrain electoral democracy to uphold nominally democratic state governance, there are certainly opposition movements that see electoral democracy as merely a stage in the ultimate suspension of democratic governance in the name of religion itself. The choices are not easy. Meanwhile, post-1989 Poland also qualifies as a secular state with religious politics. Although one might suppose it to be doubly Catholic as a reflection of both its dominant cultural religious alignment and the oftchronicled role of the church on the Solidarity side of the recent revolution, this has already begun to shift.

Many Poles are more cultural than religious Catholics, and the old patterns of opposition to ecclesiastical authority are resurfacing, especially as the church pressured the new government to outlaw divorce and abortion. The response is especially apparent in the 1995 defeat of Lech Walesa by a crypto-communist but authentic secularist - a defeat that may have occurred because of (rather than in spite of) the intercession of Cardinal Glimp and Catholic officialdom on Walesa's behalf. And just recently, the government enacted a liberalization of the church-backed abortion prohibition of 1993. In sum, while Poland currently illustrates the combination of a secular state with religious politics, it may soon join its European sisters to the West in the doubly secular category as its politics lose their religious flavour.

Locating Japan

Finally, there is one country that offers an instructive case in flux. To this point, we have not even mentioned Japan, one of the most important, dynamic, and currently conflicted countries in the world. This is partly because Japan is a country where we are still very far from being experts, though we have learned a great deal from many Japanese scholars and such U.S. mentors and sources as Winston Davis (1992), Helen Hardacre (1989), Daniel Metraux (1996), and James W. White (1970). It is also because Japan's position within our four types or categories is a matter of some doubt. In fact, at various times in its recent history, Japan has qualified for placement in all four combinations. While this is also true of many other countries - including some we have already categorized simplistically - it is worth pausing to note how the four types occur within the Japanese experience. First, one reading of the almost 250 year, pre-1868 "Tokugawa" period in Japanese history is that it combined a religious government (or shogunate) with religious politics in the jousting among various Buddhist, Shinto, and even Christian movements.

Second, it is at least arguable that the 1868 "Meiji restoration" ultimately produced a combination of a religious state and secular politics as a small elite self-consciously fashioned a new state religion out of traditional folk Shinto. The resulting State Shinto was used to define the government and to mobilize both industrialization and militarism. Opposing religious voices were stilled, at least during the war years, as the imprisoned leaders of such dissident groups as the lay Buddhist, Soka Gakkai, attest. Third, at least for the first three decades following the war and the adoption of a new constitution, the situation was more that of a secular state with secular politics. Not only was State Shinto disestablished but there was relatively little religious presence in the world of politics. Fourth and most recently, the combination of religious politics and secular state has begun to surface, however imperfectly.

Formally, of course, the state continues to be secular. Although some might argue that the Ministry of Education's 1989 requirement of the singing of the national anthem ("kimigayo") at public school graduation ceremonies and the retention of some aspects of Shinto mythology in the school curriculum marks a first step down a slippery slope toward a religious state, there remains some doubt in the courts whether Shinto itself qualifies as religious. Similar ambiguity surrounds the Cabinet member visits to the Yasukuni shrine honoring the war dead that began in the mid-1980s. And yet conservative politicians are increasing persuaded that some kind of sacred revitalization is necessary to fill the void at the nation's cultural core where a devotion to industrial capitalism and a "yen for the yen" does not suffice. Meanwhile, religious politics of a quite different sort are involved in the increasingly conspicuous role of new religious movements over the last decade.

An especially pivotal event was the 1995 nerve gas attack on the Tokyo subway by the cult, Aum Shinrikyo. The resulting trial of the leader, Asahara, has turned out to be a siege for many marginal religious movements who feel stigmatized by the same stereotypes and sanctions applied to the Aum. This is especially true of the growing Soka Gakkai, whose membership has been reckoned one-sixth of the population but whose seventy-year history has been consistently controversial because of its zealous proselytizing and its formation of the only religious political party in Japan which is now the country's largest opposition party. It is true that Komeito (or the CGP, "Clean Government Party") has not been legally linked to the Soka Gakkai since 1970, and it has recently merged with the "New Frontier" Party.

And yet there are sufficient perceived affinities remaining between Komeito and the Soka Gakkai so that discrediting one tends to discredit *the other*. This is at least one plausible motivation behind the dominant (and generally conservative) "Liberal Democratic Party's" recently successful Religious Corporation Law. The result here is partly political in applying the same brush that tars the Aum Shinrikyo to the Soka Gakkai and then Komeito in turn. But it also marks a potential sea change in state policy toward religious groups generally, especially those that are somewhat off center. The introduction of tighter reporting requirements, greater monitoring vigilance, and vague new standards of religious propriety licences the government to fish in deeper waters for its opposition prey. This might seem consistent with a secular state in the antireligious sense of the phrase. But it is an alarming departure from a secular state that is neutral concerning both religions in general and religions in particular.

It is precisely this connotation of a neutral secularity that best avoids a "religious establishment" while promoting the "free exercise" of religion. Of course, we would argue that this same combination is optimal in the long run not just for religion but for society as a whole so much for a cross-cultural reconnoitering of the various relations that exist between religion, politics, and the state. Any exercise that presumed to freeze and fit whole societies within a single simple conceptual grid would, of course, be a fool's errand. At the same time, it is sometimes useful to gain a sense of the various combinations and tendencies that exist today as a guide to tomorrow - especially since there is no more volatile intersection or one with greater consequences than the one at issue. Of the four combinations we have examined, that of a religious state combined with religious politics is certainly the most potentially violent. Unfortunately, it is also a direction in which many societies are being pressed.

By contrast, the doubly secular combination may provide political stability at the price of cultural vacuity. The conjunction of a religious state with secular politics can be either a symbolic anachronism or the result of an imposed religious orthodoxy that relies heavily on coercion and tolerates no opposition. While the coupling of a secular state with religious politics is currently rare, it is arguably the most promising type for promoting both cultural vitality and structural stability. In the final analysis, no country need be dominated either by a vacuous and a historical secularism or a raging religious current that sweeps all else before it. Let us end with a more personal postscript. Anyone engaged in comparative research learns early and often to take refuge in the phrase, "all else being equal." In addition, any American engaged in global analysis and prescription must be especially sensitive to our long tradition of triumphal "exceptionalism".

One of the problems of comparative work concerns the dilemma of dissimulating one's own values and one's best sense of what might work for others. Certainly Edward Said has alerted all Western scholars to the dangers of Orientalism and has made the term a byword for cross-cultural stereo-typing. However, as James Carrier's collection on Occidentalism implies, distorted perceptions and communications occur in both directions and are endemic in any situation in which power imbalances are compounded by cultural differences. The problem is exacerbated when one seeks not just to understand but to prescribe. But even here there are two possible errors. The first is to blunder ahead and prescribe one's own medicine for every patient, regardless of the ailments and host conditions; the second is to pull back into a benighted relativism that treats every society as only analyzable in its own terms and only changeable in its own fashion.

The latter is especially problematic when it is merely a pose - what Charles Taylor has referred to as the "obligatory hypocrisy" and false cultural respect of today's "multicultural" world. India again offers a pertinent example, as we can see in Donald Smith's magisterial volume *India as a Secular State* (1963). The definitive work on the then new constitution, the book concludes by noting some of the evidences of the religious nose in the constitutional tent cited. But the author goes on to express full confidence that India in its wisdom will work its way through or around them. One can only wonder whether that confidence was any more genuine then than it might be now. If, as Durkheim once suggested, comparative sociology is the only sociology, then a sharing of comparative assessments must be encouraged rather than censored. Both social analysis and social policy depend upon candid crosscultural exchange.

Religion and Politics

Americans embrace a role for religion in the nation's political life, but they are conflicted over the extent and contours of that involvement. Compared to a generation ago, more people are comfortable with churches expressing opinions on social and political matters, yet a solid majority of voters say they are uneasy with members of the clergy espousing their political views from the pulpit. While seven-in-ten voters believe it is important for the president to have religious faith, there is widespread discomfort over politicians who speak publicly about how religious they are. Churches, synagogues and other religious institutions are overwhelmingly seen as positive forces in addressing society's problems. Yet the public's ambivalence over religion and politics is also reflected in divisions over "charitable choice" — an initiative, approved as part of the 1996 welfare reform bill, which permits faith-based organizations to participate in government-funded social service programs.

A narrow majority (54%) supports funding religious organizations so they can run such government programs as job training or drug treatment services. There is considerably more backing (67%) when the issue is recast as allowing such groups to apply for government funding, along with other organizations, for these purposes. At a time when Joe Lieberman's appointment as the first Jew on a major party's presidential ticket has cast a spotlight on religion and politics, the latest Pew Research Center survey shows that 77% have favourable attitudes toward Jews. That rating has slipped somewhat from 84% in 1997, but the current favourability mark for Jews is virtually the same as for Catholics (78%). There actually has been no increase in the number of voters who hold unfavourable impressions of Jews; rather, slightly more voters say they are unable to give an opinion of Jews compared with three years ago. The image of evangelical Christians has improved markedly in recent years—as the political visibility, if not the influence, of Christian conservatives has waned.

Overall, some 63% of voters rate evangelical Christians favourably, compared with just 41% in 1996. Some of the biggest gains have come among Democrats and senior citizens, which are groups that tend to express the most concern about overt expressions of religious beliefs in politics. Six-in-ten Democrats now have favourable impressions of evangelicals, compared with 27% four years ago. More Americans regard the Republican Party as the protector of religious values compared with the Democrats (39% to 30%, respectively). But the GOP's advantage on this issue has declined over the past four years; in 1996, 47% saw the Republicans as protectors of religious values while just 32% named the Democrats. In a more positive trend for the GOP, fewer voters now see the party as too closely tied to religious leaders (13% vs. 20% in 1996).

Politicians and Religion

Most voters (70%) want the president to be a person of faith. But half of the electorate expresses unease with politicians, presidential contenders and others, who talk too much about their religious beliefs. Overall, women are somewhat more likely than men to want a president with strong religious beliefs (74% vs. 65%). At the same time, women are slightly less likely than men to feel uncomfortable when politicians talk about their faith (46% vs. 54%). By contrast, young people and particularly young men, are less concerned about the religious beliefs of the president. Less than half of men under age 30 (47%) say it is important that he or she have religious beliefs. While the Republican-oriented typology groups are fairly unified in saying it is important for the president to have strong religious beliefs, there are divisions among Democrats.

Fully 84% of the Partisan Poor identify this as an important characteristic for the president, and 82% of Social Conservatives agree. That number falls to 67% among New Democrats and just 34% among Liberals. Clearly, the distinction between being religious and talking about religion is more important to some groups than others. For instance, nearly eight-in-ten senior citizens (78%) say it's crucial for the president to have strong religious beliefs, but more than half (56%) also say they are uneasy over excessive public expressions of faith by politicians. Similarly, by a lopsided margin of 79%-18%, African-Americans say it is important for the president to be religious; by a narrower margin (48%-43%) blacks also express discomfort over politicians who talk publicly about their faith.

More Support for Evangelicals

While nearly eight-in-ten voters have positive impressions of Catholics and Jews, and six-in-ten feel the same about evangelicals, just half of voters see Muslim-Americans in a favourable light. Nonetheless, voters have a far more favourable impression of every religion tested than they do of atheists. Just 32% hold a favourable opinion of atheists. While, on balance, those in every major demographic group hold a negative view of atheists, they are viewed favourably by Liberal Democrats, a group that is the least religious of all typology groups. Fully 65% of Liberals have a positive impression of atheists, far more than other groups in Pew's voter typology. Evangelical Christians are now viewed much more favourably by many groups than they were four years ago while the percentage of Democrats holding positive impressions of evangelicals has more than doubled (from 27% to 60%), more Republicans and independents also have favourable opinions of evangelicals. In addition, support for evangelicals has increased across every age group.

The Industry of Manipulating Children

In recent years, children have been increasingly exposed to violence through toy manufacturers' television programs and by video games. In the early 1980s, the toy industry used violence as a marketing ingredient. In addition to advertising through commercials, companies such as Hasbro produced their own TV programs and paid to have them broadcast on weekdays and Saturday mornings. In 1984, "GI Joe" carried 84 acts of violence per hour and "Transformers". This marketing strategy was so profitable that Hasbro reused it in 1989 with "Ninja Turtles," in 1993 with "Power Rangers," and in 1999 with "Pokemon." Their primary purpose was to persuade children to ask parents and Santa Claus to give them Hasbro toys.

Most of these programs, like many video games, include fantasies and stereo types that support an aggressive culture of violence, sexism, and war. Stereotypical "real" men are strong, insensitive, and solve conflicts by exterminating their opponents. Women are docile, victims, or decorative trophies, incapable of solving problems. Gary Ruskin, executive director of Commercial Alert, explained at a 2002 World Health Organization conference:

Advertisers use many techniques to sell to youth. Mostly these involve manipulating their needs during the stages of their growth into adulthood. Some of the more common needs that advertisers take advantage of to sell products include youth needs for peer acceptance, love, safety, desire to feel powerful or independent, aspirations to be and to act older than they actually are, and the need to have an identity. Much of the child-targeted advertising is painstakingly researched and prepared, at times by some of the most talented and creative minds on the planet. Advertisers sometimes discuss it in terms of the battle over what they chillingly call "mind share." Some openly discuss "owning" children's minds.... In sum, corporations and their advertising agencies have succeeded in setting up their own authority structures to deliver commercial messages almost everywhere that children go.

Public Airwaves Controlled against Public Interests

Growing public awareness of the dangers of media violence aimed at young people has put pressure on governments to regulate it. In 1994, to prevent such intervention, Canadian broadcasters promised to regulate themselves. Six years later, researchers at Laval University noted that self-regulation had failed to reduce violence, and that violence carried by private broadcasters had increased by 432%. Two developments during this period helped to neutralize public concern. First, many broadcasters provided funding for media literacy programs on the assumption that by studying media in class, students would discover that TV violence is not "real." While such programs seem progressive and useful, they have actually been used as a smokescreen to help broadcasters project an ethical image while increasing the intoxication of children. A second development was the V-Chip.

Many parents work fulltime and cannot always monitor what their children are watching. Devices such as V-Chips were supposed to allow them to block reception of violent programs. The V-Chip system depends on ratings that are made by the broadcasters themselves. The V-Chip has helped to shift responsibility for regulating TV violence away from polluters onto parents. Those who believe that government regulation of media is an attack on freedom of speech see nothing wrong with manipulating children. They consider this form of child abuse as their constitutional right. Moreover, governments, by fear of being bullied, gave control of pollution to polluters.

Censorship

When citizens request regulation of the use of media violence in cultural products for children, the industry is prompt to consider it as an attack against freedom of expression. These corporations speak about freedom of expression as if they owned it, as if they bought it. The fact that thousands of these media belong to the same owner allows them to reach considerable numbers of viewers, listeners, and readers. They then easily make their views much more familiar to citizens and make them forget that the airwaves belong to the public. The use of violence by big media has nothing to do with freedom of speech. Media violence is the result of choices made by the industry, and it is the result of censorship controlled by the media. The use of violence to attract more children is motivated by commercial interests. Mary Megee explained why gratuitous violence on TV is a form of censorship by commerce. "In the U.S., most cultural messages are strained through a commercial filter which uses gratuitous violence as an industrial ingredient to keep viewers tuned in, ratings high, and profits up."

The first—if not the only—rule that the big media agree to respect is the market. Their argument is simple: whenever people are ready to watch violent programs, broadcasters have the right to air them and NO government should interfere. For leaders of the industry, the law of commerce is the ultimate and most natural rule. All other rules and laws are viewed as obstacles to their interest and appetite for profits. Health, safety, and happiness of vulnerable citizens never appear on their radar screen. Control of the airwaves gives them the authorization to ignore the right of children to live in a safe cultural environment. If the transportation industry acted in a similar way, there would be no speed reduction in school areas and no interdiction of carrying dangerous chemicals in tunnels. Why would own a big truck or even thousands of them give someone permission to drive on public streets and highways with no care for the public's interest? Why would the artists who build beds for babies get the freedom to space the bars so that they might turn out to be dangerous traps for small children?

The argument of airing material despite the interest of children is the opposite of freedom. If there is a choice between freedom of speech and safety for children, all civilized societies give priority to children's safety. Parents and teachers who request regulation of TV programs and video games for children quickly are stamped with the CENSORSHIP label. In 1997, George Gerbner was Dean Emeritus of the Annenberg School for Communication at the University of Pennsylvania and a pioneer of research on television violence. He had monitored television for over 30 years and found prime time television saturated by an average of five scenes of violence per hour. He found Saturday morning children's programs filled by 20 scenes of violence per hour. "When you can dump Power Rangers on 300 million children in 80 countries, shutting down domestic artists and cultural products, you don't have to care who wants it and who gets hurt in the process.

Mindless TV violence is not an expression of artistic freedom or of any measure of reality. On the contrary, it is the product of de facto censorship: a global marketing formula imposed on program creators and foisted on the children of the world." The reason why parents who request less violence in TV programs for children are labelled as procensorship is to hide censorship by the industry and to make citizens forget that they own the airwaves. Why should people who own the airwaves restrict themselves from demanding that they be healthy, free, and fair? Why would the owners be treated in such an abusive way? When any violent program is chosen to be aired, citizens are aware that censorship by the industry allowed some decision makers to eliminate other programs and films that could have contributed to their children's health and safety. The preference for violence is a decision made by somebody, elected by nobody, prisoner of a toxic culture, who knows that the authority expects him or her to give priority to cruelty, aggression, and hatred.

Why did this program selector pick these Ninja Turtles to

come and fight in our homes instead of other healthy programs for our children and their folks on our street? Did the network receive money for making that decision? Did profit increase after airing violent programs? Censorship exists; it is controlled by the industry, and millions of children pay the price today. Science also revealed that they will pay the price for their entire life, and the price becomes higher every year as increased doses of verbal and physical violence find their way into their brains.

The Purpose of Media Violence

Media violence is used by the entertainment industry for the main purpose of attracting more viewers, no matter their age, damages to their brains, or cost to society. When used by providers of entertainment products for youths, media violence has become one of the most sophisticated and cruel forms of child abuse. Pokemons, Terminators, Doom, Quake, Basketball Diaries, Grand Theft Auto, Howard Sterns, South Parks, Jackasses, all these cultural products have proven to damage children and teens across the continent. They carry and promote values that help guide and inspire children's attitudes, behaviours, clothing, and relationships with each other. Eminem, Fifty Cents, and Marilyn Manson are the products of the music industry circulating hate propaganda against women and profiting from it. These singers and characters are often portrayed as rebels. In fact, they are nothing but submissive tools for the ideology of profit. They are slaves, rich and famous slaves, but slaves anyway.

Valerie Smith monitored the music industry for decades. She wrote: "These guys would still whine in their garage if it was not for the industry that gave them a microphone, print their lyrics, sell their albums and promote them on MTV." Music videos, TV programs, and video games have become the most child-abusive babysitters in North America. Much of their audiences are young people who easily believe that rudeness is an act of courage, of independence, and of freedom. It takes experience, knowledge, critical viewing skills, and empathy to understand that these role models actually teach submission, frustration, and anger.

Verbal violence, physical violence, sexism, racism, and consumerism have nothing in common with freedom and justice—they are the opposite. These cultural products glorify violence and misogyny, although they have been the enemy of humanity for centuries, for millenniums. How would children know that? These products glamorize submissiveness of women and prostitution which have been fought by humanity for centuries, for millenniums. How would children know that? They trivialize verbal humiliations of others as if they were humoristic, acceptable, fun, natural, and entertaining. How would children know that? Damages are profound and painful.

Sophisticated Form of Child Abuse

When compared to many forms of violence against children, media violence looks minor. Many children seem to enjoy it, and parents can get more freedom as their child watches TV. When researchers studied damages made to children by media violence, they discovered that television hurts millions of them very deeply and that most damages will affect them for the rest of their lives. Parents have many reasons to consider the use of media violence as a cruel and sophisticated form of child abuse. Because media violence is primarily used in entertainment to attract human beings, particularly the youngest, we need to ask the question: Why does it work? Curiosity is not the only reason. We know for a fact that many human beings can hardly turn their head away when they witness their peers suffering or when they see pain inflicted on them. Sane human beings feel guilty to abandon their peers in a situation of danger. Using violence in entertainment for children is a very cruel form of child abuse because children cannot differentiate between fiction and reality.

The process of making that difference starts at the age of 7 and is not over before the age of 13. This is a fact despite all the spontaneous answers given by children when parents ask them if they can make that difference. For an increasing number of teens, the process of making that difference is actually completed much later than 13. The Supreme Court of Canada has analysed the issue of children's vulnerability before the age of 13 and the 83-page Irwin Toys Decision is a media literacy lesson all by itself. The use of violent fiction to lure children before the age of 13 is clearly an unacceptable lack of ethics by the most lucrative industry of the world. In the United States, marketing targeting children has gone from $100 million in 1990 to two billion a decade later. That is a 2000% increase. This appetite for reaching children has allowed advertisers to compete and try various hooking ingredients to lure children and reduce gatekeepers' authority. Violence and the nag factor are two well known marketing ingredients, the most offensive and criminal.

Multiple Victims

It is the business of television to attract audiences and to sell them to advertisers, who then find ways to manipulate their preferences and choices for goods and services. Despite children's vulnerability, violence is commonly used by both the entertainment and the marketing industries for commercial purposes. These industries have studied the psychology of children, similarly to what predators do with their prey. They scrutinized children's needs, hopes, fears, dreams, and desires. Increasing the audience means enormous monetary profits in the short term for these industries. However, media exposure also has enormous short, mid and long-term effects on children and society. Well over a thousand studies have related diseases (MRD) such as obesity, body image, self-esteem, violent crime, physical and verbal abuse, eating disorders, smoking, alcohol, attention deficit disorder and hyperactivity, compulsive consumerism, perilous driving, and so on.

What other industry can afford to generate so much damage to society without any consequences? When *ecoli* bacteria are found in water, meat, or spinach, the public is quickly informed about the risks. Why would research about MRD be deprived of similar coverage? Exposure to violent entertainment does not only show and teach how to act violently. In the child's inexperienced brain, it links pain infliction with pleasure. Violence was certainly not created by the media, but the use of violence in entertainment by the media has helped to increase the amount, the damages, and the pain for millions of children around the world. Does the industry try to prevent damages?

Unfortunately, every time accusations could incriminate them, their answer is simple: raising children is the parents' job, not theirs. Imagine any other industry (guns, alcohol, and so on) trying that line? 'I knew that kid was 10, and, yes, he walked into my pawn shop, bought a fifth of liqueur and a gun, but where were the parents? It's the parents' job to keep him out!' No other industry would try that line. The only other group of individuals who would say that are child abusers: 'I know that little girl was 8, but it's the parents' job to keep me away from her.' This (media) industry is functioning with child abuser logic, and they will pay a profound price for it." If raising a child requires a whole village, it seems that television is not a member of the village.

Size of the Effect

Research has proven that the effect of media violence is bigger than the effect of exposure to lead on children's brain activity, bigger than the effect of calcium intake on bone mass, bigger than the effect of homework on academic achievement, bigger than the effect of asbestos exposure on cancer, bigger than the effect of exposure to secondhand smoke on lung cancer. Professor Craig Anderson testified before the U.S. Senate Commerce Committee hearing in 2004. He explained that research revealed three effects of exposure to media violence.

- Short-term effects: aggression increases immediately after viewing a violent TV show or movie, and it lasts for at least 20 minutes.
- Long-term effects: children who watch a lot of violent shows become more violent as adults than they would have become had they not been exposed to so much TV and movie violence.
- Long-term and short-term effects occur to both boys and girls.

Video Games are Murder Simulators

Dr. Michael Rich testified on behalf of the American Academy of Paediatrics before the Public Health Summit on Entertainment Violence. Here is what he had to say about video games:

Video game revenues are $10 billion a year, larger than that of television and movies, and increasing. 50% of 4th graders choose "first person shooter" (FPS) video games as their favourites. The average 7th grader plays these video games for more than 4 hours each week. [...] After playing video games, young people exhibit measurable decreases in pro-social and helping behaviours, a 43% increase in aggressive thoughts, and a 17% increase in violent retaliation to provocation. Playing violent video games accounted for 13–22% of the variance in teenagers' violent behaviour. By comparison, smoking tobacco accounts for 14% of the variance in lung cancer.

Active participation increases effective learning. Video games are an ideal environment in which to learn violence: a) they place the player in the role of the aggressor and reward him or her for success at violent behaviour; b) rather than observing part of a violent interaction, video games allow the player to rehearse an entire behavioural script from provocation to choosing to respond violently to resolution of the conflict—this is more effective learning than watching or rehearsing part of the sequence; c) video games are immersive and addictive—kids want to play them for long periods of time to become better.

Repetition increases learning. While violent video games are clearly not the sole factor contributing to violence, they are clearly a factor. Other aspects of this entertainment-induced social engineering project have also come under scrutiny. Apart from the tendency of video games to arouse aggression, researchers note that these games provide little mental stimulation. Professor Ryuta Kawashima and his research team measured the brain activity of hundreds of teenagers while they played a video game and compared the results with those of other groups who did math exercises and read aloud. The researcher found out that computer games do not stimulate crucial areas of the brain, leading to underdevelopment and such behavioural problems as violence. The video game did not stimulate the brain's frontal lobe, an area that plays an important role in the repression of anti-social impulses; the frontal lobe is also associated with memory, learning, and emotions. A lack of stimulation in this area before the age of 20 prevents the neurons from thickening and connecting, there by impairing the brain's ability to control such impulses as violence and aggression.

Professor Kawashima's findings are supported by other studies: "Computer games do not lead to brain development because they require the repetition of simple actions and have more to do with developing quick reflexes than carrying out more mentally challenging activities."Lt Col Dave Grossman, a retired psychologist from the U.S. Army, co-authored with Gloria DeGaetano a book about the influence of video games on human brains: *Stop Teaching Our Kids to Kill.* Grossman knows that video games were used by the U.S. army as murder simulators for the purpose of conditioning young recruits to "kill without thinking." In many interviews and speeches, Lt Col Grossman explained that "video games give kids and teens the skill, the will and the thrill to kill."

Media Violence Linked with Bullying and Crime

Time exposure to television is actually linked with bullying. Research by Frederick Zimmerman, professor in the University of Washington's School of Public Health, found that "youngsters who spent a typical amount of time—about 31/2 hours daily—in front of the tube had a 25% increased risk of becoming bullies between the ages of 6 and 11. This is a very clear independent effect of television on children's bullying. More kids who watch a lot of TV go on to become bullies than kids who don't watch very much TV, so that's the risk. Watching a lot of TV doesn't mean that you're going to become a bully, it just means that you have a higher chance that it might happen." During the last 15 years, school authorities in the United States have noticed that violence has hit lower grades. In California, for example, the latest school crime figures show that from 1995 to 2001, rates of vandalism and other offences dropped among elementary school students, while assaults nearly doubled. In Philadelphia, the first part of (this) school year 2002–2003 brought the suspensions of 22 kindergartners.

Minneapolis schools have suspended more than 500 kindergartners over the past two school years for fighting, indecent exposure, and persistent lack of co-operation. Minnesota schools have suspended nearly 4,000 kindergartners, first and second graders, most for fighting, disorderly conduct and the like. In Massachusetts, the percentage of suspended students in prekindergarten through third grade more than doubled between 1995 and 2000. In 2001–2002, schools in Greenville, S.C., suspended 132 first-graders, 75 kindergartners and two preschoolers.

In Québec, between 1985 and 2000, the number of elementary school students with troubled behaviours has increased by 300%. Media violence is also linked with later criminal activity, as shown by this 17-year-study in which 700 young people were tracked down into their adult lives. Hours of viewing were correlated with acts of aggression. Surprisingly, viewers watching more TV as children committed more crimes as adults than those already involved in violence when they were kids. In Canada, the violent crime rate for youths is growing much faster than that for adults, and, in the Province of Québec, the violent crime rate of youths is now two times higher than that of adults.

The Social Cost of Desensitization

The most worrying effect of exposure to media violence (more than imitation) is desensitization, the reduction of empathy. Massive exposure to violent entertainment has shown to reduce the capacity of children (and their will) to rescue victims or report about them. Many young criminals often show and feel no remorse after committing horrible crimes. Increasing the punishments or judging them before a court for adults has little or no positive effect. Early desensitization of young humans will carry a heavy cost for the coming generation and the future of civilization. Massive exposure to violent entertainment reduces—if not destroys—the value of life and the power of solidarity in our societies.

Various Responses of Civil Society

All civilized societies show concern about child abuse. Concern about violence against children inspired reactions against the marketing of violence by the entertainment industry. Spontaneously, civil society across North America has developed a wide variety of promising practices to protect children from media violence. If society wants to reduce the manipulation of children by the media, and regulate violence carried by TV programs for children, increased legislation is necessary. In 2004, the U.S. Federal Trade Commission found that the entertainment industry had marketed products to children that their own ratings do not consider appropriate for them. Children under 17 could easily purchase tickets for movies, music recordings, and video games labelled as suitable "for adults only." Self regulation has clearly proven to be non-efficient.

Such marketing practices clearly contravene with the Child Rights Convention, where article 17 makes it obligatory to all States to recognize the importance of the media and protect children against "material (danger) injurious to their well-being." Despite such a clear statement, many states, including the United States and Canada, have shown reluctance to enforce it. If there are going to be attempts by decision makers to legislate this issue, successful efforts must be supported by a wide mobilization throughout civil society. Media have gradually become so powerful to influence public opinion that governments fear to intervene. Solid coalitions of parents, health professionals, education professionals, grassroots organizations, and activists could succeed where legislators alone have failed.

Parents' Education

Such wide mobilization from all sides of the political spectrum requires knowledge and motivation. In 2002, researchers Doug Gentile and David Walsh surveyed parental guidance over children's consumption of media violence and concluded that it was not sufficient. A study conducted by Joanne Cantor in 2002 revealed that most parents have little or no knowledge of the harmful effects of media violence on their child. Other Canadian and U.S. studies have revealed that parents are not aware of the amount of violence their children are exposed to on television, the Internet, and video games. It is therefore obvious that media education is needed.

UNICEF Canada also believes that "complementary regulations with parent and child education are needed. Families are important in reducing the harmful effects of media violence. Children themselves believe they should be protected from frightening television programs, websites, and video games." Many parents would be happy to learn why they should avoid purchasing toys that promote imitative play of violent programming, why monitoring their children's video game habits is helpful, why using TV as a babysitter is perilous, and why they should spend more time talking with their children.

Resistance by the Industry

History has shown that other industries have tried to oppose increased legislation to protect citizens. The automobile industry, the tobacco industry, and the food industry, for example, have spent tremendous efforts to deprive citizens and society from protection. The problem with media violence is that the industry accused of abusing children is at the same time responsible of preparing the news. Informing the public therefore becomes barely possible if not impossible. A few countries or states have succeeded in regulating the media industry targeting children: Greece, Sweden, and Québec are among them.

Legislation against Advertising to Children

The success story in the Province of Québec is interesting because it was realized right here in North America. Advertising became illegal in the province of Québec in 1976. This type of legislation requires not only courage from political decision makers but also strong support from society at large. The Québec Consumer's Protection Law forbidding advertising to children under 13 became fully enforced in 1980. The toy industry—Irwin Toys Ltd—has challenged this law up to the Supreme Court of Canada, arguing that it restricted its own freedom of expression protected by the Canadian Charter of Rights. The court declared the Québec legislation fully constitutional.

The Irwin Toys Decision takes 83 pages to describe pretty accurately (a) sophisticated manipulation techniques used by the marketing industry, (b) why any provincial jurisdiction in Canada has constitutional legitimacy to protect its vulnerable citizens, (c) why children need such protection until the age of 13. This legislation made Québec the first, and still to this day, 30 years later, the only State in North America to protect children from advertising. During the years following its adoption, lobbying by advertisers argued that the children of Québec were punished by this legislation because TV networks could not sell advertising time. Lack of income had then reduced, they said, the quality and quantity of TV programs for kids. Adopting the law supposedly punished children instead of protecting them.

Fifteen years after the law was fully enforced, the Government of Québec asked Professor André Caron, researcher from the University of Montreal, to evaluate the actual impact of the law. The study revealed that programming for children was richer, more diverse, and more educational in Montreal, Quebec, compared to Toronto, Ontario, a city where such protection did not exist. Ruling out advertising to kids has proven to be a very efficient and promising practice to protect children. The Canadian Supreme Court Decision in itself offers a rich media education lesson. An analysis of the decision gives important strategic insights for decision makers in other states and countries trying to legislate and lawyers trying to defend the legitimacy of the legislation in court.

Further research will be necessary to evaluate if regulating advertising to children also impacted child obesity and other MRD diseases. Lately, the American Psychological Association

(APA) requested a similar legislation for protecting children in the United States along with a coalition of organizations advocating in favour of children's rights. The *Washington Post* reported about the APA position. A survey conducted in 2006 showed that more than 80% of U.S. citizens agree that advertising to children under 9 should be prohibited.

Promising Practices to Protect Children

Despite powerful opposition against regulation from the media, many promising practices have been experienced in North America to protect children from media violence. A report sent recently to UN Secretary General as a contribution to the Study on Violence against Children highlights 20 such promising practices by civil society. The report was posted on the Child Rights Information Network (CRIN) Web site. Among these innovative practices, the SMART Program and the 10Day Challenge have proven to be the most efficient to help parents, students, and teachers come together and oppose the media culture of violence.

Student Media Awareness to Reduce Television (SMART)

The SMART Program was tested in 1998 by Dr. Thomas N. Robinson in two elementary schools of San Jose, California. It consists of 18 lessons for teachers preparing students and motivating them to turn off the TV for 10 days and keeping their consumption under 7 hours per week during the following months. The research was reported in the *Journal of the American Medical Association* in 2001. Reducing TV and video games helped reduce verbal violence by 50% and physical violence by 40%. The SMART Program was made available in 2004 by the Stanford Health Promotion Resource Center (SHPRC) affiliated to the Stanford University School of Medicine; CA. Information about the SMART program is posted on their Web site. Dr. Robinson also proved that reducing the time of television watched and video games played helped reduce another MRD. According to the Stanford Study reported by the *Journal of the American Medical Association,* reducing TV had a significant impact on a decrease in obesity.

The SMART Program was successfully implemented in Michigan in 2004. Principal Mike Smajda learned that one of his first-grade pupils at Lemmer Elementary School had watched *The Texas Chainsaw Massacre.* Not long afterward, the boy was playing in a leaf pile with a girl when he suddenly began kicking her in the head. Another boy joined in. "They felt it was part of the game," Smajda said. "They both kicked her until her head was bleeding and she had to go to the hospital." Smajda can't prove the R-rated slasher movie provoked the child, but the November 2004 incident reinforced his commitment to an antiviolence program getting under way at his school. It challenged students to do without TV and all other screen entertainment for 10 days, then limit themselves to just seven hours a week. Other schools joined in over the next year. Administrators and teachers say short term results were striking: less aggressive behaviour and, in some cases, better standardized test scores.

The SMART Program was successfully implemented in eight schools in 2005–2006. The school district was allowed 2.3 millions dollars for sharing the program in 2006–2007. The Delta-Schoolcraft School District, based in Escanaba, Michigan, was the first school district in the world to use the SMART curriculum across the entire district. The 10Day TV/videogame turnoff resulted in an 80% reduction in violence. In the spring of 2005, more schools participated in the program. The result was a statistically significant reduction in violence and bullying. They also witnessed a 15% increase in math scores and an 18% increase in writing scores as compared to the seven schools that did not have the program in place at that point. SMART showed to be effective at reducing violence in a double-blind, controlled experiment conducted by Stanford Medical School. In October 2006, the district had its fourth international conference to teach educators about the curriculum. All attendees were provided with the curriculum and given instruction in the implementation of the curriculum by educators and administrators who had firsthand experience with it.

The "10-Day Challenge" TV and Video Game Free

The Challenge was a success because of the media education sessions with students, teachers, and parents. It was experienced for the first time in April 2003 in partnership with the parents association of the Québec City region. It received funding from the Public Safety departments of both Québec and Canada. In May 2003, the Canadian Press (CP) covered the Challenge in St-Malachie. The Challenge was reported in the *Green Teacher Magazine*. Since then, the Challenge has been experienced in over 50 schools in the provinces of Québec and Ontario. Everywhere, the Challenge obtained huge success, as shown in the evaluation by parents, students, and teachers from six elementary schools. In April 2004, the Parents Association launched a 20-minute video (in French) telling the story of the Challenge as it was experienced in two schools.

The Canadian Observatory on School Violence Prevention (COSVP) posted the PA press release on its Web site. In all regions or cities where the Challenge was experienced, it received coverage and support by the media. In April 2005, three daily French newspapers covered the Challenge. *Le Nouvelliste* told the story in Trois-Rivières, Québec. *Le Droit* covered the Challenge in Ottawa, Ontario. *Le Soleil* made its front page with the Challenge in Québec City. In the spring of 2005, the Québec Consumers Protection Office added the Challenge to its list of recommended consuming practices and posted it on its Youth Page.

The 10-Day Challenge with Teenagers

Commemoration of the 6th anniversary of the Columbine High School shooting in Littleton, Colorado, was the opportunity to analyze the factors around this tragedy. Such an event deserves better attention than what was presented in the movie *Bowling for Columbine.* Despite efforts by the producer to take blame away from the entertainment industry, the media play an important role in the shooting as shown by further inquiry in the lives of the young killers. The preparation of the students for the 10 Day Challenge in Louis- Jacques-Casault high school, in Montmagny, Québec, showed how media education could actually help prevent teen violence. One thousand teenagers attending the high school were offered to turn off the TV and video games for 10 days. Teachers, parents, and students evaluated the outcome of the Challenge.

Interviews with teenagers who participated in the Challenge were aired all across Canada by CBC radio and TV. The evaluation below confirms the value of the 10Day Challenge as a "promising practice" with teenagers. The 10Day Challenge has shown to offer a motivating approach, an efficient way to mobilize entire communities in improving protection from media violence. As mentioned by UNICEF Canada in its consultation document, additional legislation is certainly among promising practices. However, legislation alone will be ineffective unless civil society mobilizes to counter the enormous power of the media, including the video game industry.

Independence of Media Education

Two reporters investigated the funding sources of major public health groups and found that big corporations dump big money into these groups, and pretty soon, the groups start taking the line of the big corporations. They concluded their inquiry by suggesting that such funding was causing the losing of the wars on cancer, heart disease, and diabetes. In the summer of 2006, McDonald's launched its own exercise program to prevent obesity. Again, the P. R. strategy helped take blame away from the impact of junk food on children's health. Canadians and Americans face a similar problem with media education. Organizations funded by media conglomerates were created to promote a kind of media literacy that will take blame away from the media for intoxicating kids and teens.

The funding "naturally" helps put the blame on parents; just like the food industry funding helps put the blame for diabetes and obesity on the lack of exercise. Big media corporations know how to protect their image. The media need to divert the blame for the increasing crime rate among young people for violent offences in the United Sates and Canada. During three decades, organizations were created to produce "educational material" with the financial contributions of big media. Naturally, the funding helps keep blame away from the polluters and prevent further accusations of child abuse. North American schools receive free kits, including "educational" tools, but the price is disregard for the impact of media violence on society.

Evaluation of the 10Day Challenge

In the school year of 2003–2004, 20 elementary schools in Québec and Ontario offered media education workshops to prepare students and parents to turn off their television sets. Tabulation of participation revealed that 1,354 students succeeded in saving 19,377 hours of time they would have spent watching TV or playing video games. Students succeeded in turning off their TV for an average of seven days. In April 2004, one high school did the same with its 1,000 students. In six elementary schools and this single high school, two to three weeks after the turnoff ended, an evaluation form was given to all students, parents, and teachers.

Center for Media and Public Affairs

The Center for Media and Public Affairs (CMPA) is a self-described non-partisan and non-profit research and educational organization that is affiliated with George Mason University in Fairfax, Virginia. It was founded in 1985 by political scientists Dr. S. Robert Lichter and his ex-wife, the late Dr. Linda Lichter. It publishes a bi-monthly newsletter called Media Monitor. The CMPA conducts studies of the news and entertainment media. Among its activities are a continuing analysis and tabulation of late night political jokes, an annual report on diversity among network news journalists, and a content analysis of the nightly news on the major broadcast and cable news networks.

The results of the latter are compiled in the CMPA newsletter. CMPA engages in health communication research, investigating the way in which scientific issues are conveyed in the media. CMPA also engages in survey research to determine the accuracy of media's reports of scientific opinion. CMPA conducts social scientific research on media coverage with the use of such techniques as content analysis and survey research. Its studies appear in academic journals and reference works as well as in popular media outlets. CMPA's signature activity is its "rapid response" studies of media coverage of current issues, which appear quickly enough to influence ongoing public debates, such as presidential campaigns, Senate confirmation hearings, and major policy debates in Congress.

Although CMPA avoids taking stands on political issues, its studies have sometimes become part of the public debate over the media's role in politics and society. For example, in 1992 a CMPA study found that the average length of a presidential candidate's sound bite on the evening news had dropped to less than ten seconds, down from 42 seconds in 1968. In response CBS adopted a policy requiring longer sound bites on the CBS Evening News. CMPA studies of entertainment media have been used by members of the United States Congress such as Sen. Joe Lieberman (D-CT) in their efforts to reduce gratuitous violence and sex in television entertainment. CMPA's research on entertainment media has also included studies of how various groups have been portrayed on television, such as studies of Hispanic Americans' portrayals commissioned by the National Council of La Raza and the U.S. Commission on Civil Rights.

The organization has been criticized for advancing a notion of objectivity thought to be ideologically consistent with the values of liberal democracy. Edward S. Herman and Noam Chomsky argue that the CMPA is organized around the creation of "flak," which they define as "negative responses to a media statement or program" and which they maintain is part of a project of "disciplining the media." The media watchdog group Fairness and Accuracy in Reporting (FAIR) has challenged CMPA's non-partisan claim, based on the argument that much of its funding has come from conservative sources, and that its founder, Dr. S. Robert Lichter, once held a chair in mass communications at the American Enterprise

Institute and was a Fox News contributor. After a Washington Post article referred to CMPA as "conservative," the Post published a "Clarification," which concluded, "The Center describes itself as nonpartisan, and its studies have been cited by both conservative and liberal commentators." Media Transparency documents that between 1986 and 2005 CMPA received 55 grants totaling $2,960,916 (unadjusted for inflation). The data reveals that the overwhelming proportion of CMPA's funding comes from conservative foundations.

6

Political Process in the Mediated Democracies

In October of 1968, in Rosario, Argentina, the artist Graciela Carnevale invited visitors to what would be the final opening of a "Cycle of Experimental Art" held in a storefront space in the city. Her contribution to the series consisted in luring the public inside, then slipping out to lock the door and enclose the crowd within the gallery. The visitors became the material of a social artwork. The question was: How would they react to this imprisonment? Who would finally shatter the glass to release the captives from the trap? "Through an act of aggression, the work tends to provoke the spectator to a heightened consciousness of the power whereby violence is exerted in the everyday world," wrote the artist.

"On a daily basis we passively submit, through fear, connivance and complicity, to all the degrees of violence, from the most subtle and degrading violence that coerces our thinking via communications media broadcasting false contents provided by their owners, to the most provocative and scandalous violence exerted on a student's life." In the event, the public submitted. After an hour, the blow that finally shattered the glass came from outside. A photograph shows a woman crouching down to exit through a jagged hole in the window. At the same time, Graciela Carnevale was also part of the project known as Tucuman Arde, or "Tucuman is Burning" – an experimental process of information analysis, multimedia reportage and artistic display, involving some thirty artists in an attempt to expose the conditions of exploitation, expropriation and impoverishment in an Argentinean province.

The participants, who had drawn their conclusions from the most advanced theoretical positions and technical experiments of the time, chose to break with the existing institutions in the hope of infiltrating the national information system and contributing directly to the political struggle against the Ongan–a dictatorship. Tucuman Arde is increasingly recognized as a genealogical departure point for the kinds of media activism practiced today. But can we not also read Carnevale's enclosure piece as an allegory of the way that social classes are transformed under conditions of urgency? In the late nineties, the politically involved sectors of the over-developed countries – the NGOs, the charities, the unionists, the communists and ecologists – were the people inside the glass bubble of consensus, or "civil-society dialogue."

It was the direct actionists who shattered the window. We know that the cycle of massive demonstrations that began in the years 1999- 2001 was no miracle. The impetus had come from the South, primarily from social movements in Latin America and India. The global justice campaigns, inspired by South African efforts to force debt cancellation, had built a tremendous following. Critique of neoliberalism had become a national issue in both France and Canada. The labour movements of the overdeveloped countries were ripe for radicalization. And the Zapatistas offered a new model of political confrontation, combining powerful symbolic actions with national and international networks of support. But political forces must be set into motion, passions have to catch flame. In the cities of Western Europe and North America, where the post-modern waning of affect appeared to be complete, it was the urban cultures of resistance that struck the match.

Reclaim the Streets in Great Britain, the Tute Bianche in Italy, the Direct Action Network of the Pacific Northwest United States – these were the catalysts that transformed a diffuse aspiration of isolated civil-society groups into a movement, able to take to the streets and reach beyond the specific demands of each dissenting group. A political generation is forged, not by determinants of age, but by choices of involvement and experiences of confrontation. How are such choices made? The invitation to illegal protest that sparked the current cycle of anti-capitalist mobilizations aimed to draw out the participation of social categories, particularly youth, who could no longer be lured into involvement by identity issues, parties or unions. But it also sought to bring more traditional formations into heightened conflict.

The success of the Direct Action Network in Seattle, at the WTO meeting in November 1999, was to use civil-disobedience techniques to immobilize traffic in a key sector of the city, focusing police repression and in this way creating a magnetic attractor for union members exiting from their consensually managed events but also for local inhabitants, ecologists, Third World delegations, anarchists and many others. Through that intervention a five-day urban uprising was unleashed. In a less disciplined yet equally potent way, the Reclaim the Streets carnivals offered a tantalizing cocktail of transgressive pleasure, informed political protest and direct confrontation, which radicalized the participants by exposing the structural violence of contemporary social relations. But the Tute Bianche of Italy ("White Overalls") developed the most explicit strategy.

The white overall, which could be donned by anyone, signified the permeability of a movement that was not ideological in the disciplinary sense. The use of quite ridiculous-looking protective padding created a theatrics of humour and self-derision, while allowing police brutality to be captured on video as a kind of comic spectacle. Most importantly, the duration of this movement was limited in advance by the prediction of its self-dissolution into all the colours. The release from a paralyzing consensus became constitutive of the movement. It would be misleading to claim that the direct actionists played the role of a vanguard artist, leading a naive public into an experiential trap where every participant would be forced to draw fresh conclusions. The self-transformation of society is more complicated, more multiple, than Carnevale's enclosure piece can suggest. Yet the imprint of artistic experimentation on the current political generation is undeniable.

The most obvious contribution of the visual arts to the anti-capitalist movements is the merger of community-oriented video with the distribution system offered by Internet, giving rise to innumerable non-normalized media projects that combine documentary information and expressive politics, in the lineage of Tucuman Arde. These projects carry out a specular combat with broadcast TV – that is, with the spectacle society – and in that way, they at least partially fulfill the political aspirations of the early video makers. Another, more subtle thread is the proliferation of mail art, first through 'zine culture and desktop publishing, then through the net, culminating in the mid-nineties in the widespread circulation of subversive texts and media pranks under multiple names like Monty Cantsin or Luther Blissett.

Multiple names bring the refusal of copyright and intellectual property to the very center of ego-dominated subjectivity, in an attempt to dissolve the proprietary function of the signature which has always served as the barrier between contemplative, individualistic art and collective, interactive forms of expression. Yet another artistic contribution to the movements is performance culture, with its emphasis on the embodiment of the political, played out in its inseparability from the sexual, ritual, generational, ethnic, and psycho-dramatic dimensions of human experience. One could be tempted to conceive the entire deposit if of the carnivalesque demonstration as an extension of performance to the streets. But if we stopped there we would miss the deepest commonality between experimental art and the activism.

This is the notion of process, as a value in and of itself. In the now-canonical "antiform" definitions of the sixties, process designates the temporal dimension of materials, their transformation in time, as initiated or continuously effected by the activity of the artist. But there is another definition, whose roots lie in the chance philosophy of John Cage, in the relation of prop and performance sought by Fluxus, in the interplay of score and interpretation developed in concrete poetry and vanguard dance, in the orchestrated chaos of the happenings, the improvisational work of the Living Theater or the insurgency of Provo and Situationist interventions. In these approaches, process can be defined as the generative matrix constituted by the meeting of catalytic artefacts, more or less conscious group interactions, and the dimension of singular chance inherent to the event.

This artistic understanding of the way that "social material" can proactively transform itself over time was enriched by the movements of antipsychiatry and schizo-analysis, which extended the domain of what could be accepted as self expression, and attempted to reshape institutional structures to accommodate this multiplication of subjective forms. The micropolitics of a host of liberation movements of the seventies, including the women's movements in particular, but also the local constellations of Italian Autonomia, made group processes of self-understanding and decision-making into one of the ways that adherence to a political project is developed and sustained over time. The difference of the last ten or fifteen years is that the proliferation of expressive practices in everyday life – inseparable from the rise of intellectual and affective labour – has brought the specifically artistic definition of social process back to the forefront, not within the art world but in the more open and uncontrollable space of the urban event.

The fundamental relation between post-vanguard art and contemporary social movements is here, in this resurgence of expressive and interactive process which has helped forge a political generation. What it gives us to understand is that an entire current of experimentalism has migrated outside the realm of art as defined by the signature-work. But this realization is only the departure point for a series of questions, concerning the political postures that have developed as a necessary exodus from the immobilizing transparency of the mediated democracies. The questions are these: Why was the mix of carnival and direct action so important to the protagonism of civil society? How has the situation changed since September 11? What will happen to the new political generation that emerged just before the authoritarian turn? And what roles can artists play in that generation's development?

Civil Society in a Hall of Mirrors

The idea might sound scandalous; yet just such a process lies behind the emergence of what we now recognize as global civil society. In the late seventies and early eighties, Eastern European writers like Adam Michnik, Vaclav Havel and Gyorgy Konrad used a combination of literary expression and political critique to redefine the classical concept of national civil society, and in this way, to precipitate a change in collective consciousness. No longer would civil society be simply understood as the pacifying rule of law within the boundaries of a sovereign territory; nor just as the right of citizens to engage in critical discourse. Instead it would designate the need to create an everyday space of civic engagement that effectively secedes from the totalitarian state. For Konrad, civil society was antipolitics. As he wrote in 1982, "Antipolitics is the emergence of forums that can be appealed to against political power; it is a counterpower that cannot take power and does not wish to." The Czech dissidents spoke of a parallel polis, which, as Vaclav Benda explained, "does not compete for power.

Its aim is not to replace the power of another kind, but rather under this power – or beside it – to create a structure that represents other laws and in which the voice of the ruling power is heard only as an insignificant echo from a world that is organized in an entirely different way." Because the Soviet and American blocs were widely perceived as two sides of the same coin – both threatening nuclear violence on a scale that dwarfed the traditional, nationally bounded space of civility – it was immediately considered necessary to extend the rightful space of anti-politics to global dimensions. Konrad maintained that the "existence of a world forum favours the emergence of the eccentric, those who stand out." And he continued: "The international alliance of dissenters and avantgardes takes under its wing those few people who, in their various ways, think their thoughts through to the end."

Similar ideas developed in South America, in the face of the dictatorships. The aim was to open up a myriad of divergent and ultimately uncontrollable micropolitical spaces, in order to succeed where the guerrilla struggles had failed. This conception of divergent spaces remains an important legacy for antisystemic movements, as witnessed by the Zapatista autonomous zones, the Social Forums, John Holloway's call to change the world without taking power, or Paolo Virno's notion of a non-state public sphere. But there has been a critical change since the eighties. No one today can ignore the deeply ambiguous role that civil society would play after 1989 – especially since Michnik, Havel and Konrad have all supported the invasion of Iraq.

The more recent attempts to intervene on social material have all had to respond to the bewildering metamorphosis of civil society after the collapse of the Soviet Union. The integration of a diluted concept of civil society to the reality of capitalist globalization was a consequence of the ideological vacuum left by 1989. In the absence of any coordinated oppositional force, every critique could be considered at worst harmless, and at best, profitable. The exploitation of humanitarian NGOs by the neoliberal state is there to prove it – along with the corporate patronage of critical art. Yet the nineties were also a time of opening. Air transportation, global communications and international coordination were now accessible even to informal groups. The structures of governance became more transnational but more transparent too, permeable to the public, permeated by the media, constantly overseen by innumerable observers. The paradox of civil society in the years of Clinton, Blair, Jospin and Schroeder was to sit on all kinds of official panels, to be aired on all kinds of channels and to be allowed to debate about everything, except the basic values that orient the post-'89 world-system.

Such was the Western glasnost. The hidden aims of public relations and private sponsorship, the real politics of elected office and international commissions, and the increasing insistence of the news media on the rules of a world marketplace in which they themselves are major players, all gave civil-society figures the uncanny sensation of moving in a hall of mirrors. As though transparency in the mediated democracies could only be found in a camera lens, whose function is to select and frame, even before the image is recorded, edited, repurposed and broadcast as the opposite of whatever was initially intended. In the late nineties, Havel's warning in his famous 1978 essay on "The Power of the Powerless" was timelier than ever, despite or even because of the presidential office occupied by its author: "It would appear that traditional parliamentary democracies can offer no fundamental opposition to the automatism of technological civilization and the industrial-consumer society, for they too are being dragged helplessly along by it. People are manipulated in ways that are infinitely more subtle and refined than the brutal methods used in the post totalitarian societies."

By the end of Clinton's imperial mandate, the need for direct action became obvious at least to those on the fringes. Because they did not claim to be civil anymore, deliberate gestures of disobedience could break the distorting mirror and reclaim the density and opacity of an oppositional position. Only this kind of confrontation could make activists from the South take the Northern protests seriously. But the carnivalesque dimension, the artistic treatment of information and the experimentation with social process are not just window dressing for a protestor's brick. These are the ways that participants have found to reinvent the anti-political space of everyday experience, despite full-spectrum attempts at commercial, cultural, governmental and ideological mediation.

It's often said that September 11 put an end to the effectiveness of direct action protests, by delegitimating anything that could be assimilated to terrorism and authorizing massive deployment of the police. That's true, and the strategy had already been sketched out in Genoa.

But the consequences of September 11 on the US government have had the long-term effect of demonstrating that the fusion of the state with a corporate oligarchy can produce a repressive apparatus that stretches its electronic fingers into every aspect of daily life. We are witnessing the onset of a social pathology, comparable in scale if not in nature to the Cold War. And only idealists could believe that the European bloc is not producing its own variations on this pathology, for instance in the treatment of immigrant workers and the nationalist rhetoric surrounding the presence of so-called foreigners, or in the establishment of detainment camps inside and outside the EU borders.

But to oppose the security panic and the reality of institutional racism that underlies it would mean refusing the false transparencies, escaping the co-optation machinery of parliamentary democracy itself. This is why in the very moment of their rise to visibility and to more complex forms of organization, dissenting social movements have begun to experiment once again with new forms of anti-politics, marked by the pragmatics of defection and exit, but also by the more intangible, almost mythical theme of exodus.

Re-disappearing

A strange and quite funny anecdote from the European Social Forum in Florence, in November 2002, can help make the point. Faced with an overload of slogans like "Stop this Bloody War" and "Another World Is Possible" which is like a marriage of Trotskyist populism and civil-society naivete members of the Euraction Hub network decided to intervene. They used the materials at hand. An activist in an outlandish blue wig was installed on the roof of a van outfitted with projecting pink wings; this emissary from the outside advanced within a compact crowd toward the Fortezza da Basso, a medieval castle where the main events were being held for paying admission. Vanquishing the objections of the security team, the procession entered the Forum to have a dance party right next to the circus tent where SWP Trots were bellowing out slogans from 1917. As the perimeter of the castle was crossed, the activists raised a banner that read: "Stop the World, Another War Is Possible."

The satire of consensus was perfect and so was the call for massive direct action that would paralyze entire cities. The banner in the gateway expressed the widespread desire for something more effective than the global antiwar demonstrations of February 15, 2003, which were in fact proposed at the ESF meeting in Florence. Along with this idea of mass defection from the militarized societies, it asserted the possibility of a wholly other war: a subversion that could dissolve normalized behaviours and established hierarchies. The networked activists had not forgotten that Deleuze and Guattari conceived their nomadic war machine as a potential of expressive and epistemological variance that could operate within every institution, and even at the heart of the military-industrial complexes. They had not forgotten, because the development of the Internet over more than thirty years has proved this kind of subversion to be a practical reality. Such struggles necessarily take place within the capture-devices that seek to neutralize them: thus the entry of the activists into the castle, as a way to pursue the exit from politics-as-usual that had launched the entire social forum movement in the first place.

Without a constant resurgence of the radicalizing process, grassroots mobilization can be halted by the very organizations and figureheads it needs in order to expand its field of transformation. But this is what has been learned since the early demands for the representation of civil society. The destinies of the current political generation depend crucially on maintaining the possibilities both of large-scale organized confrontation, and of direct, micro-political participation in the processes of self-government. These understandings appear clearly in the new mobilizations around precarious labour, articulated among others by the French parttime cinema and theatre workers and the Euro May Day paraders in Milan and Barcelona. These confrontational movements, which make a great use of street performance and artistic invention but also of very specific juridical and sociological knowledge, can be seen as attempts to infiltrate, destabilize and reconfigure the social state.

Not only is a new kind of labour to be considered – part-time or interim workers – but also a new set of claims, which mix wage and social insurance issues with the demand for more free time and better opportunities to use it. The treatment of casual labour becomes a question of human ecology. Thus what is ostensibly a workers' movement builds constitutive links to struggles over unemployment, education, environmental conditions, real-estate speculation and the commodification of culture. The massive presence of migrants in the circuits of precarious labour brings in concrete North-South issues of unequal exchange as well, and thereby lends these campaigns at least the potential to act with the full political composition that first appeared in Seattle and Genoa. In this way, unionizing strategies can remain part of a larger struggle, which requires a multiperspectival awareness of its protagonists. The goal is to transform the state, but without becoming it – that is, without being subjected by its market imperatives and bureaucratic categories. Only in this way can the horizons of social change remain open enough to embrace the world.

Artists and media activists participate directly in these movements and at the same time symbolize them, by condensing their experience of the radicalizing process into expressive works. The distribution of these works, through alternative circuits and then gradually through broader institutional formats, is a way to give complexity and consistency to the affects of rebellion and refusal. But the familiar limits have not vanished. The basic functions of selection and framing, editing and repurposing, are performed in perfect transparency by the gallery-magazine-museum system. As the demand for an activist aesthetic rises, the selection will almost inevitably come to focus on dramatized images of insurgency, associated with a truncated genealogy of theoretical concepts from the late sixties and early seventies. In other words, the presentations will slice out a few visual and conceptual elements from a longer, broader and more complex history, leaving the viewer untroubled by any kind of processual passion.

A new institutional critique might then arise, denouncing the failure of museums to adequately inform the public. But in reality, it is the inherent failure of representation, both in the visual and the political sense that continually leads activist-artists to abandon their works and their familiar skills and to dissolve once again into the intersubjective processes of society's self-transformation. This moment of dissolution is where one could locate exodus, not as a concept, but as a power or a myth of resistance. On the one hand, exodus is a pragmatic response to the society of control, in which any widespread political opposition becomes an object of exacting analysis for those who can afford to invest major resources in the identification, segmentation and manipulation of what we naively call the public. In the face of these strategies, exodus is a power of willful metamorphosis: the capacity for a movement to appear, to intervene and to disappear again, before changing names and recommencing the same struggle in a different way.

And this too is a process that artists can symbolize, by performing the selfovercoming of art once again – at the risk of dissolving their proper names, their trademarks and their careers. But the very statement of this tactical necessity of disappearance raises a deep anxiety, which must be familiar to all old revolutionaries, about the possible continuity of resistant culture, or the constitution over time of something like an antisystemic movement. In this regard, exodus seems to designate an existential reserve, that psychic space where fragments of artistic, poetic and musical refrains are inseparable from the wellsprings of action, but expressible only as a kind of myth.

To touch this intangible space is the ultimate intervention on social material – something no individual can do, because it is only achieved through a collective experience, by a multiplicity that has no authority, no signature. Exodus is an expression of process politics. It points beyond the distorting mediations and structural inequalities of capitalism toward a strange sort of Promised Land for the profane, which is the immediacy of the everyday, the direct experience of cooperation with others. The carnival that sometimes breaks out in the midst of concerted political action is a way to celebrate the occasional reality of this powerful and persistent myth.

Exploring Studies in Meaning

The Post-Modern Challenge to Religious Education

Over the last few decades post-modernism has influenced the way we see the world. It has moved us past a simple view of the world whereby our thoughts, ideas and theories simply mirror an objective reality. Rather, we are coming to see that reality is a joint endeavour between the external world and our own filters, perspectives and interpretations. Knowledge is the product of an interaction between our ideas about the world and our experience of the world.

Religion, Education and Post-Modernity and Gavin Flood's Beyond Phenomenology: Rethinking the Study of Religion, have begun the process of questioning the philosophical and theological modernist foundations of the way Religious Education is currently taught. According to these and other post-modern educationalists it turns out that we may have been building the foundations of our Religious Education on the shifting sands of modernity. Before we can develop a method of Religious Education that makes sense to and appeals to the current generation of students we need to consider a post-modern critique of the major methods currently used in Australian schools.

Current Methods of Religious Education

The Catechetical Approach

The catechetical approach seeks to educate students in their assumed religious tradition. It is most often used in Catholic schools where many students identify with belonging to their particular religious tradition, although it is also adopted in Islamic and Jewish schools. The focus is on the elements of being part of that religion – rituals, beliefs and scriptures – and it seeks to educate students in their faith tradition.

It is seldom used in non-Catholic private schools because of the great diversity of religious and non-religious backgrounds of the students particularly where belonging to the religious tradition is not part of the social identity as it is in Catholicism. It works to the degree to which the student does identify with the faith community but often alienates those who do not as it can foster a sense of being outside and may prove particularly difficult for young people who are testing the limits of belonging. This approach, if compulsory for students, can set up resistance among those who can feel, in this age of choices, that faith is being thrust upon them.

The Kerygmatic Approach

The key feature of the kerygmatic approach to religious education is the proclamation of the good news of the Christian gospel (kerygma). This approach is taken in many Independent Schools and some Catholic schools and a strong emphasis is often placed on teaching of scripture with the idea that scripture has the power to communicate the essence of the gospel. This is sometimes mixed with a study of religion approach in traditional church schools. This method tends to offer students a choice of one, emphasis is placed on the student's willingness to accept or reject the message of the gospel. It is clearly modernist in its approach as it presents religion as a meta-narrative, an all encompassing world view which seeks to explain everything important in life. This approach tends to assume that students will find meaning once they adopt the faith.

Many students do not necessarily feel ready to make the all or nothing choice often offered by this approach and can feel some pressure especially if this is mixed with apologetics. They are perhaps justifiably cautious in an environment where they receive a lot of mixed messages and will tend to put off decisions and commitments. This putting off of commitment often leads the students to a functional agnosticism. It can also tend towards polarization among students and us and them type of mentality. Furthermore, when students study the bible they bring with them a number of techniques and assumptions from their world view and from their other subject studies. One question they are taught to ask from their short understanding of history is, "Did it happen?"

They also bring from science a skepticism concerning what may be considered miraculous. Within an enlightenment context where the role of reason is elevated and physicalism is most dominant the miracles of the scriptures seem to belong to another world and the questions addressed by the scriptures seem far from the concerns of the students. Nor does this methodology help students understand their current unexamined belief framework. A six year study by students of Christianity is not necessarily a pretty sight. Our faith contains many moments of injustice, spiritual bullying, confusion and it requires a deep maturity to put all that in perspective. This is a task best left until later. The more appropriate task of the student should be the adoption of a personal meaning system.

The Experiential Approach

Influenced by psychology and anthropology this approach emphasizes experience; both the experience of the student and the religious practitioner are on centre stage in this methodology. Under the umbrella of this methodology the student may try meditation in the classroom, study religious experience, undertake self examination of their current belief and value system and explore the question of "Who am I?" and their own experience of prayer and faith. The danger with this approach is that it provides too little content preventing students from taking it seriously and seeing it as a soft, "touchy-feely" subject. There are also limits on how much students at their age can reflect on what is a limited experience. Furthermore it does not address the meaning gap in their lives.

Liberation and Justice Approach

Justice education takes a central place in a number of Religious Education courses. Often drawing on the work of Thomas Groome, this approach emphases filling the gap between what the gospel calls us to be and the reality of the world. Focusing on poverty, the environment and charity, this approach highlights the work of the gospel in the world. Although students can see the value of this method it often left them feeling that parts of the church weren't always on the side of justice and it had difficulty maintaining the interest of students on what is predominately ethical issues. It is very much immersed in the world of should and ought. Nor does it necessarily give meaning to their ordinary lives unless they adopt a mission to bring justice. This methodology needs to take more into account the stage of students' lives and the need to develop a meaning structure out of which they can make a contribution to justice and the world.

The Study of Religions (Phenomenological) Approach

The study of religions is sometimes called the phenomenological approach as it aims that students become familiar with the various historical manifestations of religious phenomena. Religion is situated in a cultural and historical context and one aim is to provide young people with the intellectual tools they need to understand social and political events that have religious dimensions and that are regularly covered by the media. Although phenomenology can be traces back to Kant and his contemporaries it has been made popular for Religious Education by Ninian Smart who posited seven dimensions of religion such as beliefs, rituals, religious experience, myths and rites of passages.

This approach to religion became the basis for most texts used in Religious Studies departments firstly in England where it gained great popularity and then subsequently in Australia. The adoption of this approach in schools led to students studying the myths and rituals, beliefs and religious experiences of the major world religions in class. The goals of the phenomenology of religion were the hope that students would be able to understand how religion operates in society and in the life of the individual and that understanding would foster empathy. However the attainment of these goals is now being called into question through a growing post-modern critique of this methodology along the following lines.

- Adoption of a personal meaning system is only a by-product of the phenomenology of religion and requires a high level of thinking from students, to take the phenomena, extrapolate meaning and apply within their culture. Meaning is culturally based. Students find it hard to make the shift from the phenomenological study of religion to their own existentialist situation.
- The study of religions tends to reflect the assumptions and values of modernity and specifically the enlightenment. It presupposes the neutral stance of the interpreter and seeks to suspend the judgments of the student. This suspension of judgment is not really possible nor is it desirable because the student needs to understand their own value system rather than pretend it is not there. The reasoned objective study of religion is impossible! It is enlightenment wishful thinking. The only study of religion that is possible is subjective study.
- Gavin Flood points out that in developing typologies of religious phenomena the explanatory level is usually left out is it cultural, psychological or other explanation.
- It is assumed that bracketing together religious phenomena will produce empathy on the part of the student as they will find similarities with their own experience. However this empathy may well be overstated in the case of students with their own faith who may highlight difference and absent from students without faith who often feel they are entering an alien world of religious experience and myth.
- It presupposes that the core of religious ideas is accessible through a study of their so called beliefs or rituals and that there is somehow a one dimensional thing that can

be studied called religion. It is biased towards a content approach to religion whereas religion may be just as aptly described as a process, a way of being in the world.

- The goal of religion is not religion but life. The phenomenological approach focuses too much on religion itself and not enough on how religion aids people in living their lives.
- It describes rather than analyses. Phenomenology fails to get to the underlying nature or pattern of things.
- Religious studies have withdrawn from the world's debates to study religion as an isolated topic.
- The phenomenological approach leads to a grab-bag approach to religion, many features of which are irrelevant to the hearer.

The Situation of the Student

Ninian Smart commented that the phenomenological study of religion becomes "methodological agnosticism" and this methodological agnosticism easily becomes personal agnosticism. That agnosticism tends to lead also to a sense of meaninglessness as it speaks to what the world is not rather than what it is. Flood concurs, "In the end, the discourse of religion is either from within, in which case the entailment of existence is implicitly accepted or from without in which case it is denied; there cannot be both an acceptance and a non-acceptance of an existence claim."

The phenomenological approach does not require the student to do or believe or commit to anything whereas the studies in meaning approach require them to make meaning for their lives. The kerygmatic approach shares a similar problem in that it invites the student to consider the claims of the gospel from the perspective of the outsider studying the way an insider perceives the faith – a very difficult process, the difficulty of which is indicated by the very small number of students who actually come to faith. Furthermore that outsider perspective is often the materialistic and rationalistic enlightenment attitude which the students pick up from other subjects at school. It is the perspective from which religion is studied that is reinforced not the religion itself.

Effectively the way we are teaching Religious Education currently has a strong tendency to produce agnosticism and atheism in students as it encourages either methodological agnosticism or forces students into a choice based on accepting what they have been taught conflicts with rational thinking. Flood's solution to the problem is the study of religion using dialogue in which the student recognizes their own position within its historical context and enters into a dialogue with other traditions. While this may be appropriate for the mature student, teenagers have little understanding of their own fluid personal position which is still being formed. The position that the student needs to take then is sojourner, creator of meaning – they mine religion for meaning – which requires them to understand the meaning of that faith in context. They are given a reason to visit the world of faith – sometimes they will stay.

The student learns that the meaning is dependent of the social and historical context in a way phenomenology doesn't encourage because its typology seeks to take it out of its historical context. For instance take the story of the Incarnation, from a phenomenological perspective it is studied as a myth of Christianity comparable to myths in other religions such as the avatars of Krishna in Hinduism; in that context an agnostic stance is taken toward whether it is real. In the kerygmatic approach it is taken as a central claim of Christianity to either be believed by the student or rejected. The student compares these claims with what they have learnt in history and science and often concludes that virgin births do not happen. Within Studies in Meaning the incarnation may comes up in the context of the issue of what does it means to be human, that we are both physical and spiritual, or what is God like, not aloof and distant but manifest here among us.

The step of looking at the incarnation for meaning requires the student to step inside the world view of the first hearers and assume for a while its reality. Then the student needs to evaluate the meanings – how true is it that God can be present in human form, how true is it that we are both human and physical and yet spiritual and "of God"? The issue of to what extent it happened in a historical or scientific sense is then secondary and comes under the issues of the nature of reality and is dealt with separately.

The Five Strand Approach of Peter Vardy

The most dominant approach to the religious Education in Australian independent Schools is that promoted by the theologian and vice principal of Heythorp Jesuit College, Dr. Peter Vardy. His five strand approach is not so much a new approach as a combination of a number of different approaches. It includes the study of Christian scriptures, ethics, and philosophy of religion, the study of major religions and the practise of meditation. The first strand is kerygmatic, the second and third philosophical, the fourth phenomenological and the last experiential. Vardy's approach is very traditional and its most notable feature is the combining of a number of these methodologies, however each part suffers from the critiques above and this seems a case of the whole not being greater than the sum of the parts.

Civics Education

A number of educators have advocated that the teaching of civics or citizenship as part of or an adjunct to Religious Education. If this type of citizenship is trying to merely inculcate the student into the dominate social narrative then it is going to be resisted by the student. For example Richard Rorty believes that "lower education" (primary and secondary) "is mostly a matter of socialization, of trying to inculcate a sense of citizenship." It "should aim primarily at communicating enough of what is *held to be* true by the society to which the children belong so that they can function as citizens of that society. Whether it is true or not is none of the educator's business, in his or her professional capacity."

As Baumeister points out society does not need the individual to acquire a deep sense of meaning. All that is required is enough meaning to make them a functional member of the community. In fact as there are many jobs that must be done even if they offer no meaning to the individual. Students often understand that civics may have an implied agenda that requires the sacrifice of the individual for society as a whole. Such an approach can only really succeed if a meaning system is established first. In this sense civics can sometimes be at odds with spirituality which has a questioning role toward the dominant culture and Religious Education needs to be careful not to align itself too closely with the unquestioning philosophy of teaching civics.

Furthermore young people systematically question convention from the age of about two, a tendency which is essential for cultural renewal. Religious Education should support this tendency and maximize individual meaning making. We ought not give students something to push against – it wrecks the teaching and prevents them doing any meaning or spiritual work. They become so busy being against the system that they never do the work of finding their own beliefs. We are too concerned that if given the freedom students would choose against faith and society so in our lack of trust we preach to them, get resistance and create the very thing we fear. But we have nothing to fear except fear itself! Most students when putting together their meaning system will take elements from the very pool of ideas we may wish to foist upon them anyway. Here it is important to remember that the medium is the message and if we model an open classroom we will get a student who is respectful and engaged in life's spiritual quests.

Post Modern Religious Education Programme

The Need for Meaning

Our teenagers have a great number of needs at their stage of life, a need for a sense of identity, for a competent place in world, for significant relationships and for meaning in their lives. It is particularly the latter need that a good Religious Education programme can address. All humans have a need for meaning in their lives – we are meaning making creatures.

We use meaning every time we speak or act or imagine acting. Whatever happens to us we find and assign meaning to it. Our lives are filled with attempts at giving meaning to our relationships, our work, our recreation and our difficulties. Our students' lives are bombarded with meanings from parents, media, friends, school, and the internet as well as from their own imaginations. This does not necessarily mean that students will have an integrated overarching meaning system; rather it is likely to be fragmentary and changing especially at that age.

Neither it may at that stage entail the affirmation or adoption of an already existing overarching meaning of life, a metanarrative, such as that provided by religion or a school of philosophy. Many students do not feel ready to adopt an overarching metanarrative but none the less are still engaged in putting together fragmentary meanings. Roy Baumeister in his book Meanings of Life identified four common human needs for meaning, a purpose in life, a sense of what we value, and sense of usefulness and a sense of self-worth. These he argued are essential to a fulfilled and balanced life and teenagers are constructing meanings to meet these needs continually. If a sense of meaning is so central to an individual's well being it is important for us as educators to ask where, within their school experience, students are given an opportunity to examine the meanings already attached to their lives by their society and to explore and develop their own sense of meaning. There is no doubt that values are offered in the school context often centred on honesty, respect, learning and care for others.

However these values still need a meaning structure to lend support to them otherwise they can appear arbitrary and fail to be integrated into the students own view of life. There is also no doubt that meaning is sometimes addressed in English Literature, History and Science but overall these references tend to be fleeting and occasional. Generally speaking schools have abandoned the task of exploring meaning as too hard and focused their attention on occupational subjects, the arts and literature. The two main contenders for teaching in our independent schools may be

Philosophy and Religious Education but issues of meaning are often occasional to the study of epistemology, ethics and ontology for the former and phenomenology of religion for the latter. During the first half of the twentieth century while Sartre was discussing the meaning making needs of humanity and Heidegger exploring the nature of being Wittgenstein was teaching that meaning was something which grew out of our social behaviour and was primarily a linguistic phenomenon – it seems in our schools at least that Wittgenstein won the day.

This meaning making aspect of religion is not its only one, of course. Religion is also engaged in religious experience, worship, morality and ritual. However few of these are appropriate to the classroom though some may be addressed in chapel. This can lead to a sense of disconnectedness in students: they study aspects of religion in class that they do not have access to. It is the meaning making aspect of religion that is most applicable and accessible to students and the most appropriate for the classroom. This meaning making element also runs through all other aspects of spirituality as it gives shape to and explains why rituals are formed and what interpretation is given to experience. It also adds a great deal of depth to religious education, just the study of the phenomena of religion can be frustrating to students; to describe a religion without an attempt to understand it leaves students with a sense of confusion and often alienation toward religion. They may not agree with the answers a religion gives to certain problems but they need to understand the questions and basic human needs which are addressed by that answer.

Students do not come to this search for meaning without significant presuppositions. Haing grown up in a post-modern context they tend to be attracted to what French thinker, Jean-François Lyotard, called micronarratives rather than one over arching theory which attempts to explain everything. It is my experience that they will work with the teacher who enables this search and integration of micronarratives and against the teacher who seeks to impose their own or the teacher who has none. Added to this it must be remembered that students are schooled within the enlightenment ethos where reason is seen as paramount and where there is a bias towards for physicalism (everything that exists can be explained in terms of the material world). What tends to happen is that Religious Education reenforces this Enlightenment world view as it is the critical unexamined philosophy from which religion is studied.

As the rational enlightenment philosophy starts with a view of religion as irrational, historically questionable and scientifically improvable, the whole study of religion will often be seen by the student as supporting this hypothesis. Australian social researcher Hugh McKay has labeled this generation the choices generation because in an era of pluralism and consumerism their lives are bounded by the making of choices from amongst the products, lifestyles and philosophies on offer. Furthermore they have become sophisticated consumers and choosers. They are also experts at mixing and matching and as much as their elders may want them to adopt a particular set of values or beliefs by nature they tend to pick and choose. It is not that they are not interested in issues of meaning but that they want to determine the basis on which they acquire it. As educators it is wise for us to work with our students in this task.

Studies in Meanings (SIM) Approach to Religious Education

The Studies in Meaning approach to Religious Education is based on students asking a number of significant questions and looking, with the assistance of the teacher, through the history of human thought for some answers. The basic questions addressed are of concern to most people. They can include: What happens when I die? What is the good life? How did everything begin? What is the nature of love? What is beauty? Where does human worth lie? What is mean by the idea of God? Is there any meaning to suffering? As can be seen the questions do not necessarily always appear to be overtly religious but that is because both faiths and philosophies provide the answers to many life-centered questions and not just religious questions.

This approach allows students to explore the significant issues of life and develop their own world view firmly steeped in the wisdom of the ages. For example when studying the question of what happens when we die Buddhist, Christian, Hindu, Materialist, near death experiences all need to be explored for students to get a rounded view. Because the area of study begins with a question it usually develops an open inquiring approach within the classroom. Students are encouraged to "try-on" ideas and see how they fit with their goals and with their experience so far. This approach also lends itself to a variety of teaching techniques.

These basic questions of life can be explored in film, poetry, songs as well a religions and philosophies and the way different peoples and societies have approached these questions can provide a breadth to the studies as well as the depth of the question of meaning. In a manner more reminiscent of Jesus' teaching style than St. Paul's this pedagogy is designed to confront the student with the meaning of their own lives. It seeks to deconstruct the world views that they may currently hold in a similar way in which Jesus shed light on the religious and political assumptions of his day, but not in order to disorientate his hearers but to help them confront what is important in their lives. It goes far beyond moralizing or preaching at people and helps them to sift through their inherited meaning system and make realistic choices based on considered thought and study.

The advantages of the Studies in Meaning approach:

- It changes the role of teaching from either apologist for Christianity (Kerygmatic approach) or knowledge provider and interpreter to guide.
- It is an excellent foundation for further philosophy and Religion and Society studies.
- It promotes conceptual thinking. Much of students learning is on the descriptive level or the learning of facts or techniques. Studies in meaning ask the student to

consider symbolism and meaning.

- It allows the student to explore ideas. A sense of freedom is essential in learning.
- It is the search for meaning that is itself transformative. The search for meaning is a sacred task in itself and this search may be a student's first taste of the sacred. It is not just the answers to these questions of meaning which are sacred.
- The medium is the message. Studies in meaning models a spirituality which is open to the spirit and inquisitive and is respectful of peoples' ideas and choices. Faith is a way of being in the world. It includes a radical openness to the truth.
- It engages students in the task of theology rather than in learning about other people doing theology.
- The studies in meaning approach places the student on a quest for meaning – it gives motivation and purpose to the religious Education task which is often lacking.
- It promotes continual learning. Studies in meaning promote a micro-narrative approach which considers that truth emerges out of a large number of smaller meanings. The model is the tangential circle. The more ideas that go into making up a students meaning system the closer it approximates to reality. The student is therefore encouraged to continue learning. This is in contrast to a metanarrative approach whereby once the "truth" has been ascertained no further learning is required, only a filling out of the narrative.

Studies in Meaning and Philosophy

The question arises as to what extent studies in meaning falls within the realm of philosophy. There is no doubt that meaning from time to time becomes the study of philosophy but as Baumeister has pointed out the study of the meaning of life has been out of fashion in philosophy for a long time. It is perhaps rightly an interdisciplinary concern, for philosophy has also many other interests which may only be of tangential interest to studies of meaning such as ontology and epistemology. Philosophy perhaps most naturally studies the work of philosophers which is but a part of the studies of meaning. Nor is Studies in Meaning approach is not the same as Philosophy of religion. The traditional subject matter of philosophy of religion includes arguments of the existence of God and theodicy and these usually only provide limited assistance in students finding meaning.

Studies in Meaning and Jesus' Teaching Method

Although it would be difficult to directly apply Jesus' teaching methodology to the classroom, a few observations could be made. Firstly unlike the Pharisees, to whom Jesus as a teacher was often compared, Jesus neither taught an exegesis of scripture or a systematic philosophy or theology. Instead Jesus seemed concerned to confront the meaning of the lives of those individuals who crossed his path in the light of their social and intellectual environment. What does it mean to be happy, to give taxes to Rome, to love, to be healed? Who is my neighbour, what is the truth, what makes you free, how do I live eternally? All these questions forced his hearers to look at the meanings they and others around them placed on their lives.

And as Jesus' disciples followed him they saw people who met Jesus confronted by these issues. They learnt a great amount from him, not through a systematic study of religion but through an encounter with the God and the meaning of each individual's existence. The religious Education teacher could do no better for their students than to imitate the way Jesus helped each person he met grapple with the what it means to be God's creation set into this world of meanings.

Churches have very varied attitudes towards media technologies and popular mass media. Some try, in vain, to attract young people by using PowerPoint presentations with their sermons or to display responsorial psalm verses. Others use videos for film nights or Alpha courses. Popular media, such as TV or the Internet, rarely get a mention in church services (except for youth group events). Priests and ministers extol the virtues of reading over watching TV and the values of religion over the values of popular culture. Christian media such as Bible magazines and CDs of new music are either welcomed and promoted as an alternative culture for the young, or rejected as individualistic and devoid of sound doctrine. Yet our universities are taking more and more interest in the intersection between mass media, religion and popular culture.

We are in a period of 'media convergence', a time when one form of mass media is superseded by another as the dominant cultural medium. Protestantism developed in a similar period, when the printing press became Europe's most effective mode of creating and disseminating knowledge and information. The late 20th century saw the rapid rise of television as the new dominant medium. Now television's place as our primary source of cultural information is being challenged by various forms of computer-mediated communication, including the World Wide Web, email and file sharing. Just as printing did 500 years ago, audio-visual media like TV and the Internet not only change how we think, but the places and the mess we talk about, and make decisions about, how we live as a society. Mass media, television in particular, have become the main forum for social discourse, and the place where our views on politics, government, gender roles, family life, and even religion, are shared and discussed.

In the period known as the Enlightenment scientific rationalism dominated all our social institutions. The great product of the Enlightenment was the secularisation of culture. Thinkers in this period saw reason alone as enabling right thought and right action: religion was viewed as a barrier to truth, democracy and pluralism. The result was to divide Church and State, and to relegate religious thought and practice to churches and seminaries and private life, out of the public sphere. Today the rise of audiovisual media as the dominant public media in our culture has led to the demise of secularisation, in two ways –Firstly, audiovisual mass popular media have added ritual dimensions to the communication of information, to the point of *resacralising* popular culture. We see this, for example, in the news reports of responses to the fall of the Twin Towers on September 11 2001, images of public prayer vigils, with candles and prayers pasted on billboards next to photographs of victims.

We also see it in the *Big Brother* spectacle, where contestants leave the real world by crossing a bridge over cheering, almost delirious, fans toward the BB house just as legendary heroes made their way to Mt Olympus. Audiovisual media reform and recreate religious symbols and narratives in their endeavour to portray the world's story. Secondly, audiovisual media have allowed religious institutions to reenter the sphere of public discourse. On the one hand, politicians affirm the secularization ideology by telling outspoken bishops and priests to 'stick to spiritual concerns, and leave the politics to us'. Yet when we see our Prime Minister appear at a Hillsong gathering we realise how politicians continue to rely on support from religious groups. So the role of religious institutions in public life today seems to depend on how they involve themselves in the discourses played out in mass media.

Evangelical Protestant churches appear to thrive there – they have fewer ethical concerns about borrowing from popular culture (for example, by marketing Christian mobile phone covers or iPod shuffle cases in the shape of a cross) and their mythologies and doctrines are aligned with the codes and narratives arranged in mass media. For evangelicals, the Gospel is seen as a dynamic and creative force. The dualistic theology of evangelicalism marries nicely with the symbolism and narratives of television. Evangelicals hold a utilitarian view of media, and emphasise the individual as a social unit, in the same way that TV does, focussing on an experiential and emotional communication of faith. For the generation whose aesthetic standards are shaped by a culture of sound and vision, the mainline churches seem 'boring' and 'irrelevant', constrained by the formulations and regulations of a print-based culture. This generation sees the world they live in as rejected by these churches as consumerist and devoid of meaning.

Here is a modern paradox. Those societies that have established or majority national churches (such as in Western Europe) face declining church attendances and the voice of the churches is increasingly unheard in public life. On the other hand, those nations founded on the basis of a division between church and state, such as the United States, and (to a lesser extent) Australia find that many forms of religion flourish in a pluralist, autonomous social sphere so why the churches should be concerned with mass media? We can take our cue from the Gospels. In them we see a Jesus who uses parables to explain God's purpose for the world. These stories are free from religious jargon, and use popular themes and the symbols of an agrarian society to give a picture of the Kingdom of God. And in telling these stories Jesus takes theological debate out of the Temple and into the streets and lanes, defying the authority of the religious elite.

Two thousand years later, people use mass media to construct a religious identity, unconfined by religious institutions and religious doctrine. The authority of the churches is challenged by the popularity of programs like *Supernatural, Touched by an Angel* and *Sunday Night Safran*. These explore religious issues in a language and format that is by far more accessible and attractive. People alienated by the old forms of religious expression on a Sunday morning are finding safe places to explore new symbols, stories and ways of living in community in the virtual world. The future of the Church depends on its willingness to enter this world, to explore the conversations played out there, and to accept that is no longer the single authority on religious life.

Religion and the Post-Welfare State

Over the past quarter century, deep changes in religious life and public policy have converged in ways that have transformed both. But aside from some attention to the increasing significance of spirituality and the growing political activism of religious conservatives, the news media have generally failed to grasp the scale and scope of what may be the most important and fundamental alteration in the character of American public life since the disestablishment of religion in the first quarter of the nineteenth century.

What are these changes? In religion, they involve not only intensified political engagement (including the broadening of what had been a regional movement into a national one), but also shifts in the arenas and forms of worship. Denominational structures are in eclipse. Congregations are now only one of many settings in which believers practice their beliefs. Clergy are as likely to be called to ministries in care-giving, service provision, and agency management as in traditional pastorates. On the public policy side, the barriers separating church and state have been swept aside as education, health, and human services tasks, once regarded as federal government responsibilities, have been shifted to states and localities and into the hands of private-sector—often faith-based—actors.

Why have these changes gone largely unnoticed? Since organized religion and faith communities have a long history of commitment to the needs of the dependent and disabled, the increasing importance of faith-based service provision has not been regarded as anything new or different. But there are other reasons, the most important of which have to do with the architecture of public perception. Because for more than half a century we have looked to Washington as the center and source of power, influence, and change, we are simply not equipped to monitor or assess large-scale shifts when they begin to unfold elsewhere. Information flows from the center outward, not from the periphery to the center.

Equally important is the fact that the reporters who cover politics and policy are not sensitive to or particularly interested in religion, while the reporters who cover the denominational and congregational activities conventionally supposed to comprise the sum and substance of religious life are unprepared to engage the complexities of emergent social welfare policy.

These gaps in media capacity are significant at a time when the overhaul of the social service infrastructure relies increasingly not only on traditional kinds of faith-based organizations to serve the needs of the dependent and disabled, but also on publicly funded secular agencies, many of them run by clergy, members of religious orders, and faith communities.

Despite the formidable barriers supposed to have existed between church and state, governments—particularly on the state and municipal level—have been contracting with religious bodies for more than a century. Orphaned children, nominally public charges, long have been placed in institutions operated by denominations and religious orders and, more recently, in faith-based fostercare agencies. In the 1960s, government funding of faith-based health and human services activities grew enormously. Not only did established groups like the Salvation Army and Catholic Charities become major recipients of funds under federal social programs, the Great Society's War on Poverty, with its agenda of community empowerment, began funneling economic development, housing, education, and other funds to African-American congregations and to secular corporations—particularly Community Development Corporations (CDCs)—that they controlled.

The deinstitutionalization of the mentally disabled, which began in the late 1960s, enormously increased the role of faith-based service provision. When the federal courts mandated care for the retarded and the mentally ill in "least restrictive" community settings, the states subject to these consent decrees turned to nonprofit service providers. Traditional secular and religious social agencies were reluctant to take on this task, but—thanks to the Second Vatican Council's encouragement of social ministries by members of religious orders—there was a ready supply of deeply religious men and women ready to take on some of the most arduous care-giving challenges.

It didn't take long for the names of Father Bruce Ritter and Covenant House to become staples of the broadcast and print media—whether portrayed heroically, as they were when in ascent, or villainously, when the Covenant House sexual scandal broke. But hardly any reporter grasped either the extent to which this ministry to troubled youth was part of an international human-services empire, largely supported by public monies, or the extent to which this kind of publicly funded faith-based service provision was becoming common throughout the United States. At its height, Covenant House was running an annual budget of $100 million. Only Charles Sennott, the *New York Post* reporter who broke the scandal, understood the larger implications and, as his 1992 book, *Broken Covenant: The Secret Life of Father Bruce Ritter,* makes clear, it was an uphill battle even to get his editors to publish the bare facts of the story, much less the questions it raised about faith-based service provision.

Covenant House was, in fact, only a detail in a far bigger picture of privatized faith-based service provision. But this story–particularly the national growth of a multibillion-dollar group home industry—went unreported. Some reporters, taking note of the growing ranks of homeless people, investigated the impact of court-ordered deinstitutionalization of the mentally impaired, usually focusing on the failure of state governments to establish community-based treatment and care. But hardly any noticed the extent to which the states were fulfilling these responsibilities, and the extent to which they were doing so through agencies run either by religious groups or by clergy and members of religious orders called to secular managerial or care-giving ministries.

This is no small line item. Although reliable figures are elusive, it appears that the group home industry has represented the largest outlay of public funds for any nondefense-related purpose since the construction of the interstate highway system. In Connecticut, for example, nearly 90 per cent of the state's entire economic development budget for the period 1985-1992—a quarter of a billion dollars—was used for acquiring and renovating group home properties, the lion's share going to a single politically connected consortium of for-profit and nonprofit firms, many of them faith-based. But when reporters for the *Hartford Courant,* tipped off by the release of a secret report compiled by the state's office of legislative services, brought these facts to the attention of the public, the story was not picked up by other papers, either in Connecticut or in nearby New York. (The story went unreported elsewhere even when the Courant revealed that the chairman of Connecticut's Democratic State Committee, who ran a chain of group homes as a profitable sideline to his legal practice, had massively defrauded the state.)

To be sure, the group home story was not entirely ignored. During the late 1980s and early 1990s, Michael Winerip wrote a moving, if highly partisan, series of columns on the subject for the *New York Times* that became the basis for his 1994 book, *9 Highland Road: Sane Living for the Mentally Ill.* More recently, some attention has been devoted to faith-based social-service empires like that controlled by former Congressman (Rev.) Floyd Flake, as well as to the litigation arising from use of public education and human services funds by the Ultra-Orthodox Jewish community at Kiryas Joel in upstate New York. In addition, the local news sections of daily papers throughout the country have reported on litigation between religious groups and zoning authorities. But reporters have generally failed to pursue the ways in which these stories fit into a larger pattern of fundamental institutional transformation.

The failure to see the larger significance of the increasingly frequent zoning battles involving churches—even when they led to landmark court decisions such as last summer's overturning of the Religious Freedom Restoration Act by the United States Supreme Court—is a particularly telling example of the inability of the press to grasp the significance of convergent changes in religion and public policy. Historically, places of worship have been allowed to locate almost anywhere, free from the restrictions (such as off-street parking requirements) imposed on other property owners, because traditional Sabbath-day devotional activities posed minimal burdens on the neighborhoods in which they were located and because planners assumed that most congregations drew their members from the neighborhoods in which they were located.

Today, places of worship regardless of creed have become platforms for an astonishing range of educational and social services. Church lounges serve as meeting places for self-help groups. Parish houses have been converted into child daycare centers and day schools. As social services have become more central to the ministries and finances of congregations—many of them urban bodies with declining memberships—municipal planners have noted an alarming growth in acquisitions by churches of adjoining properties not only to house service provision activities but also for church-sponsored economic development activities (job training and commercial enterprises), affordable housing, and other publicly funded initiatives.

Careful search of news databases turns up hundreds of reports of public hearings and court fights relating to churches and other faith-based entities. But the news media have yet to see these as symptomatic of more profound and far-reaching changes in religion and public policy. The failure of the media to attend to the technicalities of community-based human services provision, subtle changes in the nature of social ministries, and the minutiae of landuse litigation is understandable given the information infrastructure in the late twentieth century and the scant preparation reporters receive for dealing with religion. Still, it is surprising that when welfare reform became the battle cry of Republican congressional revolutionaries in the mid-1990s, so little attention was given to the body of ideas on which they were basing their programs.

Journalist/historian Marvin Olasky's *Tragedy of American Compassion* (1992) and *Renewing American Compassion* (1995) became the Old and New Testaments of right-wing welfare reform after receiving glowing accolades from Newt Gingrich, William Bennett, Ariana Huffington, and other leading conservative glitterati. In these volumes, Olasky sets forth a reinterpretation of the history of American social welfare policies that is unabashedly rooted in a religious vision of social change, focusing on the need to transform values and behavior rather than social conditions to break the cycle of welfare dependency.

Had journalists discerned this religious vision and understood the degree to which it led directly to the landmark Personal Responsibility and Work Reconciliation Act of 1996––which eliminated legal obstacles to the awarding of federal human services contracts to faith-based providers and mandated the availability of religious alternatives in service provision ("charitable choice")—the public would be in a far better position to grasp the astonishing but largely misunderstood institutional revolution that has taken place over the past decade.

Faith communities themselves would benefit from reporting that is informed by real knowledge of both public policy and religion. Although elements of the religious world have been actively involved on both sides of welfare reform, its implications remain largely unknown to those pursuing traditional pulpit ministries, congregational and denominational governing bodies, and people in the pews. Even as they participate in making incremental decisions about the use of church properties, they remain generally unaware and uninformed of how the choices they make are subtly but unmistakably altering the nature of religious practice and the role of religion in public life.

Finally, legislators, jurists, and policy makers at every level of government urgently need the kind of grounded and searching investigation of this unfolding story that only first-rate journalism can provide. The majority of public decision makers, even on the conservative side, have no real basis for judging the arguments of the special interest groups and lobbyists who clamor for their attention. While they may believe that they are backing policies beneficial to organized religion, because they have no clear sense of how these are actually likely to affect a religious universe which, in its increasing diversity and complexity, little resembles anything in their experience, their efforts may, in the end, have quite the opposite effect.

Many clergy and laity are in fact deeply concerned about the crumbling barriers between church and state. Looking at the disastrous consequences to secular non-profits of a half-century of large-scale government funding which has transformed a once voluntary sector into a highly regulated, commercialized, quasi-governmental domain, they worry about the ways in which such dependency may affect the freedom that American religion has traditionally enjoyed. They worry less about a "culture of disbelief" whose journalistic products marginalize religion than about a culture of ignorance that fails to provide them with vitally important information about how changes in the secular world impact on religion and vice-versa.

7

Discovering a Theory and Methodology for Studying Media and Religion

The cultural studies analysis of the media has now become a dominant paradigm of communication research, and the "Media, Religion, and Culture" focus is a central paradigm in research on religious media. For example, the biannual international conference on "Media, Religion, and Culture" usually draws from 300 to 600 people from around the world, virtually all carrying on research on media and religion from a cultural studies perspective. The cultural studies approach recognizes the importance of so-called "administrative research" used by broadcasters to measure the reach and effectiveness of programming, but argues that quantitative effects research really does not answer the central questions of religious media.

Religion is a personal response, seeking meaning in life and in one's universe. Religious expression is generally found within institutional religion, but the formal creed, rituals, devotions, and moral codes do not exhaust the personal experience of religion. The central question of the cultural studies approach is concerned with how individuals in groups use media to construct religious meaning in life and how this religious meaning relates to many other aspects of human life. This approach typically draws its theories and methodologies, not from psychology, functionalist sociology, or quantitative analysis, but from cultural anthropology, philosophy, literary studies, drama, and history. The methods of research are no less rigorous, but these are much closer to a tradition of humanities than to behavioral sciences.

Until the 1970s virtually all research on media and religion was attempting to answer the questions of religious broadcasters as to what effects they were having. Most religious programs claimed to be having large audiences-impressed with what one can do with the media compared to the Sunday sermon and they generally claimed to be "converting" many people. Others were skeptical, and the research was brought in to settle this kind of dispute. Gradually, however, researchers moved away from these "effects" questions to how people are creating meaning from media... and many other sources. How and why did this move to a new set of questions in research on religious media come about? The present essay will explore this question.

Effects Studies-background

From the time the 1920s-era Payne Studies concluded that the "impact" of film depended very much on family background, the subjective cultural background, and other factors influencing the subjective interpretation of the meaning of the film, media researchers felt that they had to use quantitative, objective methods to show the positive or negative effects of media in order to get action by governments or other public institutions. One of the typical examples was the attempt to devise an "objective" measuring scale of violent content which rated violence from the low point on the scale of a heated discussion to the high point of a bloody murder.

The researchers then attempted to show a direct correlation between the level of violent content and aggressive behavior of audiences. Coders were instructed to mark exactly what they heard or saw whether it was a Bugs Bunny cartoon for children or a portrayal of the life of Christ. Not surprisingly, humorous children's cartoons, where rabbits, pigs, and ducks were continually getting smashed about came out as horribly violent. If the quantitative interpretation of violence that some social scientists proposed were applied to the media, there obviously would be no further presentation of great works of art such as Shakespeare and even the presentation of the Bible would be questionable. What soon became evident is that the meaning construction placed on a scene or particular action can vary a great deal. The portrayal of the crucifixion of Jesus can be seen as sickeningly offensive or as a beautiful sign of enormous love depending on the meaning that the beholder places on this.

There might be wide agreement that the portrayal of explicit sexual relations is repugnant and morally offensive for many different reasons based on many different meanings. But in every case it is important to know the meaning not just for different audiences but for the writer, the producer, the actors, and a host of others who are involved in some way with producing something that does have meaning. It also became apparent that although the official practices of a religious tradition might define a devotion or action as religious, adherents of the religious tradition might have their own unique interpretations of the official practices and might have experiences which are generally consonant with the theological norms of the tradition but are completely unique for a given person.

Trying to Find the "Definitive" Proof of Effects of Religious Broadcasts

With the advent of television in the 1950s, religious television stars in the U.S., such as the evangelist Billy Graham and Bishop Fulton Sheen, began to gain top audience ratings. The mainline Protestant churches felt that they were losing out and wondered if they could not find a Bishop Sheen in the Anglican or Methodist Church. There began to be considerable discussion of whether religious television personalities were really having a significant lasting impact, whether this was drawing people away from worship in the local churches, whether it appealed to young people, and other similar questions. In 1951 the National Council of Churches in the United States funded a major study of the "effectiveness of television" as a tool of evangelization. The director of the study was one of the great personalities of U.S. religious broadcasting, Everett Parker, and the team included Dallas Smythe, who later became one of the leaders in the critical cultural studies school.

Guided by August Hollingshead, one of the top sociologists in the U.S., the study employed the best current sociological tools and behaviorist social psychological models. It remains one of the classics of research on religious media, but, unfortunately, the authors themselves suggest that their methodology raised more questions than provided answers. The study confirmed what many other surveys had indicated and others would indicate: that the main users of religious broadcasting tended to be lower status, with less education, more likely to be women and more likely to be elderly. The major conclusion was couched in terms of the behaviorist psychology model, namely, that following religious broadcasts "reduced anxiety".

The researchers admitted that they discovered that their methodology (behavioral psychology and effects models) was too limited to answer the real questions of the study, even in the simplest terms. The study did not reveal whether users of these programs become more religious, more moral, closer to their local churches, or more inspired to be involved in work with needy people. The results could say little about the relation of the broadcasts to general belief systems.

These are questions which deal with meaning. One must recognize that the researchers were using the available tools at hand in 1950. This was before the development of the sociology and anthropology of religion, before the major empirical work of Stark and Glock in the U.S., before the great theoretical advances of sociologists of religion such as Peter Berger and Thomas Luckmann or of David Martin and Bryan Wilson in Britain and a host of other major theorists in Europe. It even predated the development of "parish sociology". The 1960s, however, brought a major shift in the focus of the human sciences and in the emerging field of mass communication research in particular.

The shift from a media effects paradigm to recognition of the importance of the cultural context of media use. In the late 1940s Joseph Klapper, for many years head of the research department at CBS and close associate of Paul Lazarsfeld, did a definitive analysis (his doctoral thesis) of just what kind of effects one could expect from broadcasting. The surprising result of this analysis of hundreds of studies of media effects was that not a single study proved that the media had the powerful direct effects that broadcasters expected. The landmark book revealed that the influence of media is always limited by the subjective social context, knowledge, attitudes, motivation, and interpretation of the receiver. This suggested that broadcasters had to take into consideration the motivations, interests, enjoyments, cultural values, and the subculture of the particular audience that they sought.

Klapper and others suggested that a better approach to audience analysis was not effects research but what came to be known as uses and gratification studies. The central question was not what media did to people but what people did with the media. Peter Horsfield, in his comprehensive survey of the research on audiences of religious media in the early 1980s, found many doctoral theses and other research on religious broadcasting in the 1960s and 1970s using the uses and gratifications approach to document the now well-known patterns of religious media use. Another major influence was Marshall McLuhan's Understanding Media which argued that the most significant impact of media was not on individual psychology but on whole cultures and societies. McLuhan came to media studies from literary analysis which stressed the activity of the person in reading and interpreting a text.

Different media touched different senses-the ear, the eyes, the whole consciousness-and the person responded by constructing the meaning of the text according to the major sense influence, thereby producing an "oral culture" or a "visual culture." The perspective of McLuhan and his student, Walter Ong, S.J., also helped to shift interest of religious communicators from broadcast effects to the interaction of medium and religious cultural movements. Berger and Luckmann, in their work on The Social Construction of Reality (1967) shifted the focus away from the systemic functionalism of Parsons which made the person the result of systemic forces at the intersection of the social system, the personality system, and the economic system.

The new focus made the starting point culture, defined now more cognitively as a system of meanings produced by persons in interaction. All this was part of the great personalist movement in the late 1960s, inspired by thinkers such as Marcuse who emphasized the importance of responding to one's own identity and creativity, thereby rejecting conformity to powerful social controls. The counter-cultural movement of the late 1960s and early 1970s rejected the subjection of one's life to the mobilization of industrialization and mass consumption. All this called into question the use of media for religious persuasion and manipulation. There was awakened interest in the use of media as a context for discovering personal religious values, religious cultural identity, and an active faith expression.

The Movements of "Education for Critical Use of the Media"

In the 1950s the dominant idea of the Church's use of the media was still a powerful, dramatic speaker using a persuasive rhetoric to convert audiences to a deeper religious practice. The logic of religious broadcasts was not much different from political campaigns, advertising, or radio talks. In the 1960s, however, there was a growing critique, especially in the churches, of the harmful effects on faith and morals of the manipulation of sex, violence, advertising, and other forms of increasingly commercial "hard sell" media. This set in motion a series of efforts to introduce "media education" which assumed that the audience was not simply a passive receiver of message effects. Audiences can be critical and have their own ideas about the media.

Media education encouraged people to carefully select media use according to their personal values and to use these media to deepen one's value commitments. Media education has varied in its focus from a defensive view of media as highly manipulative to an appreciation of our benignly banal popular culture, but most approaches seek to strengthen the use of media from the perspective of one's own active interpretation and one's own cultural identity. A more important contribution, in many ways, was the movement of education for freedom which emerged in the countries of the South, especially in Latin America. The churches in Latin America, India, Asia, and Africa began a process of education of the rural and urban poor with a general educational philosophy of helping the poor and marginal form grassroots, participatory organizations to solve their own problems.

These efforts incorporated the educational methods of Paulo Freire, Badal Sircar's concepts of popular theater in India (1978) and many other popular movements. In many ways this changed the perspective on religious broadcasting and research on religious broadcasting, in large part because this emphasis was adopted by international associations of religious broadcasting such as UNDA (now SIGNIS) and The World Association for Christian Communication (WACC). First, these educational methods stressed not just new production techniques but the affirmation and promotion of the popular cultures. The media, especially small media such as group communication, popular theater, and people's radio, were the sites where the poor and marginal could develop their cultural identity.

Second, these methods saw as the reasons for poverty and oppression the passive dependence on the hegemonic culture which imposes a self-concept of "natural inferiority" and need to depend on the governing elites. Third, in the face of globalization of cultures, it is necessary for the poor and marginal to have their own media and to actively produce their own cultures. Thus, the concept of culture became central in religious broadcasting and in research on religious broadcasting. Another very important emphasis coming from education for liberation was to develop the sense of dignity, creativity and freedom of the person through dialogue in community.

These movements were far more aware of the dehumanization that comes from the concentration of power in societies and the use of media to impose that power. The ideal form of communication was a communitarian, participatory, dialogical communication, and this ideal became a central ethical and theological principle in the media, religion, and culture perspective. This value position led many doing research on religious broadcasting toward theories and research methods of "cultural studies," with its different variants in the United States and in Latin America.

The Cultural Studies Approach

Media studies began in the 1930s and 1940s in the U.S. There was virtually no communication research in Europe, at the time enveloped in total war. After the World War II, Europe began its own approaches to social studies and media. Public service broadcasting systems in Europe were much more concerned with national cultural integration and with the cultural quality of broadcasting. These systems did not need to establish the effectiveness of advertising as did the U.S. commercial broadcasters. Media researchers in Europe were concerned about the profound cultural transformations as the "welfare state" increased the incomes of the working classes and brought the working classes into a kind of broad middle status. A decisive influence was the cultural studies approach that originated in France and which was picked up by the Center for Contemporary Cultural Studies at the University of Birmingham in Britain.

The center began a program of research on the factors influencing the profound cultural changes in Britain, especially among the working classes. Not surprisingly, in contrast to the behaviorist, functionalist dependence on psychological conceptions of the individual which led to an emphasis on the blind behavioral effects of the media, the cultural studies approach borrows from the humanistic sciences of textual analysis, literary studies, semiotics, history, cultural anthropology, and cognitive structuralism. The focus was not on behavioral response but on the creation of meaning, or, more specifically, "signifying practices" which bring about "shared social meanings" in various "languages," especially mass media languages. Contrary to views of institutions such as the BBC, the popular classes were not considered "cultureless" and passive consumers of media to be reshaped in the middle-class image, but active in the creation of a rich and strong culture.

Popular novels, films, and television were sources of ideas and symbols that people used to create their own personal and cultural identities. The leaders in cultural studies were scholars formed in literary and dramatic criticism, and they saw the media as a text that both revealed and reflected the nature of the culture but that was also a source of symbols for the construction of the great variety of subcultures. What was striking about the youth subcultures in particular was the use of popular music as a symbol of resistance to the dominant, hegemonic cultures. Rather than turn their backs on their poverty and working-class status, youth took from the media images that glorified their own popular class values.

Underlying the cultural studies approach was a strong commitment to the dignity, freedom, and creativity of all persons. The individual was seen, not as an object of culture and social systems, but as the author of culture. Although cultural studies have found Marxist analysis helpful for a critical understanding of the concentration of political-economic power in the formation of cultures, cultural studies rejected the economic determinism of classical Marxism. Instead they saw the person as a protagonist in the struggle with power to define the meaning of all economic products not as hegemonic ideology but as the affirmation of the cultural identity of the subaltern classes. Stuart Hall introduced the distinction of the concept of the encoding of the preferred, hegemonic meaning of media to support hegemonic power and the decoding of the message in terms of the identity of the media user.

The studies of media fan groups have revealed how media users refashion the meaning of symbols of the media around their own person and cultural identities. Martin-Barbero's studies of the reception of telenovelas in Latin America suggested that the reading of media is a complex combination of seduction, rejection, resistance, and transformation of meaning. The American version of the cultural studies approach emphasized that media reception is a social, communitarian activity. The new religious, racial, ethnic, and gender movements in the U.S. and elsewhere, on the basis of their internal communication networks, collectively challenged the negative images in the media. Carey, borrowing from cognitive anthropologist, Clifford Geertz, introduced the ritual, communion notion of media, and Horace Newcomb and Robert Alley used the anthropologist Victor Turner's theory of ritual as the audience experience of the state between the worlds as it is and the world as the community would like it to become.

A turning point was the development of media reception theory in the late 1970s and 1980s, analyzing how audiences take media narratives, role models, and symbols as materials for constructing their own life histories. From this came a series of new methodologies of audience analysis roughly described as audience ethnography and including life histories, personal accounts through letters, observation of groups viewing television, observation of households using media, or participation in fan groups discussing programs. What has characterized reception study is the analysis of the use of media as one source of constructing meaning in a "natural life context" and a whole meaning construction process: a whole lifetime, an ongoing-friend group, a whole household, a whole community or church congregation. The purpose is to understand the role of media in a complex pattern of meaning relationships.

The Beginnings of the Media, Religion, and Culture Approach

By the early 1980s, the study of media and religion had at its disposal a new set of tools that the authors of the 1950s' study of the effects of religious television said were needed. Also emerging were new theologies of communication which defined the media as a process of bringing publics together to form dialogical communities. Evangelization was beginning to be seen, not as imposing a foreign religious culture, but as helping peoples discover and activate their best religious values. The reaching up to God is not something brought from outside, but is embedded in the nature of human existence and in human cultures. There was cross-fertilization of narrative theology, the life-history approach to moral development, concepts of faith as evolving through stages, the analysis of media reception as an interaction between media myth and narrative, and personal life histories.

Another very important influence was the new sociology of religion emerging in the 1970s and 1980s, which showed that religiosity could not be defined simply by the imposition of institutional religious affiliation. It was evident that new generations of seekers were building their own belief system from symbols from a variety of religious traditions. By the 1970s and early 1980s the prominence of the televangelists began to stimulate many studies of religious broadcasting, especially regarding the socio-cultural and political impact of new religious movements and the Pentecostals especially important were Peter Horsfield's Religious Television (1984), providing a summary analysis of research on religious broadcasting up to that point, and the Gallup survey of audiences of radio and television.

All of these studies confirmed that audiences were largely the devout church members, the elderly, less well educated, more rural, and tending to be heavier television users. Contrary to the claims of many religious broadcasters, television broadcasts made few converts among the unchurched, but television was most important in providing public symbols of identification for the new religious movements in the 1970s and 1980s. The new studies of the sociology of religion in the 1970s and 1980s were confirming that a new religious configuration was coming into existence-more fundamentalist, intensely committed, more personalistic and spontaneous, more militant against liberal religious hegemony. No sociological study suggested that the religious broadcasters were an important cause of this, but broadcasting was part of the creation of a new culture.

In the mid-1980s Stewart Hoover, drawing on the many currents of thought about religious media described above, designed a new approach to the study of religion and media which focused on the role of media in the creation of personal religious meaning and religious cultures. Also important were discussions with the Jesuit-sponsored Centre for the Study of Communication and Culture in London (the original publisher of Communication Research Trends), which was encouraging a cultural studies approach and which published his book in its Communication and Human Values series. The central question in the study was, "What kind of religious culture are we creating in this era of great social and institutional change?" Television was considered a cultural medium, a signifying practice. The study adapted the following aspects of the cultural studies approach:

- The focus was on the culture of a particular religious movement and the life context of people in this movement: their jobs, their families, the problems they faced, and their politics.
- The study focused on people involved with a televangelist movement, namely that of Pat Robertson, but looked at all the sources of religious meaning in their lives-their church, their political involvements, their general reading, their social affiliations, their many religious activities-and how they used these sources of meaning.
- The data were whole life histories and how these life experiences led up to the present searches for meaning in life, especially the precipitating factor that led to a kind of

conversion to a deeper, more intense search for meaning.

- A particular focus was on the sources of meaning for their involvement in politics and other aspects of public life.

The study revealed that following a particular televangelist was part of belonging to a particular religious subculture, in this case, a somewhat more fundamentalist and conservative religious, political, and social culture. There were many sources of information that helped those associated with the movement to define the meaning of their life situation: interpersonal contacts, discussion groups, books and newspapers, and-since television was so important a part of these somewhat elderly and more sedentary people-various television programs. All those interviewed felt that this movement had provided crucial help in defining how to make sense out of a central meaning problem in their lives: a death of a family member, a serious illness, loss of a job, family crisis, or any of the many problems that could affect a person in modernity.

Even though many did not regularly watch his TV programs, Pat Robertson was so much a public symbol of all that they believed in that they were ready to contribute relatively large amounts of money to make his voice heard. The networks of those associated with this movement included virtually all religious denominations-Protestants of all backgrounds and all social classes, Catholics, and even some Jewish people-but the "meaning problems" were sufficiently similar that all identified with what this media figure promoted and symbolized. In the highly differentiated modern societies divided into single-value concerns and single-issue politics, people of different subcultures tend to identify with different public media figures. Moreover, those who identified with a particular media figure tend to be in contact with each other and to live in a particular value world.

Formulating a Media, Religion and Culture Research Agenda

In the 1980s and 1990s religion, which many had considered a phenomenon disappearing in the face of modernity, suddenly was recognized as becoming a much more central actor in the political, economic, and socio-cultural affairs of the world. The worldwide Pentecostal, evangelical movement was one dimension of this; Pope John Paul II was another dimension; and still other dimensions were the Islamic, Buddhist, and Hindu sociopolitical-cultural revitalizations, and the evident religiosity of the people of the new nations. The literally hundreds of new religious movements and "quasi-religions" came to be considered part of the "post-modern" culture. Many scholars began to speak of the "reenchantment" of the world.

The study of media, religion, and culture also began to move out of the institutional religious base into a more secular scholarly context as it became evident that religion is a central cultural institution that is dealing with the signifying practices that link together areas of meaning. The institutional churches have ceded ground to popular culture signifying practices as the places of unifying the meaning of life. Indeed, religion is now studied more in departments and centers of the study of popular culture, although many of the centers that are part of the media, religion, and culture network still have close links with institutional religion.

This delinking of the study of religion from explicit connection with institutional religion makes it easier for the study of popular identity signifying practices to analyze critically the use of popular culture to establish cultural hegemony precisely through the commodification of objects of popular culture. In the view of some, the delinking of the study of religion from more explicit institutional definitions also helps to distance the study from more "essentialistic" conceptions of religion. Thus, the study of media, religion, and culture retains the central humanistic focus of the critical cultural studies tradition and the defense of the freedom, creativity, and sanctity of the person. The central question remains the same: what kind of culture are we creating in the context of mediated signifying practices and how do we evaluate this culture in terms of the meaning of human existence today?

The Formation of the Media, Religion, and Culture Network

By the early 1990s there was gradually forming a network of individual researchers, research centers, and research programs that identified roughly with a cultural studies approach to the study of media and religion. There are now some five or six centers in various parts of the world which generally follow the cultural studies approach to the study of media and religion. Some of the major ones are The Center for Media, Religion, and Culture, University of Colorado; Centre for Communication, Theology, and Ethics, New College University of Edinburgh; Centre for Interdisciplinary Study of Communication, The Gregorian University; the program of media and religion at Annenberg Center at the University of Southern California; and the Centre for the Study of African Culture and Communication in Nigeria. The conceptualization of the contemporary relationship of media and religion of people in this network tends to follow the lines described above.

The consensus that this focus represents an important area of research led to setting up a more formal structure of international conferences, publications, and research groups. During the 1970s and 1980s there had been a series of studies of the televangelists, but most of these were quite descriptive. It was evident that there was no coherent theoretical interpretation of the general significance of media and religion, much less a theory of media, religion, and culture. The book, Rethinking Media, Religion, and Culture edited by Stewart Hoover and Knut Lunby attempted to pull together the various strands of thought and outlined the major concepts, arguments and issues in this area of study.

The international conferences of the media, religion, and culture network have proven much more influential. The first International Conference on Media, Religion, and Culture was held in Uppsala in 1993, with subsequent international conferences in Boulder, Colorado in 1996; Edinburgh in 1999; Jyvaskyla, Finland in 2003; Louisville, Kentucky in 2004; and

Stockholm in 2006. Several collections of papers have appeared: from the Boulder conference and from the Edinburgh conference. The conferences stimulated the foundation of the Journal of Media and Religion in 2002, and a book series with Routledge Publishers, initiated in 2003.

Themes and Theses

The Interaction of Producers and Religious Culture

Much media research tends to take media messages and even the producers behind the messages as abstractions from the culture, as if a message appears from nowhere. The Media, Religion, and Culture tradition has emphasized the importance of examining how the content of religious media or religious themes emerges out of a sociocultural context. For example, when Hoover studied the influence of the televangelist Pat Robertson, he analyzed how Robertson emerged from the resurgence of the evangelical movement along with other fundamentalist movements in the American cultural crisis of the 1960s and 1970s. Robertson and others responded to a new culture of religious seekers and the desire for religious experience. Their popularity, especially in the 1980s, owed much to the capacity of televangelists to understand what people of the 1980s culture sought. With their invitation of letters from the public and the careful analysis of the voluminous correspondence, the televangelists were much more in contact with the cultural pulse of the audience they catered to and knew how to build on the cultural preferences of this audience.

The sensitivity to the cultural "feelings" of audiences and the ability to articulate the religious language of the audience explains why televangelists were able to get audiences to contribute relatively large amounts of money. This awareness of the embeddedness of producers in the culture helped to explain why the media of the mainline churches, especially the Catholic Church, which were message-oriented (especially dogmatic, propositional messages) and insensitive to the culture, virtually collapsed in the 1970s. Most of these productions were mandated by the hierarchy of the Church with relatively little audience support. Catholic productions placed little emphasis on letters from the audience, live presentations to audiences, or other forms of audience interaction that would generate audience support.

An exception is Mother Angelica's Eternal Word Television Network (EWTN), which built its relatively narrow but intensely devoted audience around its appeal to elements of Catholic popular culture such as religious habits, traditional ritual, Catholic iconography, and traditional hymns. In a more recent study, Jolyon Mitchell's analysis of the emphasis in popular West Africa home video films on witchcraft, spirits (good and bad!), and exorcisms went beyond the content to include the intentions of producers. All producers are aware of the intense interest of their audiences in the war between the spiritual powers. Pentecostal groups produce many of the films, which feature the power of Pentecostal evangelists to control this evil spirits-in contrast to the weakness of the mainline Protestant Christian churches. One of the most popular and successful producers of these films in Ghana explained that he himself did not believe much in witchcraft or the battle of the spirits, but he knew that he had to include this emphasis because this element is so central to popular religiosity in West Africa.

Bringing Theology Back

Much research on media and religion has tended to exclude theology as a valid object of study and has followed the positivist tendency toward behaviorist reduction. The Media, Religion, and Culture tradition sees the study of media and religion as an interdisciplinary exchange and insists on the inclusion of theological perspectives in its analysis. The perspectives both of popular theology-the way ordinary people explain their religious experiences and the meaning they place on these experiences-and of formal theology-the explanations in a more systematic fashion-are important. Both are signifying practices and one must be ready to accept the theological reasoning process in order to understand them.

That is, in order to enter into the meaning of a particular religious production, one must know the theology of the producers, the theology implied in the content, and the theology of the audiences interpreting and producing their own meaning.

The theologian Roberto Goizueta, argues that underlying Latino popular Catholicism is a theology of "symbolic realism." Latinos understand God as really present in the rituals, icons, processions, music, and dance of Latino religiosity and believe that these reveal the power and creative dynamism of God. As one participates with all of one's senses and corporeal reactions, one has a deep experience of an incarnate God. Medrano, in his productions for the American Latino community, felt that the programs had to reproduce the people, stories, rituals, icons, music, and dance that constitute the religiosity of the Latino in order to evoke the same experience of symbolic realism embodied in this religiosity.

Even more, he argues that, in order to truly communicate at the religious level, the producer must be part of a praying, believing community and communicate not a message but an experience of God. It is close to the experience of creators of icons who must first meditate on the subject to enter into the deep emotional full experience of the divinity in order to reproduce in form and color the experience of the divinity. Embedded in this experience is a theology, and to understand this signifying practice one must bring in the theology whole and intact.

A central premise in this approach to theology is that the lived religious faith experience of a community, the world this community attempts to bring into existence, is the most important text of reference for theologians. In today's world of large national and global communities, the interconnectedness of community occurs largely through media. Here, the Media, Religion, and Culture perspective understands media not simply as transmitters of information, but as a selective construction of the meaning of the world we live in, a selectiveness that exists by discovering the interests and desires of the audience. The religious communities of today design their construction of the future largely in terms of the materials provided by the media.

Narrative Fiction as a Space for Creating Culture

Like cultural studies, the Media, Religion, and Culture tradition takes media as a text revealing the culture. For example, German Rey shows how the Latin American telenovela provides a good indicator of Latin American religiosity in general, and the different religiosities in Brazil, Mexico, Venezuela, or Argentina, in particular. The telenovela portrays the sharp moral contrasts of good and evil, the fascination with expiatory suffering, but above all the providentialism of Latin American cultures. The telenovela shows that virtuous goodness always triumphs; separated families are always brought together; and honest, faithful effort brings results. If one compares this with Latin American reality, it is clear that a telenovela is more of a theological statement rather than a mirror of reality where brutally unjust people usually gain triumphant power.

Indeed, the Media, Religion, and Culture perspective is interested in narrative fiction or other forms of media as more than mirrors of reality, but as arenas of social discussion-what Martin-Barbero has called mediations. The meaning creating resides not in the media themselves but in the discussions about the issues that are portrayed. This may be at a more local level where housewives from the neighborhood sit together to watch a telenovela and comment together about how the protagonist handles her husband-and how they should be more independent in confronting their husbands. Or the discussion may involve a whole nation. In Chile the dominant entertainment is telenovelas that often have as many as 200 to 250 episodes and deal with major cultural, moral issues.

For example, a recent telenovela, Macho, portrayed how a family with seven sons confronted the problem that one of the sons declared himself a homosexual. Never before had the issue of homosexuality been treated so openly-and had a national discussion ensued on it. The Media, Religion, and Culture perspective finds of particular interest how audiences use the media to draw out a narrative sequence to write the scripts of their own life stories.

Often this deals with issues of ultimate, overarching meaning. In Latin America, for example, where the narrative fiction telenovela is a favourite with young people, many have noted that youth frequently find in the media a language to describe their "religious" experiences. Frequently, there is an ongoing dialogue between the television narrative and the personal life narrative. One young girl in her late teens, attempting to deal with the grief she felt at the death of her grandmother, drew strength and inspiration from how the protagonist of a telenovela dealt with a death in her life. The example of the telenovela also helped the young girl to understand better the theology of death drawn from her institutional religious affiliation.

Religion and Material Culture

The movement away from religion as institution and as dogmatic and moral propositions to religion as culture has brought much more attention to aspects of religion which are important in the everyday lives of the people. One of these is material culture-objects of everyday use that are used in religious signifying practices, from T-shirts with religious emblems to bracelets to crosses. Simple religious icons have always been important in religion, but today personal identity is established largely by mass-produced consumer items. We take on identity from what we consume; we buy and consume in order to communicate our social identity and aspirations to ourselves.

Today, both social status in the power-stratification system and social identity are communicated largely through consumer items. Marketing specialists constantly search out new uses for items people have begun to use to communicate to others who they want to become and to be recognized as. Mass advertising has played a very important role in this and the mass media also have emphasized consumer roles. The study of the subjective interpretation of popular culture has led to a deeper understanding of how popular religious art, so often relegated to a marginal role by theologically dominated institutional religion, can become the focus of stability for the emotional life throughout the life course. The visual symbol often functions as a point of integration of meaning in life, and a popular devotional icon becomes the organizing principle of personal identity. In this, the study of religions, previously limited to the analysis of print media and print-based messages, becomes more open to the role of the visual.

The Role of Popular Culture in Religious Education

The Media, Religion, and Culture focus has privileged popular culture, a culture very largely constructed in the media experience, as a source of religious meaning for a series of reasons. Fundamentally, it sees religion as the construction of limit experience or ultimate, overarching meaning; this is a construction of meaning that is continually shifting. The greatest problem for any religion is that its interpretation of the meaning of reality does not relate to the contemporary problem of the meaning of life. For this reason, all religions display a series of continuous new religious revitalization movements, new saints, new prophets, and the continuous generation of sacred founder texts.

Popular culture is created largely by contemporary "entertainers," those who, in the words of Horace Newcomb and Robert Alley, can take us out of the present world and hold us between a world of the past and a world that could come into existence. These entertainers live by being able to articulate the way the world makes sense right at this moment. As John Shea once argued, the popular artists are the first to sense the new, emerging religious meaning, even if it is too new to be given sanction by religious institutions as truly "religious". Entertainers also appeal to the authenticity of audiences with texts that lie closer to the way people feel at a particular time, and they also strongly invite the audience to listen to their own construction of meaning for that text. This experience of being entertained includes the discovery of more of one's own personal existence.

Religious educators, then, take responsibility for what might seem an impossible task, helping a new generation to assume the responsibility for the tradition of values of a religious community. Mary Hess, in her reflections on the task of religious education feels that religious education should be a process of dialogue in which the educator representing perhaps more centrally the tradition of the community listens to the way a young generation is constructing a contemporary meaning of the sacred text and lived tradition of the community by their authenticity. From this dialogue, which is both confrontational and discerning, emerge broader symbols with which all involved in the deliberation can identify? The discernment sets up a mutual critique of the tradition and the emerging culture. The partners in this dialogue feel that these symbols evoke what is most authentic about their honest desire to give witness in the culture to the values of the tradition in the language of contemporary popular culture.

The Role of Culture in the Formation of Religious Institutions

Many analyses of the formation of contemporary religious institutions such as the Pentecostal movements have tended to explain the theologies, language, and practices of these movements in terms of "strange theologies," ideologies, or simply personal greed. Although personal beliefs and personal motivations certainly operate in the actions of the founders of Pentecostal or other religious movements, local cultures, and especially local religious cultures, are important factors. For example, the Pentecostal movements sweeping Africa and parts of Latin America owe much of their power to attract adherents to the cultural institutions already strong among young Africans.

Many of the founders and leaders are well educated and some are former university professors with doctorates in business, management, or engineering. African religion has a strong orientation toward getting practical outcomes. Pentecostal leaders see their well-organized churches as bringing some rationality and principles of good management into the chaos and corruption of African societies. Pentecostal churches in Africa offer services of employment, special education, and contact with the most influential people in the industrial world. They appeal to the desire for modernity of many young Africans by borrowing many of the techniques of mass media hype from the American Pentecostals and ultimately from the American advertising and public relations experts. At the same time, they call on the Pentecostal theology of powerful evil spirits to respond to the belief in witchcraft and pervasiveness of evil spirits common in African cultures. Pentecostal pastors present their superior power over evil spirits as an example of their general superiority.

The literal appeal to the biblical text convinces young Africans that this religion has clearly indicated foundations in tangible evidence. They appeal to upwardly mobile young Africans, especially young men, with their messages of capacity building, empowerment, and realization of potential. To many, all this provides evidence of insincerity, greed, and an offer of false prosperity, but this conclusion provides no real explanation of the powerful attraction of these new religions. The young Africans drawn to these churches and movements experience liberation and strengthening of their desires for modernity. Increasingly, many of the leaders in business and the professions find in these churches the integration of their personalities around their religious values.

Religious Seeking and the New Internet Media

Many in the Media, Religion, and Culture perspective subscribe to the thesis of major sociologists of religion such as Wade Clark Roof that many people now tend to pull loose from institutional religious systems and respond more to their own personal project of identity and self construction. There is less a conscious process of identity building and more one of simply responding to what an individual enjoys, doing what makes him/her feel good, or what makes sense in one's own personal life. Religious seeking is rooted in a person's internal emotional structure. Religious seeking may always have emerged from internal motivational dynamic, but today people around the world experience more socio-economic and political freedom in their own life context and less institutional constraint. There is a much wider range of educational and occupational opportunity. If marriage does not bring internal emotional satisfaction, people tend to move into other relationships.

The research of Roof, now and many other sociologists of religion confirm the broader theory of sociologist Anthony Giddens that late-modern consciousness now finds itself in a more or less constant quest to construct an ideal "self." Religion and much seeking of meaning that is quasi-religious is a project of self construction. The Media, Religion, and Culture research methodology has sought to trace these self-building, seeking accounts of stages of life-course development, focusing on the moments of much more intense seeking of meaning and the factors that are involved in this. Internet use is a particularly interesting case because it leaves the subject a great deal of freedom to respond to one's own internal motivations. The now voluminous research on religious use of the Internet has now categorized many different types of persons and uses.

Hoover and Park refer to Christopher Helland's discussion of two major types of religious presence in the Internet: "religion online" where institutional churches provide information services of publicity, education, and outreach to their committed members and "online religion," which is open to the subjective construction of religion of seekers. Whereas religion online is self-consciously controlled by the church authorities, online religion responds to the nature of the medium, unstructured, open, and non-hierarchical. What Hoover and Park found is that those who have a religious seeker personality or were in a phase of life when religious meaning systems were shaken tended to use the Internet for a religious quest much more. Individuals who were satisfied with their present experience in an institutional religious community were much less likely to use the Internet to construct a religious self. This confirms earlier research on religious life histories that the use of religious media is much greater in times of less religious certainty.

Family Processes of Constructing Meaning in a Media-Saturated Family Context

Most studies of construction of meaning in the media experience are based on an individual telling the story of how he or she individually constructs life meaning. Other studies report that individual young people construct meaning through interaction with their peers. The Centre for the Study of Media and Religion at the University of Colorado, working with the team of the "Symbolism, Media, and Life-course" project, took on a far more complex research task: how families-parents interacting with each other and with their children of various ages- construct meaning of media.

In other words, to understand meaning making practices, research must "simultaneously" take into consideration both "micro" and "macro" aspects of cultural construction. What emerged in this research involving some five or six associates and graduate students at the University of Colorado was the realization that a very complex set of factors influenced media practices among families of the United States in the last 10 years. The research attempted to take into consideration the extremely diverse understanding of what is a family or household in the U.S. at present: not just traditional nuclear families, but various forms of single parent and companionship families and many types of dysfunctional families with, for example, an alcoholic husband-father. Most of the families approached, in some form, the classical modern nuclear family and virtually all were attempting to assume some set of norms of good parenting. Thus, family values and some ideal of the kind of values adults desired for their children entered into the picture. Good parenting included guiding the media use of the family.

Regarding media use, one of the central findings is that most families apply what Carey called "public scripts" about media and values in America or what Ellen Seiter has termed "lay theories of the media." The common public script or lay theory is that the "sex and violence" of the media are harmful to all in the family, especially to children. This may prompt the question: Why does a nation tolerate a media system that virtually all agree is harmful to its people? Here enters another set of factors: the sacredness of freedom of expression, the assumption that "the buyer must beware," and the view that the entrepreneurial drive for profits in the capitalist system is necessary for the political-economic well-being of the nation. Another set of factors are the parents' religious world views, which often dictate a more or less strict view of parental guidance. The script which parents used was often their memory of how their family of origin had experienced the media and the view that the media had become less favourable to parenting. In the background, too, lies the assumption that every person is entitled to his or her sense of self realization.

Children were often aware that they were entering a very different technological and political-economic world than their parents had known and that they had to chart their own script for use of media. Most parents experience the tension of trying to protect their children and, at the same time, allow the children to respond to their own sense of self and personal identity. Finally, it was apparent that the media practices varied considerably according to the socio-economic status and disposable income of the families. Given the complexity of the factors influencing family media practices, it is not surprising that no unifying theoretical perspective emerged in the research. It is evident that neither sociological theory-in its general theory and variants of family theory-nor media theory seem capable at the present date of providing the materials for formulating this general theory. Much intellectual work remains to be done.

The International Study Commission

In 1996 the Porticus Foundation initiated the International Study Commission on Media, Religion, and Culture made up of 15 scholars and media producers to carry out a more focused study of the emerging shape of religion in the media-dominated age and how the institutions of religion should respond to these challenges. The commission has met with local religious leaders and scholars in Asia, Africa, Latin America, Eastern Europe, and Australia to interchange perspectives on media and religion in those parts of the world. In 1999, to encourage more research and scholarship on media and religion in countries of the South, the commission began a program of scholarships for Catholic doctoral candidates from Africa, Latin America, Asia, and Eastern Europe.

The scholarships are granted by the Porticus Foundation under the title "International Catholic Fellowships for Research in Media, Religion, and Culture." The program does not simply pay tuition but attempts to bring together the approximately 30 fellows in roughly yearly meetings to discuss their research among themselves and with senior scholars in the field. The commission has also been interested in reaching church leadership and leadership in seminary formation. For this audience Peter Horsfield has prepared The Mediated Spirit, a CD that traces the role of media in the development of Christianity. The CD-ROM has proven to be a very useful resource for researchers, teachers, and youth leaders, or those simply interested in understanding the nature and reasons for the changes in religious faith and practices taking place today. Horsfield has also assembled a comprehensive bibliography of publications of the members of the commission which, when complete, will appear on the commission website. Over the 10 years of its existence the study commission has attempted to explore the following questions:

- In what ways can we say that the media have come to occupy the spaces traditionally occupied by religion?
- What is the relationship of religious authority to modes of symbolic practice?
- How must we rethink the relationship between religion and media?
- What does this new situation imply about epistemology?

In the background of these questions lies the emergence of global cultural and religious contact, the disappearing vestiges of collective nationalistic-ethnic definition of religious identity (the tradition of cujus regio, ejus religio), the personalization of religious choice, and the recasting of social relationships and information-seeking in the moulds of communication technologies. Perhaps a good way to close this review and to bring together more briefly the current thinking of the Media, Religion, and Culture approach is to sum up the evidence about the interaction of media and religion emerging from the numerous studies of people using the more open-ended ethnographic interviews of the cultural studies methods.

The situation in which people are increasingly cut loose from the institutional religious framework that structured the parameters of their cultural beliefs and values provides the backdrop. At one time an institutional religious framework structured the way people perceived their world, their standard questions about this world, and the standard answers to these questions. These religious institutions were often closely associated with national and ethnic geographical territories. As people have moved out of these structured social contexts through globalization and physical and intellectual migration, they have had to piece together their own coherent world views, their own definitions of the key questions, and their own answers.

The Media Gets Religion

Students in a single college class could advance the debate on a major media issue. The issue is how the press covers religion. A class in religion at the University of Rochester did a detailed study of top newspapers and concluded, based on empirical evidence, that the media's performance on religion is woeful. The press plays up the negative (radical Islam, for example), largely ignores many faith groups, and fails to tap into the advice of experts. Pollster John Zogby says the findings validate what he already knew or suspected about religious coverage. The findings ring true to me as well. "When it comes to religion, the press seems at odds with itself," the study found. "On one hand, religion pervades America's newspapers as part of the background on topics from politics and economics to sports and the arts. On the other hand, stories about religion itself infrequently address religion's beliefs and values."

The study, dubbed "Religion in American Newspapers: A Critique and Challenge," was conducted by a senior seminar for religion majors at the Rochester school. The 29 students were led by professor William Scott Green and Curt Smith, a former speechwriter for the first President Bush, radio commentator, and author of numerous books on baseball. The papers scrutinized for the month of February were the New York Times, Washington Post, Los Angeles Times, Chicago Tribune, Dallas Morning News, Boston Globe, Atlanta Journal-Constitution, Denver Post, Wall Street Journal, Seattle Post-Intelligencer, USA Today, and Rochester Democrat & Chronicle. Thousands of stories were examined.

Though the students didn't say so, I suspect the findings apply to coverage of religion, period, not just to newspaper coverage. It's not a pretty picture. So what were the specific findings? For one, more often than not religion is fleetingly mentioned rather than being the subject of a story. Two, religion stories are mostly about how some faith deals with political or legal issues. Most of the attention paid to Catholics dealt with the sex scandal involving priests. Coverage of Protestants, Jews, and other religions is more balanced. The study also found that while religion is often used to identify people, it is done haphazardly. Senator Joe Lieberman is frequently identified as an orthodox Jew, while other politicians with strong religious beliefs are not identified by their faith. No politician is ever identified as an atheist. Coverage of the religious lives of Latinos, blacks, and women gets little media attention. And as you might expect after the September 11, 2001, terrorist attacks, the coverage of Islam is disproportionate and heavily slanted toward "criminality and bad deeds."

Another finding: The religious left's opposition to the war with Iraq got a lot more attention than the religious case for the war. Finally, here is what I think is the most important conclusion: The bad-news bias so prevalent in the media today also permeates the coverage of religion. "All the papers studied devote more coverage to religion in the context of bad deeds than they do to the good deeds religions do in their communities." Why is this? The study doesn't say, but I believe it's the case because most reporters at large papers—or TV networks or magazines, for that matter—are secular in the extreme and regard religion with disdain. The recommendations in the study are fairly tame.

The press should "make a clear distinction between religion and criminals or criminal groups associated with that religion," the students say. It's hard to argue with that. Coverage should be balanced, the study also declares. One way is for the media "to help readers achieve an accurate perspective on the communities... [by reporting on] the ways religions actually improve society." And so on. For those who claim the American press is being taken over by the political right, there's nothing in the report to buttress their claim. The right in America is often seen as more hospitable to religion, particularly Christianity. If that's true, then the media is more hospitable to critics of religion and, by extension, opponents of the political right.

The Skewed Representation of Religion

It would surprise few people, conservative or progressive, to learn that coverage of the intersection of religion and politics tends to oversimplify both. If this oversimplification occurred to the benefit or detriment of neither side of the political divide, then the weaknesses in coverage of religion would be of only academic interest. But as this study documents, coverage of religion not only over represents some voices and under represents others, it does so in a way that is consistently advantageous to conservatives. As in many areas, the decisions journalists make when deciding which voices to include in their stories have serious consequences. What is the picture of religious opinion? Who is a religious leader? Whose views represent important groups of believers? Every time a journalist writes a story, he or she answers these questions by deciding whom to quote and how to characterize their views.

Religion is often depicted in the news media as a politically divisive force, with two sides roughly paralleling the broader political divide: On one side are cultural conservatives who ground their political values in religious beliefs; and on the other side are secular liberals, who have opted out of debates that center on religion-based values. The truth however is far different: close to 90 percent of Americans today self-identify as religious, while only 22 percent belong to traditionalist sects. Yet in the cultural war depicted by news media as existing across religious lines, centrist and progressive voices are marginalized or absent altogether. In order to begin to assess how the news media paint the picture of religion in America today, this study measured the extent to which religious leaders, both conservative and progressive, are quoted, mentioned, and interviewed in the news media.

Among the study's key findings:

- Combining newspapers and television, conservative religious leaders were quoted, mentioned, or interviewed in news stories 2.8 times as often as were progressive religious leaders.
- On television news—the three major television networks, the three major cable new channels, and PBS — conservative religious leaders were quoted, mentioned, or interviewed almost 3.8 times as often as progressive leaders.
- In major newspapers, conservative religious leaders were quoted, mentioned, or interviewed 2.7 times as often as progressive leaders.

Despite the fact most religious Americans are moderate or progressive, in the news media it is overwhelmingly conservative leaders who are presented as the voice of religion. This represents a particularly meaningful distortion since progressive religious leaders tend to focus on different issues and offer an entirely different perspective than their conservative counterparts. If one were trying to assess the state of religion in America today by examining the major news media, one would be forgiven for believing that religious Americans are primarily concerned with a small subset of issues, chief among them ending legal abortion and opposing gay marriage. One might also believe that a handful of vocal religious figures advocating extremely conservative political views, many with close ties to the Republican Party, represent the face of religion in America today.

Since the 2004 election and the allegedly heightened influence of "values voters" itself a term the media usually use not to mean voters who have values, but voters who are both religious and conservative — there has been a notable increase in coverage of religion, particularly as it intersects with political debates. Consequently, *Media Matters for America* undertook this study to assess just whom the media turn to when they want to represent religious opinion. We found that conservative religious figures dominate the media's coverage of religious issues, while religious progressives and representatives of mainline religious institutions, who regularly make statements on controversial issues, went relatively ignored. The actual data on religious belief and observance in America illuminates a picture at odds with the media's representation. According to a 2006 survey by the Center for American Values in Public Life, only 22 percent of Americans are traditionalist in their religious beliefs, whereas a full 50 percent of Americans can be classified as centrist in their religious orientation, 18 percent as modernist, and 10 percent as secular or nonreligious.

According to the Pew Research Center, in 2004, evangelicals represented 23 percent of Americans, the same percentage as reported in 2000. Furthermore, despite media depictions, evangelicals are a heterogeneous group with varying priorities: For example, in 2006 only 10 percent of evangelical Christians said abortion and gay marriage would be the most important factor in determining their vote. This heterogeneity of political views among religious Americans applies across varied religious denominations and traditions.

Other studies further demonstrate the diversity of views among religious Americans. A Beliefnet.com study by John Green and Steven Waldman based on data from the Pew Forum on Religion and Public Life classified 24 percent of Americans as either "Religious Right" or "Heartland Culture Warriors," while 17.9 percent were classified as the "Religious Left" or "Spiritual but not Religious."

That 17.9 percent did not include Latinos and African-Americans, most of whom are politically progressive. But something significant happened when exit polls taken on Election Day 2004 showed that more people chose "moral values" as the most important issue on which they based their vote than any other issue. On the basis of this single vaguely worded question, many media outlets delivered a verdict that it was "values voters" - - defined as individuals driven by opposition to abortion and gay rights based on religious belief - that won the 2004 presidential election for George W. Bush.

In fact, national post-election surveys have shown that gay marriage and abortion were far from the most important predictors of vote choice: These issues had no effect on votes among Independents, respondents in battleground states, or respondents in states with antigay marriage initiatives on the ballot. Opposition to abortion and gay marriage did have an effect in the South, albeit minimal in comparison to that of attitudes toward the economy, the Iraq war, and terrorism. An exit poll taken by Zogby International in 2006, furthermore, showed that the "moral issue" cited most by voters was the Iraq war, and that more than twice as many voters cited greed and materialism or poverty and economic justice as "the most urgent moral crisis in American culture" as those who cited abortion or same-sex marriage.

Nonetheless, whether it sprung from a misinterpretation or not, the media's increased focus on religion after November 2004 might have been a good thing — had the balance of voices they presented accurately represented the American public. But that has not been the case. Religious coverage as it exists today does a disservice to the public in two major ways. First, the distorted picture allows a vocal minority to exercise an outsized influence on the issues and politicians that shape the direction of the country.

The second disservice is in the opportunity cost of neglecting to offer a more accurate picture of religiosity and its effects on political views: More than eight in 10 Americans, consistently across virtually every religious tradition, agree that too many leaders use religion to talk about abortion and gay rights, but don't talk about more important things like loving your neighbour and caring for the poor. This is particularly notable in a country with higher rates of religious observance than nearly any other industrialized nation.

Principal Finding

Since the media increased their focus on religion and politics after the 2004 election, we decided to examine the period beginning on the day after that election and continuing through the end of 2006. The data demonstrate that conservative religious leaders comprise the overwhelming majority of religious perspectives presented in news coverage. For this time period, we examined print media coverage in major newspapers and televised coverage on the three major networks, three major cable channels, and PBS. We looked at all news stories that included mentions, quotes, or interviews of 20 major religious leaders — 10 conservative religious leaders and 10 progressive religious leaders. For the purposes of this study, we defined "religious leaders" as clergy or officials of religiously based organizations with clearly identifiable ideological positions who are called upon to comment on political issues and events and offer a religious perspective. This meant that certain individuals were outside our main focus, particularly those who can be considered political actors in their own right.

We offer three kinds of data for the religious figures: the number times each person was interviewed, the number of times they were quoted, and the number of times they were mentioned. The unit of analysis here is the news story; each number represents one story, even if the figure in question was quoted or mentioned multiple times in the same story. These codes were applied in a hierarchical fashion: If a story contained an interview, it was coded as an interview, whatever else it contained; if it contained quotes and mentions, it was coded as a quote; finally, the "mention" category covers stories containing at least one mention of the religious figure but no quotes or interview.

Religion in the Media Age

Religion and the media are today linked in powerful and profound ways. The sex-abuse scandals in the Roman Catholic Church, the consecration of a gay bishop in an Episcopal diocese, the Ten Commandments monument in the Alabama Supreme Court building, and struggles over the constitutionality of" faith-based initiatives" are only the latest ways that religion has emerged into public debate. Religion seems to be a subject that is vitally important and yet little understood. And the media, which are both the context of such conversations and the central source of our information about religions other than our own, seem often illprepared for the role they play.

In the media age, religion can no longer control its own story or its own symbols. In times past, clerical authority could more or less dictate where, when and how religious ideas, symbols and claims would surface. Today, the pope can't control the way Madonna or Sinead O'Connor use or abuse religious symbols. Muslim clerics can't stop portrayals of Islam that it does not approve of. No one can control what the news media will cover and how they will cover it. What once was a bright line drawn around religion, shielding it from secular scrutiny, has long since been dissolved by universal, instantaneous and increasingly visual media experience.

As the Catholic and Episcopal churches have learned, it is not just a matter of controlling their own stories. It is no longer possible to have things remain private, either. In an era of global news on a 24-hour cycle, anything that happens "here" is known about "there" in real time, and vice versa. In another time, news of the consecration of a gay bishop here in the United States might eventually have filtered to Africa. Today, Anglicans in Africa feel that they are part of the story because the live pictures are there, instantly. The conversation is not limited to that church, either. Nigerian Anglicans are keenly aware of how things might be interpreted by their Muslim neighbors in a context where those two religions share an uneasy coexistence. This local competition for the moral high ground is an important explanation for African opposition to the consecration, and is a microcosm of the emerging global confrontation between Islam and the West.

The various "fundamentalisms" worldwide have been described by scholars as modern movements. Christian, Hindu and Islamic traditionalists wish to realize, in the context of modern life, visions of an imagined past that was less complicated and more pure and authentic. For these movements, the media provide a prime source of information about other religions and about the sins of modernity and secularism that they hope to confront. It is clear, for instance, that the Islamist critique of Western culture that provided part of the "justification" for the Sept. 11 attacks is rooted in ideas about the West derived from our own popular culture.

The best and the worst of American film, television and popular music is readily available throughout the Middle East. Imagine your impression of the values of our culture if you had only those sources to rely on. In this, and in more mundane ways, nearly all of what any of us knows about the values, spiritualities and religious beliefs of others comes from the media. We may have the time or interest to delve deeply into the tenets or practices of one or two other faiths or faith traditions, but can we do justice to more than just a few? In an era when immigration is shifting the American religious landscape, it is through the media that we will come to know our new neighbors. The fact is that the media are moving to the center of American religious experience and at the same time religion is becoming a central part of media culture. Of course, the kind of religion we see there is varied and clearly not limited to what we think of as traditional. The CBS show

"Joan of Arcadia," for example, portrays God, but does so in distinctly nontraditional ways.

But that is the reality of contemporary American religion. More and more of us are exploring a variety of spiritual and religious paths, and the media are happy to go along for the ride. At the same time, we should not forget that the media are also sources of some very traditional representations of religion, as in Mel Gibson's controversial new film, "The Passion." Religious groups and organizations also have realized that the media must be a central focus of their efforts in the social and political spheres. Christians on the right and the left, as well as other religious traditions, are increasingly active in efforts to project their messages into the media.

Media are at the center of American religion in another important way. Our civil religion used to be something that was a homogeneous set of commonplace rituals and expressions such as prayers at football games, invocations of a generic God in political speeches, and so on. In the years since the Kennedy assassination, a newer, more authentic civil religion has emerged, one that centers the media as the place where we share common experiences of shock, grief, loss, and mourning. This reached a certain pinnacle on Sept. 11 and in its aftermath, and we now expect that at such times we will gather in front of our television screens and that it will be more than just information that we are getting there.

This role at the center of contemporary American civil religion is not a comfortable place for journalists to find themselves. Religion has always been a difficult beat because of the expectation among journalists that it was both too soft and potentially too subjective. It has never been thought of as" hard" news. However, it is becoming both increasingly "hard" and increasingly difficult for news people to ignore. We are all participating in the evolution of new forms of religion and new ways that it will be understood and experienced through the media. As a society and a culture, we need to take the resulting challenges seriously.

8

Media's Influence on Society

It probably goes back to our earliest ancestors. When something horrible happens in our community, we want to find a reason, an explanation for the horror. Because if we don't, that means that somehow things happen to us over which we have no control and no understanding. So, when a couple of teenagers kill at random, we have to find an explanation. In the 20th century, the explanation for such behavior always has been the media—from the tabloid press to the dime novels to silent films; then sound movies, radio, comic books, television, and now video games and the Internet. In addition, adult entertainment, sometimes labeled pornography, is always one of the usual suspects.

The ritual is so familiar that any viewer or reader knows it by heart—the horror occurs; the reaction sets in. For years, comic books were the great villain blamed for all of society's ills. Today, video games seem to be the main culprit and if not video games, movies and TV. Some blame the individuals involved, the society that created those individuals, the parents or friends or teachers involved. Others blame religion or the lack of religion. In shooting incidents, many blame the National Rifle Association and the easy accessibility to guns. But the main brunt of any criticism is often focused on the newest and most technologically advanced piece of the media—violent movies, violent television shows, violent video games, and violent web sites.

What few seem to realize is that the reason the Colorado shootings became news around the world—the reason newspapers, magazines, television, and the Internet were saturated with the killings of 13 people in a typical American high school—was the rarity, the unusual how-could-this-have-happened nature of the story?

One of the traditional definitions of news is that it means an extraordinary event: a plane crash; a massive earthquake; a devastating storm; a serial killer; a football hero on trial for murdering his ex-wife; the kidnapping of a rich family's son; and, yes, the killing of innocent high school teenagers by their peers. When that rare occurrence takes place, we are shocked, mystified, and saddened, and then angry. We must find a reason why.

Logic dictates that, if movies, television, video games, and the Internet are responsible for this kind of behavior, then why is this event so unusual? If these media so corrupt the minds and hearts and souls of America's young people, then why doesn't this kind of activity happen every day? Why is the event itself so bizarre, so unfamiliar that it grabs the headlines of news media around the world?

An aberration such as this cries out for a reasonable explanation even when such an explanation is impossible. You can blame the individuals involved; you can blame their genetic structure; you can blame the environment that taunted them; you can blame their parents and their teachers; you can blame the new and the old media, but none of this finger-pointing has any meaning.

Because if we could figure out why one individual who plays violent video games or goes to violent movies or watches adult tapes or creates angry, illogical e-mail or web sites does not go out and hurt anyone else and why another goes out and kills and rapes, then perhaps we could figure out why these aberrations take place. But we cannot. And blaming the now popular forms of media for creating these damaged, pathetic human beings only clouds the issue and creates the kind of censorship which in the past has watered down and destroyed our forms of communication.

The Colorado shootings made most Americans forget that the United States' President joined with NATO to order bombs to fall on innocent people in Yugoslavia and unilaterally in Iraq. The reasons put forth by Pres. Clinton and the U.S. allies make sense to the majority of Americans—to force dictators to come to their senses and act like civilized human beings. But those familiar with such bombing strategies conclude that they do little good and that the so-called "smart" bombs—a hideous phrase coined by Pentagon spin doctors and taken up by the news media—don't just destroy buildings, they kill and maim human beings.

When three American soldiers were captured by Yugoslavia, Clinton and the American people were furious. Yet, one old man sitting in the ruins of his neighborhood was quoted by an American reporter as saying, "What about my neighbors? What about the hundreds of Serbs you are killing with your bombs? Why should I care about three Americans?" In Clinton's view, the horror that the dictators of Iraq and Yugoslavia do is reason enough to bomb the people they rule, even if the people themselves are not responsible for the dictators' brutal actions and is often the subjects of that brutality.

To those who suffer under this policy, Clinton and his allies seem as abnormal and irrational as the two teenagers who went on a rampage because they believed their peers' actions were brutal and inhuman. It's a matter of perspective. Are presidents who bomb other countries conditioned by the war films they saw while growing up? Are the media that influenced them responsible for their decisions to go to war? To those in Iraq and Yugoslavia who suffer the loss of people they love, America and its allies are devils and evil incarnate.

They do not understand how the destruction of everything they love and care about will help get the dictator out of his bomb shelter and into the conference room. They are just as confused, sad, and angry as the parents of the slain teenagers in Colorado. To anyone who suffers the consequences of what seems to them to be irresponsible actions, to those who see a loved one destroyed at the hands of another, an explanation is essential if they are once again to find meaning in their lives. Any explanation will do even if it is one that defies logic.

Teenagers, the Media, and the Supernatural

As American society continues toward religious pluralism—and becomes less reliant on religious sources for ultimate truth—youths have more options to reach conclusions about spiritual matters. However, because the American experience is so grounded in the country's Christian heritage, teens must make options fit the mold of tradition. How teens integrate spirituality and religion, particularly as it is portrayed in popular culture and television, is the subject of *From Angels to Aliens: Teenagers, the Media and the Supernatural.* The text seems geared toward graduate students interested in media effects, cultural research, and teen psychology.

Author Lynn Scholfield Clark sheds new light on a broad research topic: media effects. While research into media violence and behavioural studies have long been a topic of debate for researchers, Clark looks at the idea of media effects from a spiritual plane, a vein of research not mined as deeply. The final result is a groundbreaking and ambitious work on the subject of media effects. Yet Clark, an assistant research professor at the University of Colorado's School of Journalism and Mass Communication, states several times that while her research is thought-provoking, it is only a beginning, and more research needs to be done to understand how teens integrate popular culture experiences with religious or spiritual experiences.

And what are the findings? Here's the short version: the youth get it. Teens, overall, are media savvy. Clark states that teens from all backgrounds know that stories of the supernatural–stories of angels and aliens and vampires–portrayed in the mass media are entertainment and should not be taken seriously, particularly when applying them to their belief systems. However, since popular culture feeds off the stories of the larger, shared culture and the past, and since shared culture and the past are steeped within religious tradition, the distinction between entertainment and religion becomes blurred. Teens deal with this blurring by what Clark identifies as an "openness to possibility" theory.

While teens bring to their media experiences certain beliefs about the spiritual world, and are not likely to have their minds changed about what they believe by what they see, they are influenced by a learned culture of tolerance and openness to religious and spiritual differences. When teens come across something in the media about spiritual matters that differ from their own, they do not immediately discount it, but leave it open to possibility. Clark leans heavily on the "culture as toolkit" model theorized by Ammerman, Swindler, and others, where people pick and choose how to react to certain cultural phenomena based on whatever fits their situation and what they have experienced in the past.

But within this overall "openness," there lie varying shades of belief and interaction with spiritual elements. The bulk of the book is devoted to ethnographic stories that shed light on teens working through the belief systems they were taught, their current belief system, and the portrayals of the supernatural in the mass media. Using television shows such as *Buffy the Vampire Slayer*, *Charmed*, and *Touched by an Angel* as starting points for conversations, Clark found that teens can be classified into five different categories: teens who interchange stories of religion and fantasy in part as a form of rebellion against dominant culture (the Resistors); teens who saw a big difference between their beliefs and what they saw in popular culture (the Traditionalists); teens who dabble in the supernatural either to bring their religious beliefs into the context of activities (the Mystical Teens), or as a way to foster their interest in contacting the realm beyond (the Experimenters); and teens who found it difficult to understand the distinction between the mediated supernatural and their beliefs (the Intrigued).

Clark makes sure teens from every economic and racial category, and nearly every major religious movement, are represented in the ethnographic stories, which gives it a broad appeal and is the beauty of ethnographic research. However, the overall result can seem somewhat limited. The research is based on a relatively small sample (250 or so) and a relatively limited location (the southwestern United States) that Clark says is home to a lot of differing belief systems, from the mystical (Wiccan) to traditional Protestant denominations. Replicating the study in another area of the country would add validity to her findings.

Also, the wide representation of different religious beliefs limits the scope of the results. Since no one type of belief is central, the teens represented in the ethnographic studies become archetypes for all teens that come from that background. Would the results be the same if the research focused solely on youth from the mainline Protestant or Reform Jewish denominations? Would the openness to possibility that Clark found still be as prevalent if the study were limited in this way? That is open to debate, but what this book does is offer a blueprint for future research. In that way, this study is a great success. The results, while admittedly limited, suggest rich areas for further research.

Religion Reporting in India

The word *diversity* best describes India. In his book *The Argumentative Indian,* India's Nobel Prize-winning economist Amartya Sen says, "India is an immensely diverse country with many distinct pursuits, vastly disparate convictions, widely divergent customs and a veritable feast of viewpoints." The diversity offers excellent potential for reporting religion, but it also poses many challenges, as realities change from rural to urban areas, from one state to another, and even from one region to another within a state. Given that India has 28 states and six Union territories, one can understand how diverse the realities must be.

It would be safe to assume that reporting of religion and religion-related issues in such a situation will not be homogeneous by any stretch of imagination. An endeavour to identify blanket trends will be a futile exercise. Therefore, my primary focus is the English national media — whose reach is a little lower than the Hindi media, though I have also made an attempt to uncover a few common features in the Hindi media. Although a majority of the 1 billion-plus population of India is Hindu, there is a sizeable number of Muslims, Christians, Buddhists and people from other religions — even atheists, who have coexisted with the people belonging to the "majority" religion for centuries.

In *The Argumentative Indian,* Sen points out that while most of Catholic Europe was given over to the Inquisition, and in Rome Giordano Bruno was being burned at the stake for heresy, in India the 16th-century Mogul emperor Akbar was declaring, "No man should be interfered with on account of religion, and anyone is to be allowed to go over to a religion that pleases him." Today, India has the world's third-largest Muslim population, after Indonesia and Pakistan. In addition, about 2.2 million people in India follow the Bahá'í faith, forming the largest community of Bahá'ís in the world. India is also home to followers of Zoroastrianism, who in India are called Parsis. They represent about 0.006 percent of the total population, with a concentration in and around the city of Mumbai, the capital of the western state of Maharashtra.

According to the 2001 Census of the Government of India, this is the religious population of the country:

Religion	*Population*	*Percentage*
All	1,028,610,328	100
Hindus	827,578,868	80.456
Muslims	138,188,240	13.434
Christians	24,080,016	2.341
Sikhs	19,215,730	1.868
Buddhists	7,955,207	0.773
Jains	4,225,053	0.41
Others	6,639,626	0.645
Not stated	727,588	0.07

These statistics do not give the extent of demographic diversity in the country, as the presence of religious minorities differ from state to state, and in some states it even exceeds the number of Hindus. In fact, the government is presently contemplating a Constitutional amendment to define minorities' state wise, rather than at the national level — a move that many rights groups are opposing.

Christians account for 64.58 percent, 85.73 percent 87.47 percent in the northeastern states of Meghalaya, Mizoram, and Nagaland respectively. Besides, in the states of Arunachal Pradesh, Goa, Kerala and Manipur, they comprise 10.29 percent, 29.86 percent, 19.32 percent, and 34.11 percent of the total populations respectively — much higher than the national average.

Though Muslims do not form a majority in any state, there are Muslim-dominated regions within some states—for instance, the Kashmir valley in the northernmost state of Jammu and Kashmir.

In addition, the number of Muslims is more than the national average in some states, including Assam (28.43 percent), Kerala (23.33 percent), Uttar Pradesh (17.33 percent) and West Bengal (23.61 percent).

Indian Religiosity

Religion plays a key role in the lives of Indians. Rituals, worship, and other religious activities form a very prominent part in the daily life of an individual. Religion also organises social life, especially in rural parts of the country.

India hosts numerous pilgrimage sites for almost all religions. Most festivals are celebrated by people of all communities, irrespective of which religions these festivals belong to. Unlike the West, where a drift away from religious orthodoxy is a visible trend, the people in India are generally drawing closer to traditions in search of their identities in the wake of globalization.

The number of Hindu gurus (and of their followers) is

increasing. The number of temple goers is also on the rise. Even in the national capital, Delhi, young and old Hindus can be seen going to a temple barefoot and carrying a bowl of milk as part of a religious ritual. People prostrating themselves in front of a temple on a busy road has also become commonplace. Generally speaking, people in smaller cities and rural places are more religious than in bigger cities. Sections of the upper middle class are also drawing closer to materialism and the New Age, like in the West. However, it must be acknowledged here that Hinduism is conglomerate of diverse beliefs and traditions, and not a "religion" as understood in the West, and therefore the diversity within it is so immense that any generalization is extremely difficult.

Indian Muslims and Christians too have started asserting their religious identities, perhaps as a reaction to the rise of Hindu extremism, because Muslims are seen with suspicion in the wake of the "Global War against Terrorism." On Fridays, Muslims can be seen kneeling publicly on roadsides or in parks to offer "Namaz." Similarly, Christians too can easily be identified as most of them owning a car will either have a cross hanging in the car or a Christian sticker on the back screen. There are at least 14 religion channels in India, and the number is growing by the year.

The Centrality of Religion in Indian Politics

Religion also dominates the Indian political scene. India's numerous political parties can broadly be divided into two categories: "secular" and "communal." Secularism, according to the Indian definition of the word, does not mean complete detachment from religion, but fair and equal treatment of all religions and religious freedom to all communities. On the other hand, "communalism" means religious sectarianism or creating, promoting and highlighting the clash of worldly interests among religious communities, mainly between minorities and the "majority."

Parties in India's ruling alliance, United Progressive Alliance (UPA), which is led by the Indian National Congress (also known as the Congress Party), are by and large considered secular, while some of the allies of the opposition coalition, the National Democratic Alliance (NDA), whose leader is the Bharatiya Janata Party (BJP), are known to be communal in their ideologies — the BJP is regarded as the principal communal party. Communist parties most of which support the UPA from outside, are also secular. Both secular and communal parties have managed to influence the public opinion to such an extent that if you know which party a person votes for, you can safely assume what his or her opinion will be on a plethora of religion-related issues facing the country.

Print and Electronic Media in India

There are close to 6,000 daily newspapers published in over 100 languages, in addition to more than 40 domestic news agencies in the country. The reach of the press medium (dailies and magazines combined) has increased from 216 million to 222 million during the last year. The number of readers in rural India (110 million) is now roughly equal to that in urban India (112 million). Similarly, there are more than 100 TV channels, and the number of news channels is growing. Satellite TV has grown considerably in reach — from 207 million watching in an average week in 2005 to as many as 230 million in 2006 — further expanding its lead over the number of readers.

Religion-Related Political Issues in Indian Media

The fact that religion and issues related to it take center stage in politics is naturally reflected in the mainstream media, both electronic and print. Secularism, communalism, "saffronization" of education, quota, Dalits, caste conflicts, anti-conversion laws, conversion, "reconversion," uniform civil code, adoption rights, and "Ram Janmabhoomi" are a few words that regularly feature in the media. The numerous issues surrounding these words can be classified into three broad categories: "caste system" political ideologies, and legislation, though there may be many overlaps.

An Oppressive 'Caste System'

The term "Dalit" appears daily in Indian newspapers and news channels in different contexts. Dalits are "untouchables" who have traditionally occupied the lowest place in the caste system of Hinduism. They are classified in the Indian Constitution as "Scheduled Castes." They were called "untouchables" because they were considered to be outside the confines of caste by so-called high-caste Hindu *Brahmins*, the priestly class, thousands of years ago. Their impurity derived from their traditional occupations, such as the taking of life and the treatment of bodily effluvia.

India's Dalits remain on the margins of society and face discrimination. Atrocities on Dalits meted out by higher-caste Hindus are commonplace in the country, mainly in rural areas. There are also instances of Dalits being killed if they dare to enter a Hindu temple or marry a person from a "higher caste" – although there is a special law with stringent punitive provisions to protect Dalits from atrocities. The extent of the discrimination can be ascertained with a recent development in the Jagannath Temple in Kendrapara district of Orissa state early this year. Sections of temple devotees went on a "strike unto death" when Dalits were allowed to enter the temple by an order of the Orissa High Court in November 2006. The tussle was finally over after a compromise was reached between the higher-caste devotees and Dalits in July 2007.

The caste-based problem is so pervasive that it has even seeped into the psyche of other religious communities. In the western state of Goa, for example, sections of the Catholic community whose ancestors converted to Christianity through Portuguese missionaries in the 16th century still assert their *Brahmin* background. In the matrimonial sections of regional newspapers, one can invariably find advertisements for a groom or bridegroom by a person who self-identifies as a "Roman Catholic *Brahmin*." It may be surprising, but there are caste-related problems also in Sikh, Buddhist and Muslim communities in India, though doctrinally there is no caste hierarchy in these religions.

Affirmative Action for Dalits and Others

Article 15(4) of the Constitution provides for positive discrimination in the nature of special provisions for the benefit of certain marginalised sections of the Indian society, of which Dalits and Tribals form a major portion. The term "tribals" or "Scheduled Tribes" (STs), as given in the Constitution, refers to the aboriginal people of India. About 16 percent of India's population is Dalit, and 8 percent is Tribal. Based on this provision, 27 percent of government jobs and admissions in educational institutions run or aided by the government have been "reserved" for SCs and STs. This reservation is referred to as a "quota" in the newspapers.

The UPA government recently proposed an additional 27 percent "quota" for some more backward castes, classified as "Other Backward Classes" (OBCs), for their uplift. This is being fought tooth and nail by the opposition NDA, mainly through its leader, the BJP, saying it is "murder of merit" and appeasement of caste communities. A case about this proposal is also pending before the Supreme Court of India. Some states, mainly in the south, are planning to provide a quota for members of religious minority communities, mainly Muslims, in institutions run by the state government and in state government jobs — in addition to Dalits and Tribals.

Affirmative Action and Dalits from Non-Hindu Religions

In 2004, the Supreme Court of India accepted a plea for extension of affirmative action rights to Dalits who have converted to Christianity or Islam, which revived the debate whether only Hindu Dalits are eligible for affirmative action. The case is still pending in the apex court. A clause in the Constitution, known as the Presidential Order of 1950, says that only Hindu Dalits are entitled to reservation. Thus a Dalit who converts to Christianity or Islam loses the status of SC. The order, which was based on the premise that non-Hindu religions do not have any caste system, and therefore do not need any special privileges or protection, has been amended twice to include Dalits from Sikh (in 1956) and Buddhist (in 1990) faiths in affirmative action benefits.

Christians say if Dalits from Sikh and Buddhist backgrounds can be part of the reservation, why should Dalit Christians be excluded? Besides, sections of Christians also openly acknowledge that even in some churches Dalit converts are discriminated against. Right-wing parties, mainly the BJP, and Hindu extremist organisations have opposed the demand of Dalit Christians, arguing that such a move would encourage religious conversions of Hindu Dalits, as the exclusion of Dalit converts from SC lists acted as a deterrent. Approximately 65 percent of Christians in India are believed to be Dalits.

Issues Related to Political Ideologies

Although India chose to be a secular nation when the Constitution was adopted by national leaders and thinkers of the time in 1950, there have been continual and aggressive efforts to create a "Hindu nation" and oppose secularism.

Secular State or Hindu Nation

Hindu nation is the dream of the Rashtriya Swayamsevak Sangh (RSS), which is the parent organisation of a plethora of Hindu extremist groups such as the Vishwa Hindu Parishad (World Hindu Forum or VHP) and Bajrang Dal, VHP's youth wing, which are collectively referred to as Sangh Parivar by the Indian media. The BJP is its political wing. The RSS, registered as a cultural and charitable organization, believes in and promotes "Hindutva," a Hindu nationalistic ideology that proposes a nation ruled by those whose ancestors were born in India and who belong to religions that originated here, namely Hinduism and its offshoots. It allows religious minorities to live in the country, but in subordination to the majority community.

Hindutva (meaning "Hinduness") is a term coined by Vinayak Damodar Savarkar in 1923 through a pamphlet, "Hindutva: Who is a Hindu," which claimed that the Indian subcontinent is the homeland of Hindus while Christians and

Muslims, being "outsiders," are its enemies.

The Sangh Parivar allegedly indulges in making antireligious minority statements, launching violent attacks on members of minority communities, training its supporters in handling arms, and organizing antiminority hate campaigns. Through its political wing BJP, it has enacted anti-conversion laws in some of the states it rules and sought to amend school textbooks to promote its ideology. Whenever any move related to these activities is made by the RSS, it makes a headline.

School Books and Hindu Nationalism

In 2000, the BJP-led NDA federal government revised social-science textbooks of the National Curriculum Framework for School Education evolved by the National Council of Educational Research and Training (NCERT). The move was called "Saffronization of education" (the color saffron is associated with Hindu religion in India). This was allegedly done to condition the thought process of children in favour of Hindu nationalism and to drive a wedge between the majority community and the minorities of the country. When the Congress party-led UPA came into power, it brought in the new National Curriculum Framework for School Education 2005.

However, some states ruled by the BJP rejected the new framework and introduced other textbooks. For instance, the BJP in Rajasthan state introduced a Class X Social Sciences book prepared by a state body. The book equates "Indianness" with the Hindu identity and excludes Muslims and other communities. Some of the objectionable content includes portrayal of India as superior to other countries; description of Hindu deity figures, religious festivals, and places of pilgrimage covering three-fourths of the book; identification of a Muslim community "pampered by both Pakistan and India" as India's enemy and a comment that the growth in population of this community needs to be monitored closely.

Religious Conversions: Boon or Bane

The issue of religious conversions has been a subject of

debate for a very long time. It continues to surface at the national level from time to time. For instance, in 1994, Arun Shourie (a BJP leader and former editor of The Indian Express newspaper) brought out a book, *Missionaries in India: Continuities, Changes, Dilemmas* (ASA Publication, New Delhi), which took the issue to new heights. The issue surfaced at the national level again a few years later after another BJP leader and the then Prime Minister of India, Atal Behari Vajpayee, called for a national debate on conversion in the wake of a spate of anti-Christian attacks by Hindu extremist groups in Dangs district of Gujarat state from December 25, 1998, to January 3, 1999. Vajpayee once again called for a national debate on conversions after Australian missionary Graham Staines and his two young children were burned alive by a mob led by a Hindu fundamentalist, Dara Singh, in Orissa state on January 22, 1999.

Hindutva sees Christianity as a Western religion, brought to India mainly under British colonial rule in the 19th century. Under this policy, the anti-British sentiments held by many Hindus are extended towards the whole Christian community. The RSS says India's minorities need be "Indianized." The RSS also claims that missionaries are part of an international conspiracy to convert and overtake India. It alleges that Western missionaries use material bribes or force to convert poor and illiterate people. When the Sangh Parivar fails to prove its claims of conversion by the use of force, fraud and allurement, it quotes some Hindu sages who were opposed to even voluntary conversion. They argued that conversion to other religions, mainly Christianity, is destructive to the Indian culture. In their view, Indian culture is so rooted in Hinduism that one cannot exist without the other.

Swami Dayanand Saraswati, an eminent Hindu philosopher and the founder of the Arsha Vidya Hindu study centers in the U.S., believes every conversion is an "act of violence." In an open letter to Pope John Paul II in 1999, Saraswati said conversion would ultimately lead to the destruction of the entire Indian culture. "Religion and culture are not often separable," he wrote. "This is especially true of the Hindu religious tradition. [For instance,] the greeting word, *namaste,* is an expression of culture as well as religion." He also referred to the *bindi,* a mark worn by women. "Even though a... mark on the forehead is purely religious, it is looked upon as an integral part of Hindu culture." He said culture often disintegrated after conversion, "leaving only dead monuments." In other words, some Christian converts still followed cultural traditions but abandoned the religious meaning behind these traditions.

'Reconversion' Conversion or Mere 'Homecoming'

Hindu nationalists oppose Christian conversion on the one hand, but organize "reconversion" of Christian converts on the other, maintaining that it is mere "homecoming." Newspapers and local regional news channels report on reconversion of converts to Hinduism from time to time. Reconversions normally take place en masse in special ceremonies organised by Sangh Parivar groups, mainly the VHP. The reconversion movement was launched by Dayanand Saraswati, who founded a Hindu reformist organisation known as the Arya Samaj in 1875 during the British rule in India. Christened as "Shuddhi" (purification), the movement aimed at bringing back those who had converted to Islam or Christianity, mainly the former, back to Hinduism.

Post-independence, Raja Vijay Bhushan Singh Judeo, the last king of Jashpur, which is now a district in Chhattisgarh state, adopted the Arya Samaj model to reconvert tribal people in the region in 1952. Judeo termed it as "Ghar Vapsi" (Homecoming). In 1990s, Judeo's son Dilip Singh Judeo, former federal minister under the erstwhile BJP-ruled coalition government and presently a member of parliament, gave a new thrust to the movement.

The movement was later extended to other parts of the country, mainly Madhya Pradesh, Uttar Pradesh, Orissa, Bihar and Maharashtra states, by Sangh Parivar organisations. In 1999, Judeo claimed that he had reconverted at least 165,000 Christians in several tribal areas. It is estimated that around 2,300 people were reconverted to Hinduism in 2006.

Spontaneous Clashes or Organized Pogroms

Although religion-related violence has been a part of India's history, its incidence with focus on religious minorities — mainly Muslims and Christians — suddenly rose to new heights after the BJP came into power at the national level in 1998. According to the figures of India's home or internal ministry vis-a-vis anti-Christian attacks, between 1950 and 1998 there were only 50 recorded cases. However, the number shot to 100 in the year 2000 and from 2001 to 2005 at least 200 incidents of anti-Christian attacks were reported every year. However, it is the Muslims who face the brunt of communal violence in the country. In Gujarat state in March 2002, members of the VHP and its youth wing Bajrang Dal led the killing of more than 2,000 Muslims— according to unofficial counts given by rights groups — after a few VHP workers were killed in a train fire in Godhra district, which the VHP claimed was an act of terrorism by Muslims.

Although the BJP-led NDA lost the 2004 general elections and the UPA, led by the "pro-minorities" Congress Party, formed the government, the incidence of attacks on minorities continued to increase. According to the 2005-2006 annual report of the Ministry of Home Affairs, 779 incidents of religious identity-related violence were reported in 2005 in which 124 people were killed and 2,066 injured. In 2003, during the BJP regime, 711 such incidents occurred, claiming 193 lives and injuring 2,261 people. A visible crisis in the RSS and the BJP — after the latter's defeat in the 2004 general elections — is compelling them to fully exploit the issues of Christian conversions and "Islamic terrorism" so as to revive their pet slogan, "Hinduism is under threat."

Most anti-minority attacks are organised by the Sangh Parivar under these two pretexts, and attributed to public anger against the members of the minorities, suggesting that it is not possible for different religions to coexist peacefully — as Samuel Huntington sought to prove in *The Clash of Civilizations.* It must be acknowledged that Christians and Muslims are not the only communities that face religious persecution in India. For instance, sections of Hindu pundits in Kashmir region in Jammu and Kashmir State are also victims of discrimination and harassment.

'Ram Mandir' or 'Babri Masjid'

On December 6, 1992, VHP extremists demolished, Babri Mosque, which was built in the 16th century, in the city of Ayodhya in Uttar Pradesh state, and installed an idol of the Hindu god Rama. The demolition was the culmination of BJP leader L.K. Advani's Rath Yatra (chariot rally) to the city, to remind Hindus of the claim that the spot where the mosque stands is Ram Janmabhoomi, the birthplace of Rama. The Sangh Parivar had been making the claim since 1984 that the Muslim emperor Babur had demolished a temple of Rama to construct the mosque, and that the "historical injustice" must be reversed, allegedly in an attempt to polarize voters along religious lines.

An enquiry commission is investigating the charges against top BJP politicians, including Advani, in connection with the demolition of the mosque. The demolition of the mosque, which was symbolic of the creation of a Hindu nation, led to numerous incidents of communal violence in different parts of the country. It also resulted in polarization of sections of the people along religious lines. Political analysts attribute the success of the BJP in forming the federal government, for the first time in 1998, to this communal division. Neither Muslims nor Hindus are allowed to worship in the mosque/temple site, but from time to time, mainly at the time of elections, the BJP reassures Hindus of its promise to give them "back" the "Ram Mandir" (Temple of Rama).

Legislative Issues

Issues related to legislations regulating religion or civil affairs of religious communities also feature in the media regularly.

Personal Laws or a Uniform Civil Code

India has personal laws, for Hindus, Muslims and Christians, dealing with civil matters, such as marriage, divorce, and succession – though subjection to these laws is optional in certain matters, as there are also special civil laws meant for people of all communities. However, Article 44 found in Part IV of the Indian Constitution, which is not binding, says that India should endeavour to adopt a uniform civil code throughout the country. The objective of adopting a uniform code is national integration, according to the Supreme Court of India.

Many rights groups are in favour of a uniform code as they believe Muslim personal laws in particular are oppressive for women. The BJP too advocates for it, but seemingly with a different objective. It is believed that the party is pro-common code because it can make life difficult, especially for conservative Muslims and the clergy. However, the Congress and other secular parties are of the opinion that adoption of a uniform code must be preceded by a national consensus, especially among the Muslim community.

Following a pro-common code observation by a judge of the Supreme Court of India in September 2003, the then President of India, Dr. A.P.J. Abdul Kalam, stated that law in the country had to be uniformly implemented, reviving the debate on a uniform civil code. Issues arising out of the uniform civil code debate include what will be the content of the common code, in what areas of life will it apply and whether religious customs will be exempted from the common code. There is a fear among minority communities, mainly Muslims, that a common code will be misused to impose the principles of the majority religion on the minorities in the name of uniformity without respecting their beliefs.

Laws Banning Conversion Constitutionally Valid

Although the Indian Constitution provides for religious freedom to all communities, India has seven states with special laws banning conversions. Commonly known as anti-conversion laws and christened as Freedom of Religion Acts, these laws have been implemented only in three states – Madhya Pradesh, Chhattisgarh and Orissa – while they remain on paper in Arunachal Pradesh, Gujarat, Rajasthan and Himachal Pradesh.

Many political analysts in India link the enactment of anti-conversion laws to the Hindu nationalistic agenda of the BJP, which supposedly uses these laws as a tool to institutionalise Hindutva, and to divide voters along religious lines before elections. To defend the various anti-conversion laws, the BJP cites a Supreme Court's 1977 judgment upholding the Madhya Pradesh Dharma Swatantrata Adhiniyam (Freedom of Religion Act) 1969 in the *Reverend Stanislaus vs. State of Madhya Pradesh* case. According to the verdict, the right to propagate does not include the right to convert another person to the former's faith on the premise that the latter is equally entitled to the freedom of conscience. Not all in the legal fraternity agree with the judgment, though.

However, in 2006, two members of the National Commission for Minorities, Harcharan Singh Josh and Lama Chosphel Zotpa, acknowledged that Hindu extremists frequently invoke the anti-conversion law in the BJP-ruled Madhya Pradesh as a means of inciting mobs against Christians or having them arrested without evidence. Christians also allege that these laws define "force," "fraud" and "inducement" vaguely, which can restrict Christian work and allow anti-Christian forces to levy false charges on Christian workers. They also object that these laws require that all conversions be reported to the government, failing which both the priest and convert can be imprisoned or fined like criminals. Although the law has been in force in some states for close to four decades, not even a single person has been convicted of wrongful conversion by any court thus far.

In India, there is no provision for religious minorities to adopt children. Under the Hindu Adoption and Maintenance Act (HAMA), 1956, only Hindus can adopt legally. Muslims, Christians, Parsis and Jews can only become the guardians under the Guardians and Wards Act (GAWA), 1890, which does not confer the status of a biologically born child. However, as per the high court rulings of Kerala and Maharashtra states, Christians can apply for conversion of their guardianship to full adoption.

The Juvenile Justice (Care and Protection of Children) Act (JJA), 2000, does provide for the adoption of abandoned and abused children by all religious communities, but its implementation vis-à-vis adoption remains only on paper. Under the JJA, only the Juvenile Justice Boards, after they are empowered to do so by way of notification in the official gazette, can facilitate adoptions. However, no state government has issued any notification to empower the boards to deal with adoption matters. A case related to absence of legal provision for religious minorities to adopt children is pending before the Supreme Court of India.

Trends in Reporting of Religion-Related Political Issues

Following are a few trends in the way various religion-related political issues are reported in the media. There are several factors behind why issues related to the Muslim community generate news stories on a daily basis. Being the largest minority community in the country, Muslims get the attention of almost all major political parties. Consequently, the welfare of the community features in both national and state governments' policies.

Indian Prime Minister Dr. Manmohan Singh appointed the "Rajinder Sachar Committee" to evaluate the social, economic and educational status of Muslims. The report was tabled in Parliament on November 30, 2006. Based on the report, the UPA government in January 2007 directed all banks to provide preferential loans to minorities. The government is contemplating more sops for Muslims based on the report. Besides, Muslims are the main target of the Sangh Parivar, which leads to numerous incidents of anti-Muslim violence. Further, misdeeds of a very small section of the Muslim community, both in India and in other countries, have put the whole community under suspicion.

"We should not fix labels like Muslims or non-Muslims; it won't help us in understanding the situation or dealing with it. A terrorist is a terrorist; he has no religion or community. As a Sikh, I understand the trauma (of being labeled)," said Prime Minister Dr. Manmohan Singh in the wake of the July 6 Glasgow bombings in Australia. The statement underlines the plight of a common Muslim. In fact, what the Muslim community in the West is facing post-9/11 has been a tragic experience of the community in India for the last few decades, thanks to the Sangh Parivar's anti-Muslim campaign.

Most newspapers and TV news channels assume that the reader or viewer understands major issues facing the country, and therefore very few stories explain the background. This is true also in reporting of religion and religion-related issues. For instance, stories related to the Muslim and Dalit communities feature daily in the media, but without bringing out the religious dimensions of the issues. Perhaps, because the incidence of such stories is so high, explaining the background will inevitably become too repetitive. However, foreign news agencies and organizations, such as the BBC, Reuters and AP, and Indian agencies that have foreign clientele, such as the Indo-Asian News Service (IANS), do carry a background each time a religion-related story appears. In fact, IANS is among the very few Indian news organizations that have religion as a separate column.

Coverage of Communalism is Dynamic

It is unfortunate that for the Indian media the politics behind communalism is more important than its effects on society or the plight of the victims of communal violence. Near the time of elections in states or at the national level, the coverage of Sangh Parivar's communal activities or incidents of violence increases in the media, to highlight BJP's attempts to divide people along religious lines. The rest of the time, only "large-scale" violence is reported, while many sectarian activities — which happen almost regularly — go unreported. Also, for the same reason, communal incidents are given greater coverage if the states where they take place are ruled by the BJP. The truth is that such incidents also take place in the states ruled by other parties.

In fact, the overall coverage of communal issues by the national media was much higher during the rule of the BJP-led

NDA at the federal level, from 1998 to mid-2004. After the NDA lost the general election in May 2004, the coverage fell visibly.

In the third week of July 2007, *The Indian Express* sponsored a debate on whether excellent journalism is bad business. The editors and CEOs of *The Times of India* and *The Hindustan Times* newspapers and the IBN 7 Hindi news channel, which is in partnership with the U.S.-based CNN, publicly and explicitly admitted that for them becoming popular was a major factor in determining what is covered or what goes on air. While the commercialization of the media must be criticized in light of the fact that it is considered one of the pillars of democracy, this development has made the reporting politically more neutral as a byproduct.

For example, *Aaj Tak*, considered the most popular news channel in Hindi with a pro-BJP slant, on April 29, 2007, showed a Christian pastor in Jaipur, the capital of Rajasthan state, being beaten up by Hindu extremists of the VHP. This was the first televised anti-Christian attack in the country. As a part of the coverage, the channel interviewed VHP leaders actually putting them to national shame. In contrast, the IBN 7 Hindi news channel, which is seen as anti-BJP, exposed corruption in sections of churches in India and aired the views of VHP leaders on the same. The channel showed some pastors accepting money for fake baptism and church membership certificates for admission purposes.

Another factor that has contributed to the reduction of political biases is the large number of news channels, newspapers and other means of mass communication, such as the Internet. As a result, any attempt to hide information from the readers or viewers or to twist the truth gets noticed and exposed when other newspapers, channels or websites show the truth — which is not affordable at this competitive stage. In fact, news channels and newspapers are trying to beat each other in exposing failings of (or corruption in) the governments, irrespective of which party rules them.

Reports on Christian missionaries indulging in "conversions" are commonplace in Hindi newspapers. The largest selling *Dainik Jagran* daily is the best example of this trend. The local edition of *Dainik Jagran* in Himachal Pradesh state has been carrying provocative stories maligning the local Christian community for the last two years. It has been publishing a series of reports with the same headline, "Isaiyon ka gorakh dhanda" (Misdeeds of Christians), each time carrying a picture that shows a *trishul* (trident, one of the signs of a Hindu god) piercing the cross and stains of blood.

Several *Dainik Jagran* stories have alleged that Christians eat beef (the cow, considered a holy animal, is worshipped by Hindus) and "forcibly" convert Hindus, identifying Christian workers with their names. According to local evangelical Christian organisations, the extremists somehow get hold of their inhouse magazines and misquote from these publications in the newspaper to support their allegations. In fact, there is a feeling among local Christian workers that it is a result of the anti-Christian campaign in the local media that the Congress Party government in Himachal Pradesh Assembly passed an anti-conversion bill on December 30, 2006, alleging that "conversions" were happening, leading to law and order problems in the state, and the local people wanted a law to ban "forcible" conversions.

Internet Material is Quoted out of Context

An Islamist terrorist group on May 22, 2003, attacked Christians for the first time in Kashmir valley, a region in the state of Jammu and Kashmir that is infamous for persistent bloodshed due to conflicts between India and Pakistan. The attack on a Christian school in Nai Basti in Anantnag district, Saint Luke's Convent School, followed media reports alleging that some Christian groups were using money to convert Muslim youth in the Valley. An opinion article in *The Indian Express* daily by BJP legislator Balbir K. Punj said: "The Vatican and allied Christian groups make no bones about using money as their primal leverage for 'harvesting souls'... And it's no surprise that the Campus Crusade for Christ could afford to pay every fresh recruit in the Valley Rs.2, 000 per month, plus perks and other expenses... Would this then not appear to be a more lucrative career choice for some Kashmiri Muslim youths – with hard cash which not even a terrorist organisation would have paid him for picking up an AK-56 against the Indian Army?"

Such newspaper reports merely reflected what the three-part investigation report in *The Indian Express,* on April 6, 7 and 8 (2003), claimed. Titled "It's conversion time in Valley," the report stated, "At least a dozen Christian missions and churches based in the U.S., Germany, the Netherlands and Switzerland have sent evangelists to the Valley and are pumping in money through intermediaries based in New Delhi... Christian groups are putting the number of neoconverts at over 10,000... and a Sunday Express [the Sunday edition of the newspaper] investigation confirms that conversions have been taking place regularly across the Valley."

The newspaper's idea to conduct the investigation originated out of a claim made in a website by the U.S. evangelical magazine, *Christianity Today,* which said that thousands of Muslim youth were accepting Christ in Kashmir. Titled "Harassed Kashmir Christians reach out to discreet Muslims," the article appeared on the website on September 9, 2002. "Thousands of mostly young Kashmiri Muslims, disillusioned by Islam, are seeking new ways to resolve Muslim-Hindu violence.... Wearied by violence, thousands are interested in the Prince of Peace," it said. BJP leader Punj also quoted from other Christian websites in his article. He said, "The World Evangelisation Research Centre estimates that it takes 700 times more money to baptise a convert in rich countries like Japan and Switzerland than in a poor country like Nepal."

In February 2004, an 11-page cover story in the weekly *Tehelka* carried another article quoting from Christian websites. Titled "George Bush has a big conversion agenda for India," the article was based on material available on the websites of the "AD 2000 and Beyond" movement and "Joshua Project" I and II. The authors of the story sought to portray Christian missionary work in India as a "sinister and disturbing phenomenon" that should "ring alarm bells within the intelligence agencies in India." They misunderstood, or maybe misused, the term "spying of the land" done by Joshua in the Old Testament, which Christians understand in a spiritual context, to mean spying in a political context. They alleged that the Central Intelligence Agency (CIA) was behind the preparation of data about postal codes of India by Christian missions.

Most English national newspapers in India have special religion columns, but there is no regular, dedicated program on religion in news channels. However, the news channels, mainly Hindi, do like to highlight people's superstitions. Hindi news channels' obsession with spiritual healing and occultism is easily perceivable and reporting on such practices features in almost every news bulletin. To give an example, the *Aaj Tak* channel on July 28 showed a "healer" stepping on young children to "heal" their diseases. The coverage lasted for more than 15 minutes, and the clip repeated several times in the day.

TV channels showed devotees of the Hindu god Ganesha in Delhi and other parts of the country offering milk to the idol, claiming that it was actually drinking. The coverage was shown the whole day after short intervals, and Hindu priests were interviewed on the possibility of an idol drinking milk. A few days later, the channels showed a clip of devotees of a temple on seashore in Mumbai, the capital of Maharashtra, drinking sea water, which had reportedly turned sweet.

The devotees attributed the "miracle" to their god. In fact, there are special half-hour programs on most Hindi channels showing the fame and claims of occultists claiming to have supernatural powers. English news channels also report on incidents related to people's superstitions, but the frequency is way lower than their Hindi counterparts. From time to time, superstitions do figure in debates on English channels. The media can blame the viewers for this trend, as such coverage does increase the TRP (Television Rating Points) of a channel, but it is also true that this is promoting superstitions among the people.

Most newspapers have special religion columns, but they lack serious content. *The Hindustan Times* has a column called "Innervoice" which appears each weekday. "Innervoice" normally features articles on the philosophy of religion written mainly by the readers. Till last year, it carried contributions from popular Hindu gurus, clergy from different religions and freelance writers. Of late, the policy of the newspaper changed and the column was made open to readers' contributions. The flip side of this policy is that it has brought down the quality of the articles.

On Saturdays, the newspaper features a special page on religion, "Faith on Saturday," which carries four columns. These columns normally feature "entertaining" stories related to religion, like the beauty of the building of a temple, with almost half the page devoted to graphics. One does not find spiritual articles meant for followers of a religion, except some quotes from various scriptures on a topic. *The Times of India* has a column, "Speaking Tree," which appears from Monday to Saturday. The articles in this column mainly talk about Hindu scripture Vedas or Reiki, Feng Shui (an ancient Chinese practice of arranging space to achieve harmony with the environment), and Vastu Shastra (traditional Hindu canons of town planning and architecture), etc.

The daily also carries a special page on Sundays, "Mind Over Matter," which normally features articles by famous New Age gurus like Deepak Chopra or those who advocate using spirituality for enhancing management skills and success in worldly matters. *The Hindu*'s column, "Religion," also runs from Monday to Saturday. The newspaper has its own writers for this column, which invariably talks about Hinduism. The articles do not carry a byline. Only on festivals celebrated by other religions does it feature articles by clergy or writers from other religions. Until recently, *The Indian Express* had a biweekly religion column "Faithline," but as of now, it does not have any religion column.

The trends in the way religion and religion-related issues are reported in India give us at least three inferences:

First, the Indian media give substantial coverage to religion and religion-related issues, but highlighting mainly the negative and divisive aspects—which perhaps is the case in general reporting too. For instance, many religious communities are doing commendable social work, but their work rarely gets the attention it deserves. This is perhaps a result of most media being market-driven, rather than having an agenda, which compels them to use only stories that are potentially sensational and can sell. Second, there is a decline in seriousness in the various religion columns in newspapers. Maybe this only reflects popular Indian religiosity, which seems to lack spiritual substance. Third, generally speaking, the Indian media promote false spirituality. Perhaps the popular Indian gurus, who seem to be very shallow in the spirituality they preach and practice, are good in public relations skills and are aggressive evangelists.

Bibliography

A.H. Armstrong, ed., *Classical Mediterranean Spirituality*, World Spirituality 15, New York: Crossroad, 1989.

Armstrong, Karen, *Muhammad: A Biography of the Prophet*, Victor Gollancz Ltd.: U.K. 1991

Babin, P., *The New Era in Religious Communication*, Minneapolis, MN: Fortress Press, 1991

Brasher, B., *Give Me That Online Religion*, San Francisco, CA: Jossey-Bass, 2001

Buddenbaum, J., *Reporting News about Religion: An Introduction for Journalists*, Ames, IA: Iowa State University Press, 1998

Coleman Barks, trans. *The Essential Rumi*, new expanded edition (San Francisco: Harper San Francisco, 2004

Daniel Chanan Matt, ed., *Zohar: The Book of Enlightenment*, Classics of Western Spirituality, New York: Paulist Press, 1988

Eichhoefer, Gerald W. *Enduring Issues in Philosophy*. San Diego: Greenhaven Press, Inc., 1995.

Geertz, C., *The Interpretation of Cultures*, London: Hutchinson, 1975

Hunt, Stephen J., *Alternative Religion: A Sociological Introduction*, Aldershot: Ashgate, 2003.

Jenkins, H., *Textual Poachers: Television Fans and Participatory Culture,* London: Routledge, 1992

Khan, Muhammad Zafrulla, (trans.) *The Qur'an,* Olive Branch Press: NY, 1997

Kintz, L. and J. Lesage, *Media, Culture, and the Religious Right,* Minneapolis, MN: University of Minnesota Press, 1998

L. S. Clark (eds), *Practicing Religion in an Age of Media,* New York: Columbia University Press, 2002

Malise Ruthven, *Islam: A Very Short Introduction,* New York: Oxford University Press, 2000

Mircea Eliade, ed., *The Encyclopedia of Religion,* 16 vol., New York: Macmillan, 1987

Nouwen, Henri J.M. *The Road to Daybreak: A Spiritual Journey.* New York: Doubleday, 1988

O'Flaherty, Wendy Doniger (ed. and trans.), *The Rig Veda: An Anthology.* Penguin Books, NY, 1981

Pritchard, James B. (ed.), *The Harper Concise Atlas of the Bible,* HarperCollins: NY, 1991

Roleff, Tamara L., ed. *Satanism.* San Diego: Greenhaven Press, Inc., 2002

Silk, M., *Unsecular Media,* Urbana, IL: University of Illinois Press, 1995

Steven Heine and Charles S. Prebish, eds., *Buddhism in the Modern World: Adaptations of an Ancient Tradition,* New York: Oxford University Press, 2003

Sushil Mittal & Gene Thursby, eds., *The Hindu World,* New York: Routledge, 2004

Takeuchi Yoshinori, ed., *Buddhist Spirituality I: Indian, Southeast Asian, Tibetan, and Early Chinese,* World Spirituality Series 8, New York: Crossroad Publishing, 1993

Tu Weiming & Mary Evelyn Tucker, eds., *Confucian*

Spirituality, World Spirituality 11, New York:.Herder & Herder, 2002

Veer, P. van der, 'Transnational Religion', paper presented at the Conference on Transnational Migration: Comparative Perspectives, Princeton, 2001

Warms, Richard, James Garber and Jon McGee, eds., *Sacred Realms: Essays in Religion, Belief & Society*, New York: Oxford University Press, 2004

Wilkins, W.J., *Hindu Mythology: Vedic and Puranic*, Rupa and Co.: Calcutta, 1986

William C. Chittick, *Sufism: A Short Introduction*, Oxford: One World, 2000

William C. Chittick, *The Sufi Path of Love: The Spiritual Teachings of Rumi*, New York: SUNY, 1983

Wise, Michael, Martin Abegg, Jr., Edward Cook, *The Dead Sea Scrolls: A New Translation*, HarperCollins: NY, 1996

Wuthnow, R., *Rediscovering the Sacred: Perspectives on Religion in Contemporary Society*, Grand Rapids, MI: Eerdmans, 1992

Xinzhong Yao, *An Introduction to Confucianism*, Cambridge: Cambridge University Press, 2000

Zaehner, R.C. (translation), *Hindu Scriptures*, J.M. Dent & Sons: London, 1966

Zaleski, J., *The Soul of Cyberspace: How New Technology is Changing our Spiritual Lives*, New York: HarperCollins, 1997

Index